EDMUND BURKE FOR OUR TIME

EDMUND BURKE

FOR OUR TIME

Moral Imagination, Meaning, and Politics

William F. Byrne

Northern
Illinois
University
Press
DeKalb

© 2011 by Northern Illinois University Press

Published by the Northern Illinois University Press, DeKalb, Illinois 60115

Manufactured in the United States using postconsumer-recycled, acid-free paper.

All Rights Reserved

Design by Shaun Allshouse

Library of Congress Cataloging-in-Publication Data

Byrne, William F.

Edmund Burke for our time: moral imagination, meaning, and politics / William F. Byrne.

p. cm.

Includes bibliographical references and index.

ISBN 978-0-87580-649-5 (clothbound: alk. paper)

1. Burke, Edmund, 1729–1797—Political and social views. I. Title.

JC176.B83B96 2011

172—dc22

2011001149

For Gretchen, Martha, and Katie

Contents

Acknowledgments

As Burke would no doubt appreciate, I cannot conceive of myself as the sole creator of this book. Although I take full responsibility for all that is in it, I am deeply indebted to many others. They are too numerous to list individually, but a few of those most directly involved must be acknowledged. I cannot convey enough gratitude to Claes G. Ryn of The Catholic University of America, who not only helped spark my interest in Burke but guided me through the initial stages of this project. He offered wisdom, knowledge, and encouragement, while recognizing the importance of freedom to the writing of political philosophy. David Walsh and Dennis J. Coyle of The Catholic University of America likewise provided invaluable wisdom and support in making this book a reality. Joseph L. Pappin III of the University of South Carolina and of the Edmund Burke Society of America has exhibited kindness and generosity to me in many ways, one of which has been his helpful commentary on this manuscript. The blind reviewers have also done much to make this a better book; their task is an important but largely thankless one, for which I convey my thanks. I also thank the directors and staff of Northern Illinois University Press, especially Amy Farranto, for believing in this project and helping bring it to fruition. And I greatly appreciate the past financial assistance provided to me by the Earhart Foundation and by the Intercollegiate Studies Institute, which ultimately helped make this book possible.

I would like to thank the following publishers for permission to include in this book material adapted from that included in several previously published articles of mine: The Edmund Burke Society of America for use of material from "Imagination and the Good in Burke" in *Studies in Burke and*

His Time, 21 (2007); the Intercollegiate Studies Institute for use of material from "Edmund Burke and the Politics of Empire" in *The Political Science Reviewer*, 37 (2008); and the National Humanities Institute for use of material from "Burke's Higher Romanticism: Politics and the Sublime" in *Humanitas*, 19, nos. 1 and 2 (2006).

EDMUND BURKE FOR OUR TIME

Introduction

IT IS OFTEN ASSERTED THAT we live in a "postmodern" age. The term "postmodern" has varied meanings, but is generally understood to indicate either a reaction to the modern or the fulfillment of it. In either case, traditional sources of order and meaning have lost much of their salience. This poses fundamental problems for politics, for society, and for one's own personal search for the good life. To complicate matters further, it is also widely noted that ours is a "multicultural" age; not only does intense interaction occur on the global level among states with highly distinct cultures, but the populations of individual states and societies have themselves become extremely diverse culturally.

The effect of all of this is to make political discourse and decision-making much more difficult, since people no longer share the same "thick" understandings of what life is about. In 1776, the U.S. Declaration of Independence could speak of "truths" that we hold to be "self-evident." Today there is less consensus about what truths we should believe in—or even if there is such a thing as truth at all. And even when a consensus appears to exist among the general public—such as when the bulk of a population acknowledges the legitimacy of particular statements of rights—it quickly becomes evident that great disagreement exists regarding precisely what those "truths" mean in practice.

The political and ethical challenges posed by this late-modern or postmodern era are daunting. However, they are not entirely new. One of the first thinkers to recognize and confront in a significant way the kinds of problems now associated with late political modernity—and, to a degree, to confront problems of multiculturalism as well—was Edmund Burke. The Irish-born, eighteenth-century British statesman and writer has been the subject of much interest and scholarship in a variety of fields, including politics, history, aesthetics, and literature. In particular, there has been a considerable volume of scholarship on Burke's political philosophy. Yet there are important aspects of Burke's thought that have been inadequately recognized, appreciated, and explored. It is argued here that from some of these neglected dimensions we can recover from Burke a path to addressing fundamental problems of order and meaning in the contemporary world.

Edmund Burke was keenly aware of the potential precariousness of political and social order. Burke was born around 1729[1] and died in 1797; his life roughly coincided with the height of the Enlightenment and with the flowering of the modern political order. He had the opportunity to take in the French Revolution, an event widely regarded as a milestone of sorts in political modernity. Burke is justly famous for his perception of the significance of the Revolution and of the peculiarly modern ideological thought associated with it; indeed, his writings on the Revolution have long been his most well-read works. Although Burke is a modern, in that he lived in the modern age and was steeped in its intellectual life, there is also something premodern and, one may argue, postmodern, about his thought that gives him a particularly insightful perspective from which to critique modernity. His significance, however, does not begin with his commentary on the particularly modern French Revolution. From his earliest writings Burke displayed a strong interest in the cultural and social underpinnings of morality and politics. The philosophical themes and ideas that appear in the *Reflections on the Revolution in France* and in other late writings and speeches are the same as those that illuminate his earliest works.

Increasingly, scholars have noticed relationships between particular aspects or strains of "conservative" thought and postmodern thought. Political theorist Peter Augustine Lawler argues that "conservative thought today is authentic postmodernism."[2] All political labels can be problematic, and "conservative" is perhaps especially so. Nevertheless, although he was very much a reform-oriented politician and a prominent member of the Whig Party, Burke has come to be widely associated with forms of thought commonly identified as conservative. One prominent mid-twentieth-century conservative thinker strongly influenced by the thought of Burke is Russell

Kirk; in a recent book on Kirk the scholar Gerald Russello maintains that Kirk possesses a "postmodern imagination."[3] The kind of postmodernism to which commentators like Lawler and Russello refer is of course quite different from what has commonly been thought of as postmodernism; for one thing, it seeks to recover, rather than abandon, traditional sources of order and meaning. Like other postmodernism, however, it is quite different from typical modern thought; Lawler and Russello would, in fact, probably maintain that it is more different from typical modern thought than are the usual forms of postmodernism, which really amount to a sort of hypermodernism. Unlike this self-defeating hypermodernism, Edmund Burke, it is argued here, offers us ways of thinking about political order, about morality, and about "reason" and human thought and emotion that may serve as a corrective to some of the fundamental problems that have emerged or become more acute in the contemporary world.

In any polity, the institutions, laws, and power structures represent only part of the basis for order. Underlying these elements is what is commonly called a political culture. "Political culture" is in turn linked to a broader culture or worldview encompassing a whole range of norms and predispositions covering many areas of behavior. The sorts of behaviors that we tend to view as particularly political, including political participation, the adoption of specific public policies, and the strictness or looseness of adherence to stated laws and policies, can be seen in part as products of the worldview, predispositions, and character of a people. It is in such elements that important roots of political and social order lie.[4]

In the context of modern liberal democracy the question of sources of political order takes on added importance.[5] In premodern societies human behavior and human relations were bound fairly tightly by tradition, custom, and religious belief. In some cases, norms were largely unspoken; in other cases, fairly explicit teleological frameworks, or conceptions of the good life, were emphasized. Either way, shared understandings of the meaning, purpose, and structure of human life and society, whether explicit or implicit, provided a basis for order. As the world became more modern, such as in Europe's long transition from the Middle Ages to the Enlightenment and beyond, traditional frameworks were, to some degree, discarded. This movement away from tradition sometimes occurred inadvertently, as a by-product of changing conditions. At other times, individuals rejected tradition quite deliberately and self-consciously, often in the name of "reason," which came to be understood in opposition to tradition-based (or similarly, religion-based) norms. The contemporary philosopher Alasdair MacIntyre refers to "the Enlightenment project to discover rational foundations for an objective morality."[6] This project was, in MacIntyre's view, doomed to failure.

The concept of "The Enlightenment" is a bit fuzzy and problematic; it is difficult to define or date with precision, and it was not some sort of highly unified movement. Great differences existed between, for example, the French Enlightenment and the Scottish Enlightenment, and even within the French Enlightenment there were diverse and conflicting strains of thought. However, a broad sense certainly existed among intellectuals of the latter eighteenth century that Europe had entered a new "enlightened" age that stood in sharp contrast to the medieval period, now labeled the "Dark Ages."[7] One may argue that, in moving away from tradition, the Enlightenment— and, in fact, the development of political modernity from the 1500s onward—set up a dynamic in which explicit formulations regarding human nature and the good order actually became more important. That is, as tradition, religious piety, and unspoken common understandings faded, it became more necessary to identify and articulate bases for political order, and perhaps for good behavior in general. The search for a moral grounding for the political order led to the rise of social contract theory based upon a highly abstract and arguably imaginary "state of nature" and a questionable conception of human beings as atomized rational actors. It also led to the development of natural rights–based frameworks, in which a political order is understood in relation to particular universal rights that are posited as existing independently of that order.

Without a strong traditional order to back them up, however, such rights-based formulations have developed an increasingly hollow ring. The political philosopher Richard Rorty points out that "about two hundred years ago, the idea that truth was made rather than found began to take hold of the imagination of Europe."[8] The truths proclaimed by Thomas Jefferson to be self-evident are, in fact, not always so self-evident, particularly if one attempts to move past generalities and vague ideals and to identify the specific real-world meanings of the "truths." Truths increasingly appear to be subjective or culturally specific, not universal and binding. Liberal democracy poses a special problem because of its professed cultivation of "neutrality" with regard to conceptions of the good. Under liberal pluralism there is little assertion of a common ethos, but without a common ethos, liberal society disintegrates. Without a meaningful shared sense of human nature, liberalism itself becomes difficult to justify.[9] Why must we be free to make choices if all choices are of equal value?

Burke offers us his own brand of "Enlightenment" thought, which can serve as a corrective to the sort of thought that most commonly springs from the Enlightenment. His pursuit of stable, effective, humane, and reasonably liberal political order incorporates within itself a partial response to the fundamental problem of order and meaning in human life, with special reference to political life. His approach to this problem involves a number of closely related themes, which are identified and brought together in this book under the concept of the "moral imagination." The term "moral imagination," though often incorrectly attributed to later writers, is first known to appear in Burke. He uses it just once, in one of the more prominent and important passages in the *Reflections*. Burke does not highlight the concept or develop it systematically, but, given the fact that his later writings were all geared toward pressing political issues and not philosophical explorations, this is not surprising. The term nevertheless signals a set of ideas that is central to Burke's thought and underpins his politics.

Although the term "moral imagination" originated with Edmund Burke, much Burke scholarship fails to mention it. Two notable early and mid-twentieth-century thinkers, Irving Babbitt and Russell Kirk, do pick up on Burke's concept and consider it very important, but they offer relatively little explication or philosophical development of it.[10] Since that time the term has appeared more and more frequently, but has received even less serious attention from those writing on Burke. Ironically, the importance of the imagination, and to some, even of the moral imagination to Burke is often recognized, but in a vague way, and its real significance in his thought is rarely explored.[11] In overlooking the importance of the concept of the moral imagination, Burke scholarship has actually overlooked an entire complex of ethical, epistemological, and social ideas that may in fact represent Burke's most important contribution to political and philosophical thought.

From his earliest writing Burke displayed a strong interest in how people learn, think, and develop their opinions and views. He emphasized the ways in which people make judgments without the deliberate exercise of conscious rational thought or conceptualization. Before turning his attention to politics, Burke took a strong interest in literature, theater, history, aesthetics, and philosophy, and he saw how thought, morality, and, ultimately, politics are shaped in myriad ways through cultural elements and other aspects of life. Morality has for Burke a large imaginative component. Through the imagination, we build up a sense of the world with the aid of symbols, metaphors, images, and associations of various sorts. The characteristics of the imaginative whole or framework that we build up influence profoundly how we think and act, including how we think and act in the moral sphere. This makes up an important part of what we commonly call character.

For Burke, the problem of good politics is inseparable from the problem of how to make people good. In his early years Burke tended to focus on how aesthetic and cultural elements such as art and literature shape intuitive understandings of the world. After entering Parliament in 1766 his interest expanded to how such perceptions interact with public policy and with other aspects of life. In responding to political issues Burke took pains to consider how the particular worldviews of the affected parties would influence their reactions to the policies employed. And his policy choices were often driven in significant part by his concern over how particular political actions might shape—for better or for worse—the perspectives of the public. He also came to place great emphasis on the role of traditional cultural elements—customs, manners, established social structures, religion, and so on—in addition to ongoing cultural developments, such as those in literature and the arts, in shaping character and influencing society and politics.

For the most part, Burke does not develop the philosophical dimensions of his thought in a highly explicit, systematic way. Burke was well read and, as a young man, he engaged in philosophically oriented writing with his *A Philosophical Enquiry into the Origin of our Ideas of the Sublime and Beautiful* (and, perhaps, with his satire *A Vindication of Natural Society*). But for the vast bulk of his career his energies were taken up by everyday British politics, and his writings and speeches were of a polemical sort; although there is great depth to them, his concern was not with writing philosophy, but with making the sorts of arguments most effective in advancing or blocking various political initiatives. This book is an effort to draw out and develop from Burke various ideas that are implicit in his thought. These ideas have been grouped with reference to Burke's concept of the moral imagination, although they go beyond the meaning of the term as explicitly used by Burke. What is offered is an application of Burke's ideas to some of the political and, perhaps, existential problems of the contemporary world; in the process, it is hoped that this book helps recover a sophisticated political philosophy in Burke.

Burke's thought represents an alternative to the kinds of modern thought most associated with the Enlightenment. A sophisticated thinker, he employed his own modern thought to understand and, he hoped, preserve what was best about premodern thought into the modern age. Burke largely embraced the eighteenth-century British political order, including its liberal and republican elements. He sympathized with the Americans' perspective at the time of their Revolution, and his efforts to improve the treatment of Ireland's Catholics and to reform British colonial rule in India were major defining elements of his career. He was no reactionary, at least of the stereotypical sort. Yet he perceived dangers in the modern order as well. He offers a perspective that is distinctly different from those typically associated with the Enlightenment era. In particular, Burke's thought offers a wider and richer understanding of human reason or thought. Linked to this understanding is a different approach to ethics and, more broadly, to questions of order and meaning. While the universal and the particular tend to be sharply distinct in most modern and contemporary thought, Burke's approach offers a glimpse of an unchanging reality within the flux of daily life. It is argued here that Burke's approach offers a more effective and more solid grounding for ethics and politics than does the mix of abstract ideals and crude "pragmatism" that characterizes most contemporary politics.

In offering a broader and richer understanding of judgment, Burke's thought also addresses tensions and distinctions between reason and emotion. Along with its sharp distinction between the universal and the particular, popular modern thought tends to distinguish sharply between reason and emotion. Reason, very narrowly conceived, is often assumed to be the correct basis for judgment. It is "objective" and offers a sound perception of reality, while emotion is "subjective" and distorts reality. The effect of this is a false objectivity that actually distorts judgment. When combined with other characteristics of modernity, this helps give rise to political thought driven by the secular religions (and sometimes not-so-secular religions) of ideology. Political actors claiming to be simply following a scientific or "rational" approach to the world may actually be slaves to unrecognized passions and to idiosyncratic prejudices. In the same context, political actors may, alternatively, actually embrace emotion and subjectivity, but do so in a way that yields irresponsible or unjust political action. In contrast, Burke's approach to politics is one that not only recognizes a proper role for emotion (and helps to promote sound emotion), but also leads to a different conceptualization of judgment in which the old distinctions between reason and emotion lose much of their meaning. The result, it is argued here, is a more sound approach to political decision-making and social life, which leads to a politics that is at once less shrill and more effective and just.

Indeed, the value of Burke's thought today extends far beyond esoteric dimensions of political theory and into practical politics. For example, often in political discourse we find that no mustering of evidence, no matter how extensive, will change a viewpoint; in conversation, the most persuasive arguments are frequently simply dismissed. The problem may not be that one side is being "irrational," but that each side's rationality is operating within a different construction of reality. Likewise, in public discourse and politics we find that debates on public policy questions tend to be subsumed under more amorphous conflicts of "values." None of this would seem terribly new or strange to Edmund Burke. His understanding of politics, culture, and meaning has much to offer us in our efforts to address problems of contemporary liberal democracy. Burke demonstrates how concern for the moral imagination can shape politics and public policy for the better. He displays remarkable cultural sensitivity, and his approach offers insights that may be useful in addressing contemporary issues of multiculturalism. Above all, this examination of Burke reveals how the liberal order—with all of its freedoms and benefits—rests upon an imaginative framework that must be carefully maintained if that order is to survive.

In recent years concerns have grown in the United States in particular about an erosion of political discourse and behavior, with a growth in naked power politics and the rise of an "anything goes," us-versus-them mentality that increasingly justifies the bending or breaking of rules and norms. This also would have been unlikely to surprise Burke. His project was, to a great extent, one of preventing such developments. He was concerned about preserving and building up the right kinds of norms, the rule of law, and the basic sense of fairness and justice required for a stable and free polity to survive. The insights that can be developed from his thought are needed today more than ever.

It was mentioned that there is something postmodern about Burke. If one sees the modern in part as the casting off, or loss, of rich traditional social and moral frameworks and their replacement by more clearly articulated, but "thinner," political/social frameworks grounded in "rational" precepts, then the postmodern can be seen as a recognition of the potential hollowness or bankruptcy of those precepts, and as an attempt to respond to this situation. Nietzsche's proclamation that God is dead and "we have killed him" is a recognition of this loss, and of the precarious position in which this places humanity.[12] This is what some call the modern crisis. A sense of arbitrariness sets in; nothing really means anything, and there are no standards by which to judge right and wrong. One postmodern response is a sort of embrace of this arbitrariness and contingency in the form of an ironic or "playful" approach to the world.[13] Burke was postmodern in that he was aware of the potential hollowness of political or moral precepts, and of the potential for a crisis of order and meaning in the emerging new era. His response, however, is in some ways the opposite of that of many postmoderns in that he positions himself against arbitrariness or, to use a term of his, caprice, and strives to recover the sources of order and meaning necessary to maintain sound standards. Burke does this partly by recognizing the importance of developing and maintaining the right kind of moral imagination. As will be shown, Burke offers an approach to morality and to reason that avoids some of the pitfalls of contemporary debates regarding normativity, because he recognizes universality while rejecting an emphasis on a priori principles. His manner of doing so is one of the most important and valuable aspects of his thought.

A central question of much contemporary political-philosophical discourse is that of norms. That is, we debate not only which ethical laws should be controlling in particular circumstances, but also the existence of such laws themselves. Are they absolute and universal? Where do they come from? Who has authority to interpret or pronounce them? What, ultimately, should guide our behavior? The question of norms has also been central to much Burke scholarship. That is, scholars have debated whether or not norms are for Burke universal and God-given. While specific interpretations of Burke will be addressed in greater detail later, it can be noted here that an important approach since the mid-twentieth century has been the "natural law school" of Burke interpretation.[14] This "school" argues, essentially, that Burke believes that a universal order exists, that this order is of divine origin, that it can be perceived through the use of reason, and that moral and political conduct should be in conformity with it. There is nothing unusual about this formulation, and there is nothing unusual about it being ascribed to a man of the eighteenth century; even today it is sometimes taken for granted that people think this way. What makes the application of this model to Burke significant is that many commentators have not understood Burke to be thinking in this manner at all. Much of Burke scholarship has interpreted him as some sort of utilitarian, or proto-progressive, or historical determinist, or pragmatist, or even nihilist, and has either lauded or faulted him for rejecting more traditional approaches to morality and politics.

The natural law school approach to Burke was to a great degree a reaction and rebuttal to such (self-described) "modern" understandings of Burke, which were most dominant in the late nineteenth and early twentieth centuries but are still widely found today. The fact is that some aspects of Burke's writing may invite "utilitarian" interpretations of various sorts, but such interpretations all have glaring weaknesses when examined in the context of his work as a whole. With its emphasis on Burke's search for order and meaning, this book is, in a broad and general sense, sympathetic to the natural law approach to Burke. However, if understood in the usual way, the natural law interpretation is also problematic and cannot be accepted in a strict form. The more rigorously such a model is applied to Burke, the less appropriate it seems and the less useful it becomes for developing an understanding of his thought. For one thing, Burke uses very little traditional Thomistic or natural law language in his writings. And given that Burke is famous for disparaging "reason," and even appears at times to disparage "truth," how can he be a natural law thinker in the usual sense? Elements of Burke's aesthetic thought and this tendency to blur lines between aesthetics and ethics are additional stumbling blocks to the application of this model, since they seem to contradict the usual natural law approaches to morality.

Reading Burke, it is hardly surprising that no broad consensus interpretation of his thought is found among scholars. When placed under philosophical scrutiny Burke's writings can be so problematic, mysterious, and apparently contradictory that some commentators maintain that he has no underlying philosophy at all. Burke, it is argued, simply responds pragmatically to individual political problems and circumstances as they arise.[15] The exclusion of Burke, despite his stature and influence, from some introductory political theory texts is in part a reflection of this view that he is not a "real" political thinker or a "real" philosopher. It is difficult to believe, however, that a statesman like Burke, who wrote so prolifically in a variety of fields, who read so much philosophy and literature, and who was so highly regarded, possessed no overarching philosophical framework, even if that framework was not clearly and systematically articulated. This book maintains that Burke is very much a "real political-philosopher" in that he thought profoundly and insightfully about core issues of the human condition, and that his thought is reasonably consistent and coherent. He was, however, not a "metaphysician," to use his own term; his focus was on immediate human concerns rather than on abstract or conceptual philosophy.

By explicating and clarifying those ethical, epistemological, and aesthetic dimensions of Burke's thought revolving around the idea of the moral imagination, one develops a framework that is not only highly applicable to problems of contemporary politics but helps make sense of much that is confusing, or that appears contradictory, in Burke. For one thing it offers a way in which one can recognize that Burke's approach to morality is broadly theocentric, that he believes in a universal order and that he believes that we have some ability to perceive that order, without encountering the pitfalls and limitations that have accompanied the more customary natural law interpretations of him. A central concern for Burke is *how* we perceive moral order, and one may argue that it is actually the sophistication, subtlety, and uniqueness of his thought in this area that contributes to the confusion among many of his interpreters. What may appear in Burke to be a rejection of universals is actually a reflection of the fact that he is much more sensitive than most thinkers—in his time or in ours—to the basic problem of recognizing universals, and to the problem of knowing right from wrong in both theory and practice. He rejects the arrogance and naiveté of those who simply assume that they possess unimpeachable knowledge of truth. Burke's response to the epistemological problem is not some sort of radical skepticism or nominalism or nihilism, but a humble search for a path to the true and the good.

Since this study is built in part around the concept of the moral imagination, it is appropriate to provide a brief discussion of the term before proceeding further. Despite its use in the early twentieth century by American scholars, largely in the field of literary criticism, and its prominent use by social commentator Russell Kirk at mid-century, it is only since the 1970s that the term has become more widely prominent. Since the 1990s in particular, its use has mushroomed; many books and articles in fields as diverse as public policy, literary criticism, popular moral philosophy, and business ethics include "moral imagination" in their titles or otherwise make prominent use of the term. Of the many books and articles in diverse fields that have appeared with "moral imagination" in their titles, relatively few credit Burke for the term or associate it with him. More important, these books tend to include little or no rigorous or systematic discussion of the concept. The ubiquity of "moral imagination" in titles suggests that the concept has strong appeal. The relatively modest role that the concept actually seems to play in most of these works suggests that, while it may be long on appeal, it tends to be short on meaning. It is hoped that this book will give a more clear meaning to the term by examining it in the context of the thought of its original user, Burke. It is argued that his usage of the term has connotations that are broader, deeper, and more precise than those found in most contemporary literature, and that have important implications for politics and for moral life. In uncovering and developing the Burkean roots of the concept of the moral imagination, this book will perhaps be a contribution of some use in the diverse fields in which the term has been employed.

This book will begin its approach to Burke's thought by addressing problematic aspects of two of its widely recognized elements: the outlook that is commonly identified as "Burkean conservatism," and his related emphasis on "prejudice." These are important both for developing a correct understanding of Burke and to finding correctives to some of the problems of our late-modern age. Chapter 2 focuses on relevant dimensions of Burke's aesthetic thought and shows that Burke's aesthetics offers important keys to approaching problems of politics and ethics. Chapters 1 and 2 lay the groundwork for the development of a moral-epistemological framework from Burke, which offers a path to addressing problems of politics, society, and meaning today, while also helping to explain much that is going on in Burke. This material is pulled together with additional material in chapter 3, to explicate and develop these key aspects of Burke's thought with some assistance from contemporary political and philosophical thinkers. Chapter 4 addresses the question of what, in practical terms, constitutes for Burke an imaginative grounding for a sound interior life, and explains how culture, the interior life, and politics interact. Chapter 5 focuses explicitly on Burke's political activities, bringing to bear the understanding of his thought developed in chapters 1 through 4 in interpreting key elements in the historical record of his statesmanship, thereby demonstrating the political application and practical effectiveness of the ethical-epistemological framework developed here. Chapter 6 plumbs more deeply into the moral underpinnings of Burke's thought, particularly into the basic problem of doing right. Through the concept of the moral imagination Burke's "pragmatic" focus on real-world concerns is united with a belief in universal standards, and he is seen as emphasizing a particular kind of movement toward the true and the good that transcends the usual categories. The Conclusion pulls together the material in the preceding chapters while further exploring the relationship of Burke's thought to fundamental problems of order and meaning in liberal-democratic society in our late-modern or postmodern world.

1

The "Burkean" Outlook and the Problem of Reality

The Problem of "Burkean Conservatism"

One way to begin to get at some of the moral, political, and epistemological insights yielded by a study of Burke is through some attention to that outlook that is commonly referred to as "Burkean conservatism." This book is not the place to attempt to locate Burke at a particular point within conservatism broadly, or to articulate his role, versus that of others, in anything identifiable as a "conservative tradition"; treatment of problematic labels such as this, and of the ideologies they represent, will be left to others. Instead, the aim is to develop a proper understanding of what is commonly called Burkean conservatism as a key to some of the most important ideas that can be drawn from Burke for application in today's world. Specific interpretations of Edmund Burke's underlying political philosophy vary greatly, but most people who possess at least a passing familiarity with him believe that he was in some manner a conservative. Even Harold Laski, who at times gushes with praise for Burke, and who particularly likes what was sometimes called (in the conventional language of some commentators) "modern" and "utilitarian" about him, sees Burke as, ultimately, a conservative.[1] In Laski's case, Burke is faulted for being conservative; for many other commentators this has been a source of Burke's appeal. Indeed, one of the more interesting and significant developments in Burke's legacy has been his embrace by American conservatives since the mid-twentieth century. The 1950s and '60s saw the rise of a self-consciously conservative intellectual movement in the United States. This movement was in search of a coherent, sophisticated political philosophy of conservatism, and it saw the makings of such a philosophy in the writings and speeches of Burke. Russell Kirk is probably more responsible than anyone for this heightened awareness of Burke's value as an intellectual justifier of conservatism.[2]

This rise of affection toward Burke among some on the political right probably contributed to the development of a distinct lack of interest in, and sometimes outright hostility toward, Burke on the left, at least in the United States. (In contrast to the United States, in the British Isles Burke has not been so closely associated with a particular contemporary ideology, and interest in him has generally lacked a partisan tinge.) The situation in the United States may be changing, if a clue is provided by the reappearance of favorable treatments of Burke by American scholars who do not see themselves as conservative.[3] Although it is increasingly recognized that the simple label "conservative" does not adequately capture the thought of Burke, the term "Burkean conservatism" is still widely employed—sometimes positively, sometimes to denote an object of criticism. The meaning of this term, however, is more problematic than one would guess from the extent to which it is used.

The most common view of Burke—and the view usually given when he is treated in broad political theory survey courses and books—tends to rely very heavily upon his late writings, especially *Reflections on the Revolution in France*. This view often emphasizes Burke's "doctrine of prescription."[4] Burke himself never referred to his thinking on this subject as a "doctrine," but the general idea can be legitimately drawn from his writings. This "doctrine" is a general preference for the old over the new, and a sense that legitimacy is conferred upon practices that have existed for a long time. The doctrine of prescription is found alongside an emphasis on the limitations of human reason in the face of the complexity of life. Within the Western tradition a strong sense of such limits is perhaps most associated with classical thought and traditional Christian thought, but some can still be found in contemporary writers such as Friedrich Hayek and Michael Oakeshott. It is often invoked as a caution against excessive rationalism or planning in politics, against highly optimistic expectations regarding human perfectibility, and against the ability of a small number of people to change or to manage a society effectively.[5]

Because of the limitations of human knowledge and rationality, our best bet is sticking with the tried and true. One of the most oft-cited Burke quotations is on this subject; he states that "we are afraid to put men to live and trade each on his own private stock of reason, because we suspect that this stock in each man is small, and that the individuals would do better to avail themselves of the general bank and capital of nations and ages."[6] Our own individual knowledge and experience is limited, so we must draw upon that of society as a whole. This implies that we must respect practices that have been built up gradually over time and that have enjoyed widespread acceptance over a long period. These practices have been adapted to human nature and to human needs, and even if they are imperfect, they have proven their effectiveness and workability. We change such practices at our peril, because it is unlikely that we know enough to do better.

Burke does, of course, make a case for this sort of conservatism; the above quote is evidence of this, and there are other passages to back this one up, although they tend to be concentrated in just a few of his many works. An emphasis on this idea as representing the essence of Burke is, however, highly problematic. For one thing, by itself this sort of conservatism provides no guidance as to when change is appropriate; the suggestion seems to be that it never is. Taken to the extreme, this yields a rather dubious political-philosophical model in which past changes are accepted and, if they are old enough, revered, but no further change is permitted. This would presumably result in efforts to freeze the current order in place, or to restore the political and social order that existed at an arbitrary point in the recent past, without assessing the desirability of the various different aspects of that order. Over the years a few commentators have in fact claimed that Burke deliberately takes such a position because he is enamored with British political life as it existed in the period immediately after the Revolution of 1688, and wants to keep Britain in a late seventeenth/early eighteenth-century mode as much as possible.[7] A more common, and perhaps more realistic, interpretation of Burke's conservatism is that he believes in slow, incremental change only. There is definitely an element of truth to this. Burke falls very much within the British gradualist tradition, and can in fact be seen as one of the great articulators of this tradition. However, this interpretation is still somewhat problematic since it is not consistently supported by Burke's own political record. As a member of Parliament he often took positions that are difficult to characterize as representing slow or incremental change. As will be shown, on some occasions Burke opposed even relatively modest changes, but at other times he supported changes that would have been quite dramatic.

It is very difficult to characterize Burke's parliamentary record simply as that of a conservative as this term has typically been understood. An examination of the whole of his writings and speeches suggests that, most of the time, he was much more interested in promoting change than in thwarting it. If a political label had to be applied to Burke as an MP, he would perhaps be best characterized as a "liberal reformer" or something along those lines. This was, in fact, how he was generally regarded in his own time; his almost violent reaction to the French Revolution surprised many, including Thomas Paine and Mary Wollstonecraft, who had assumed that Burke was an ally. As has been noted, Burke was a Whig. The division between Whigs and Tories in eighteenth-century Britain was not a division between "liberals" and "conservatives"; the ideological divisions between them, to the extent that that term can even be used, most explicitly focused on the scope of the king's power, although there were other components as well, such as their level of comfort with the emerging commercial society. The Whigs, as opponents of overreaching by George III and his court and, usually, as supporters of free markets, could generally be characterized as the more rights-oriented and democratically inclined camp. The Whigs also tended to stand more with change, in part because of their association with the emerging bourgeois commercial order, while the Tories were associated more with the older agrarian and aristocratic order.

There were, of course, Whigs of different types. In some ways, the older "Rockingham Whigs" like Burke bore a closer resemblance to Tories than to the newer Whigs who came to dominate the party in Burke's later years. Some Whigs, such as Charles Fox, were quite radical and populist, and greeted the French Revolution enthusiastically; such positions were of course not shared by Burke. Samuel Johnson famously denounced "Whiggism," yet he and Burke were friends and mutual admirers, so, presumably, Burke could not have represented the brand of "Whiggism" that Johnson detested.[8] Burke was brought into Parliament under the auspices of Lord Rockingham, and the Rockingham Whigs were generally a rather aristocratically oriented group. Burke was, however, a believer in popular government, properly understood and under appropriate circumstances. Although he strongly opposed radically majoritarian democracy, commentator James Conniff maintains that "Burke's greatest contribution to modern politics lies in his role as a theorist and practitioner of representative government."[9] Burke is also widely viewed as one of the originators of the concept of party government, due to his efforts to organize and solidify the Whigs in Parliament so that they could stand against the King and the Tories.[10]

In addition to his friendship with Johnson, complications arise in identifying Burke simply as a "Whig" because near the end of his parliamentary career he broke with the Whig Party. This was actually a part of a splintering within the party; in this splintering, Burke represented what one might label the more "conservative" brand of "Whiggism." It could be argued, however, that it was the more radical Whigs who moved from the Whig mainstream, not Burke; as an organized political force the more radical Whigs would in fact end up disintegrating rapidly. At any rate, before this breakup began, Burke was not on some conservative fringe of the Whig party, but was one of its central players. In fact, he sometimes staked out positions that were more reformist or radical than those taken by many others in his party. Among Burke's positions that were controversial even among his fellow Whigs were his support for greatly easing the laws against Catholics in Ireland and his support for freer trade. When Burke first moved toward advocating dramatic changes in British rule in India, his views were directly contrary to the long-established position of the Whig Party, which had opposed even very modest reforms of the East India Company.[11] So Burke himself was not especially "Burkean," if "Burkean" is to indicate simple conservatism.

Conserving a Moral Imagination

To the extent that there is such a thing as "Burkean conservatism," we can get a glimpse of its true nature from a passage in the unfinished *English History*, a writing project that Burke undertook when he was about 28. Compared with Burke's other writings, this work receives little attention from scholars, and indeed much of it may be seen as less important than his more directly political or philosophical writing. Still, aspects of it yield vital insights into Burke's thought, and into central questions about knowledge, morality, and politics. Especially noteworthy is Burke's recounting of the conversion of England to Christianity. In this animated passage he relates the story of how Pope Gregory took care to accomplish the conversion in as gradual a manner as possible.[12] Rather than destroying pagan temples, they were slowly converted to Christian practice; long-standing pagan practices, such as the slaughtering of oxen, were deliberately continued near the new churches. Ceremonies and even doctrines were changed gradually. Burke explains:

> Whatever popular customs of heathenism were found to be absolutely not incompatible with Christianity, were retained; and some of them were continued to a very late period. Deer were at a certain season brought into

St. Paul's church in London, and laid on the altar; and this custom subsisted until the Reformation. The names of some of the church festivals were, with a similar design, taken from those of the heathen, which had been celebrated at the same time of the year.[13]

Burke clearly approves of the manner in which the religious conversion was accomplished; he goes so far as to state that the pope's policy revealed a "perfect understanding of human nature." If anything, Burke may actually overstate the seamlessness of the transition to Christianity and the melding of the Christian and the pagan; this subject clearly captures his imagination. Why should this be so? For one thing, the incremental change involved in the conversion would seem to fit in well with the usual idea of "Burkean conservatism." But a problem exists in that "Burkean conservatism" is typically associated with the belief that traditional knowledge and practices are, as a general rule, superior to new schemes. It is certainly not the case here that Burke could believe that the old paganism was superior, or even equal, to Christianity. His belief in and support for Christianity are evidenced throughout his works. While a few commentators have questioned the sincerity of Burke's religious convictions, the vast majority have not; J. G. A. Pocock for example maintains that "the point at which his thought comes closest to breaking with the Whig tradition to which he deeply belonged was that at which he articulated his concern for clerisy. Burke's religiosity—his awareness of the sacred, of the need for transcendent moral sanctions—was real."[14] Moreover, just a few paragraphs earlier in his discussion of the conversion of England Burke remarks that Christianity confers "inestimable benefits on mankind" and that it helped change the "rude and fierce manners" of the Anglo-Saxons.[15]

Of course, one may construct an argument that belief in the superiority of Christianity to paganism is not inconsistent with Burke's approval of the gradualness of the transition. Such gradualism appears to be a key component of "Burkean conservatism." Because of the limitations of human reason, we cannot be sure how new schemes will play out; therefore, change should be incremental. However, a problem exists with this model as well. The standard "limitations of human reason" argument is generally used to oppose the sudden adoption of new, untested rationalistic schemes. That is, the model is generally understood to argue for respect for tradition, and for caution regarding the implementation of new plans or ideas for society. Christianity, however, was no new scheme; it was, in fact, a tradition, with centuries of experience behind it by the time of its introduction into England.

It had been time-tested and, to a degree, had evolved and developed over time. Since Christianity had already been long proven and was not some new idea that had just been thought up by armchair philosophers, there would presumably be no reason why it should be introduced into England in a cautious, incremental manner. Why then should Burke take a conservative or gradualist position regarding the introduction of Christianity, and even approve of the admixture of presumably inferior pagan elements?

Fortunately, Burke states quite plainly why it was desirable to ensure a gradual transition and to retain aspects of paganism wherever practical. Abrupt changes were avoided "in order that the prejudices of the people might not be too rudely shocked by a declared profanation of what they had so long held sacred."[16] The danger Burke perceived lay not in Christianity itself as an untested scheme, but in the possible effects of *any* attempt to disrupt the pagans' existing worldview. The "prejudices" of the people had grown up over a long period of time in the context of belief in a particular cosmological order and in the context of specific practices related to that belief. Consequently, the sudden profanation of the sacred would have wreaked havoc on the community by undermining its basis for order and meaning. Pope Gregory, in Burke's eyes, understood the importance of preserving the old framework, and took pains to minimize the disruption that would occur as a result of the change in belief system. This argument, it should be made clear, is quite different from the usual understanding of "Burkean conservatism." Burke's focus is not on the objective problem of whether or not the innovation is "good," or even whether the change is suitable for the circumstances at hand. His focus is on the subjective experience of the people. This emphasis on subjectivity is one key to Burke's approach to fundamental problems of order, meaning, and the good.

What informs Burke's discussion of the conversion of England informs his politics and writings in general. This is a concern for what contemporary writers such as Charles Taylor have referred to in other contexts as "horizons of significance."[17] Taylor's term, however, might be understood as referencing explicit religious, moral, or teleological beliefs only, and Burke has much more than this in mind. In the above discussion Burke's concern is not limited to the gods in which the pagans believed and any explicit moral codes that may have been directly associated with that belief. He is concerned about the rites, the practices, the physical structures, the geographical locations, the calendar, and various other elements that were present in the pagan religious culture. All of these elements worked together to give the pagans a sense of the sacred and to form a framework of order and meaning, which shaped their lives. Without this framework the ordered lives and society of the pagans would presumably collapse.

The retention of so much paganism, which Burke regards so positively, might make some Christians uncomfortable. Objections could be raised that it would compromise, corrupt, or at least needlessly encumber Christianity. If Christianity's truth and benefits are acknowledged, then, one might argue, it must follow that only the "purest" form of it should be pursued. Burke, however, sees things differently. For him the approach to the true and the good is not simply intellectual in character but broadly experiential, and involves much more than a conscious rational assent to certain propositions. This favoring of the experiential over the "rational" should not be taken to suggest that Burke is a radical skeptic, that he rejects reason or universals, or that he is less than fully committed to the true and the good. This subject will be taken up in some detail later, when it will be argued that Burke in fact possesses a greater sense of the sacred and a deeper appreciation of the search for what is true and good than do many of his critics.

The way in which the various elements of the pagans' religion shapes their lives is through the feeding of the moral imagination. The term "moral imagination" does not appear in Burke's early *English History*, but much later in the *Reflections on the Revolution in France*. Burke uses it when he is bemoaning the spread of the radical and rationalistic worldview of the French Revolution:

> All the pleasing illusions which made power gentle and obedience liberal, which harmonized the different shades of life, and which, by a bland assimilation, incorporated into politics the sentiments which beautify and soften private society, are to be dissolved by this new conquering empire of light and reason. All the decent drapery of life is to be rudely torn off. All the superadded ideas, furnished from the wardrobe of a moral imagination, which the heart owns and the understanding ratifies as necessary to cover the defects of our naked, shivering nature, and to raise it to dignity in our own estimation, are to be exploded as a ridiculous, absurd, and antiquated fashion.[18]

Although the phrase "moral imagination" appears in Burke only this one time, it alludes to a set of concepts that are compactly present in his thought, that may be employed to help make sense of politics and of his writings in general, and that, when developed, yield especially important and useful insights into the sources of political order. Burke never develops a detailed philosophical explication of his approach in one place; this is partly because, once he entered Parliament, his concern was much more for matters of practical politics than for speculative philosophy. The philosophical tools and language available to him were also different from those available today, and this may also have contributed to his difficulty in fully articulating his relatively novel perspective. However, the existence of this important and sophisticated, if somewhat compactly held, philosophical framework is readily apparent from an examination of the body of Burke's writings.

In the particular context of the above reference to the moral imagination, Burke is defending traditional elements of society—customs, manners, ritualized behaviors, common beliefs, symbols, and so forth—which some would "explode" as "ridiculous" and "antiquated."[19] These elements are for Burke necessary to the maintenance of civilized society. This is because they serve as reference points that constitute a kind of framework of meaning that underpins morality and order. The manner in which this underpinning occurs is complex, and will be explored throughout this book. To start, it may be observed that the source of any particular political or social order is found, to a significant degree, in the hearts and minds of the individuals who make up that society. Societies work (or fail to work) in particular ways because their members tend to think in certain ways. That is, they tend to frame questions in particular ways and tend to be inclined toward particular inferences, conclusions, and ultimately, actions. These inclinations are partly culture-specific. The difficulties that often arise from attempts to duplicate a particular political system and legal structure in a context that is culturally different from the original, such as failed attempts to export Western European or American democracy to emerging third-world states, attest to the importance of these learned inclinations. For a stable and liberal state to work, people need to possess worldviews and habits that promote the kinds of behaviors that make it possible for such a state to work in the context of the particular physical conditions and other circumstances at hand. One commentator on Burke's speeches, Stephen Browne, finds that "for Burke, the question of order is very much a matter of public virtue."[20]

Related to Burke's concern regarding character is his emphasis on prudence. A great many commentators have remarked on Burke's emphasis on prudence in place of any particular conceptual formulas for politics. Most have viewed it favorably, but some have seen it as a weakness. In his introduction to a collection of Burke's letters, Harvey Mansfield complains that Burke emphasizes "a moral prudence. . . . But he does not say how to be sure of the morality of prudence."[21] While Mansfield may seem to be making a good point, it is important to step back and ask how one is "to be sure of the morality" of anything. What if Burke had instead emphasized liberty, or equality; how would we be sure of the morality of liberty or equality? How would we be sure even of the precise meaning of "liberty" or "equality," in various specific circumstances? How, in fact, can we be sure of anything? Many people have been "sure" that the sun revolved around the Earth, or that bloodletting would cure disease, or that the abolition of private capital would lead to a workers' paradise. There is always a problem of certainty of knowledge. The problem of moral certainty—which is in some ways a special case of the problem of certainty of knowledge—is perhaps especially acute. Consequently, there is always a problem of knowing the right thing to do. We are groping along in partial darkness.

What distinguishes Burke is not that he is unaware of this problem of knowledge but that he is so keenly aware of it, and that he approaches it with a relatively sophisticated moral and epistemological outlook. He knows that the adoption of certain political ideals or formulae such as the "rights of man" does not solve the basic problem of how to do the right thing. This does not mean that, in the proper contexts, formulae and ideals of various types cannot be helpful. But, they are not self-executing, and they are only partial expressions of complex truths. Likewise the adoption of particular political structures or rules will not necessarily yield good government, although such structures or rules may play an important role in promoting sound politics by interacting with other social and cultural elements in a desirable manner. Burke's call for prudence is not meant to be understood as a simple formula that one can quickly adopt for automatic success. The development of prudence is a problem of both morality and knowledge—or wisdom—which takes time and effort to address. It is in part a function of the character, or thinking patterns, or inclinations, of a people; this is why Burke demonstrates so much concern for cultural elements and their role in shaping a citizenry.

For example, for Burke the "most important," and most dangerous, aspect of the French Revolution is its "revolution in sentiments, manners, and moral opinions."[22] It is this cultural revolution, not the political revolution per se, that threatens to send Western civilization on a downward spiral into chaos from which it may lack the resources to recover. In the most extreme case, what is at risk is nothing less than our humanity. We need "the superadded ideas" because they are "necessary to cover the defects of our naked, shivering nature, and to raise it to dignity in our own estimation." They make us who we are. And for Burke, our ability to perceive reality, and consequently, our ability to act ethically and effectively, is a function of who we are. Who we are, in turn, is in part a function of the kind of imagination we possess.

A good example of how the imagination shapes our actions is provided by the idea, or complex of ideas, of chivalry. In Burke's time many historians and philosophers, especially those of the Scottish Enlightenment, took interest in the historical phenomenon of chivalry and credited it with helping to bring about modern Western society, which they generally considered to be less brutal and tyrannical than the societies of the East.[23] With its philosophically problematic yet effective mix of Christian principles and warriors' code of honor, chivalry promoted self-restraint, loyalty, protection of the weak and of noncombatants, gallantry towards women, and a host of other good manners and actions. It encouraged people to act in certain ways because it taught people to see themselves and those around them in certain ways. That is, it helped to shape their perception of reality, and it provided motivations for them to act in an upstanding manner. They rose to the occasion, so to speak, or at least they often tried to. By providing a particular imaginative framework chivalry helped to underpin morality and to promote desirable social and political behavior. In so doing it helped Europe become less barbaric. Of course, as Burke himself remarked, by his day the age of chivalry was gone. However, chivalry had evolved into the concept of a gentleman. Burke famously gives credit jointly to the "spirit of a gentleman and the spirit of religion" for "our civilization, and all the good things which are connected with manners and with civilization . . . in this European world of ours."[24]

In Burke's time many gave commerce much of the credit for the civilizing of Europe, but Burke changes the formula.[25] He argues that

> If, as I suspect, modern letters owe more than they are always willing to own to ancient manners, so do other interests which we value full as much as they are worth. Even commerce and trade and manufacture, the gods of our economical politicians, are themselves perhaps but creatures, are themselves but effects which, as first causes, we choose to worship. They . . . may decay with their natural protecting principles.[26]

Commercial activity is a function of the underlying culture and its imaginative frameworks. The "natural protecting principles" of a healthy commercial society are the various "sentiments, manners, and moral opinions" that are in place. Today we are familiar with discussions of cultural factors that influence the development of economics and politics in a particular country or region.[27] We cannot be fruitfully engaged in comparative politics or economics without becoming acutely aware of the fundamental role played by the "sentiments, manners, and moral opinions" of a people. Burke knew that the economics and, especially, the politics of a nation rested upon such elements, and that public policy must take this into account.

In his passage on the moral imagination Burke refers to its elements as ideas "which the heart owns." We can become strongly attached to certain ways of thinking about things, and these attachments can be powerful drivers of behavior. In his *English History* he remarks upon the role that customs and traditions have played in traditional societies: "if people, so barbarous as the Germans, have not laws, they have yet customs, that serve in their room; and these customs operate amongst them better than laws, because they become sort of nature both to the governours and the governed. This circumstance in some measures removed all fear of the abuse of authority."[28] As will be seen, such early sociological observations will still be animating Burke's politics many decades later. Burke clearly places great emphasis on the fact that customs are internalized in such a way that they become a natural part of one's character and operate as an internal constraint on behavior. In this particular instance they deter the abuse of authority. Interestingly, Burke biographer Conor Cruise O'Brien (who does not discuss the *English History*) finds opposition to the "abuse of power" to be the key overriding theme in Burke.[29] What O'Brien fails to recognize fully is the importance that Burke places on custom and the like in constraining such abuse. For, even in a society like Britain with a highly developed political and legal system, Burke considered such extralegal elements to be of prime importance. The very liberties that the British enjoy are for him dependent upon tradition and upon other moral-imaginative elements that act to constrain and direct the behavior of both the governors and the governed.

Burkean Prejudice

Burke speaks at one point of man's "nature as modified by his habits."[30] The second nature that the old Germans gain from custom, and which helps constrain and otherwise influences their behavior, is closely related to what Burke refers to elsewhere as "prejudice." It will be recalled that when discussing the conversion of England to Christianity he speaks of the need to ensure "that the prejudices of the people might not be too rudely shocked." Depending upon the specific usage, a particular "prejudice" can be seen as either a function of a particular moral imagination or as a label for one of the elements that constitute the "wardrobe of a moral imagination." In either case, a close relationship exists between "prejudice" and the idea of a moral imagination. It should perhaps be made clear at this point that the moral imagination is by no means made up exclusively of old prejudices, or of traditional ideas and customs that have been handed down; it is shaped by other influences as well, including contemporary politics, literature, and the arts, and indeed, all life experience. Because Burke provides more extensive explicit discussion of prejudice than of the moral imagination, his treatment of prejudice offers important clues to his political, ethical, and epistemological thought. It also leads back to a more direct discussion of "Burkean conservatism."

In championing "prejudice" Burke is deliberately staking out a controversial and provocative position. Although in his day the term did not carry connotations of racial or ethnic bigotry, it was still usually understood to be a negative term. "Prejudice" refers, of course, to a "pre-judgment," which implies a decision made unthinkingly, without full and careful employment of one's reason and knowledge in assessing all of the available information. Besides being an MP, Burke had spent some time in law school, and he probably would have most frequently encountered the term in its legalistic usage, which is particularly negative. At any rate, in going out of his way to mount a defense of prejudice Burke is prompting his readers to radically reshape their thinking.

Burke's most famous discussion of prejudice occurs in the *Reflections*. He informs the reader that, unlike the French *philosophes* and Jacobins, and those who take after them, the British (really, most of the British) have the good sense to cherish old prejudices. The passage begins with a sentence quoted earlier:

> We are afraid to put men to live and trade each on his own private stock of reason, because we suspect that this stock in each man is small, and that the individuals would do better to avail themselves of the general bank and capital of nations and ages. Many of our men of speculation, instead of exploding general prejudices, employ their sagacity to discover the latent wisdom which prevails in them. If they find what they seek, and they seldom fail, they think it more wise to continue the prejudice, with the reason involved, than to cast away the coat of prejudice and to leave nothing but the naked reason; because prejudice, with its reason, has a motive to give action to that reason, and an affection which will give it permanence. Prejudice is of ready application in

an emergency; it previously engages the mind in a steady course of wisdom and virtue and does not leave the man hesitating in the moment of decision skeptical, puzzled, and unresolved. Prejudice renders a man's virtue his habit, and not a series of unconnected acts. Through just prejudice, his duty becomes a part of his nature.[31]

In this important passage Burke makes a number of different observations about prejudice that should be identified and distinguished from one another. First, Burke says that prejudice incorporates within itself the wisdom of the ages. This is his most familiar argument regarding the benefits of prejudice, the value of tradition, and the limits of individuals' reason. Because life is so complex it is unlikely that innovative schemes or approaches will be successful; one is therefore better off sticking with the tried and true. The old ways have proved themselves over time and are therefore worthy of respect. Consequently, old prejudices should be maintained.

Because this line of argument regarding prejudice is most clearly articulated by Burke, and because it is relatively easy to understand, it is sometimes taken to be the sole rationale behind Burke's evident conservatism. This can lead to an understanding of Burke's traditionalism as a sort of proto-Darwinian theory in which various practices arise at random over time, those that work survive and are duplicated, while those that do not work well disappear. Under some versions of this model, human reason essentially vanishes as a force for creating good in the world, and humanity is seen as the passive victim of historical forces beyond its control. Leo Strauss comes to adopt a perspective on Burke that is along these lines. Picking up on Burke's tendency to disparage "reason," Strauss concludes that "the sound political order for him, in the last analysis, is the unintended outcome of accidental causation."[32] This is a wholly inadequate characterization of Burke's position. A full refutation of Strauss's view requires an explication of Burke's understanding of the sources of "the sound political order," which cannot be made briefly; in fact, it requires this entire book. But for now it can be pointed out that, far from arguing on behalf of "accidental causation," Burke in fact makes a point of bringing up the qualities of the "true lawgiver," explaining that he "ought to have a heart full of sensibility. He ought to love and respect his kind, and to fear himself. It may be allowed to his temperament to catch his ultimate object with an intuitive glance, but his movements toward it ought to be deliberate."[33]

The "ultimate object" and "deliberate movements" favorably referenced by Burke would seem to contrast sharply with a supposed belief in the merits of the "unintended outcome of accidental causation." Burke's views on reason and its application in politics and morals will be unpacked over the course of this study, but for now one can state in simple terms that his real disagreement is not with those who advocate the use of "reason" per se, but with those who disregard the fact that more than instrumental reason is involved in good judgment. He argues that in contrast to the self-styled "philosophers" or "metaphysicians" of his own time, "the legislators who framed the ancient republics knew that their business was too arduous to be accomplished with no better apparatus than the metaphysics of an undergraduate, and the mathematics and arithmetic of an exciseman."[34]

Since the "metaphysics of an undergraduate" cannot serve as an adequate basis for the establishment and maintenance of a sound political order, what can? Part of the answer to this question is suggested by the remainder of Burke's brief passage on prejudice. Returning to this passage, we learn that reason should not be disengaged from prejudice because prejudice "has a motive to give action to that reason, and an affection which will give it permanence." That is, it is not enough for one to decide through one's rational faculties that a particular course of action is appropriate or desirable. One must also have the motivation, or the *will,* actually to do what one thinks is right. As many who have attempted diet or exercise regimens will attest, one must train one's will if one is to carry out a desired plan. It should be noted that Burke rarely discusses the will, and then usually in negative terms; reflecting the common language of lingering natural law rationalism he tends to refer to the will when discussing arbitrary action, just as "willful" is sometimes used today as a synonym for "capricious." Nevertheless, an awareness of the key role of the will is central to his thought, even if much of this awareness is rather compact and is not systematically articulated. As will be shown, some commentators on Burke have in fact pointed out his emphasis on will. For Burke, prejudice, when desirable, represents in part a tendency toward the right kind of *willing.* As the result of various inclinations that have become second nature, one "naturally"—or, one could say, unreflectively—wants to do the right thing.

Once again Burke makes a case in favor of prejudice and tradition and in opposition to a heavy reliance upon abstract reasoning and radical innovation. It is very important to note, however, that he never claims that prejudice necessarily embodies greater wisdom than "reason" or deliberate reflective thought. It is certainly possible that one might rationally formulate a new way of doing things that is better than the accustomed methods. If the subject at hand is, say, a manufacturing process, effective implementation of the new scheme may be relatively easy. But in many situations, including most cases of human interaction, a conscious rational plan alone is unlikely to result in desirable behavior, since it is difficult for "reason" alone to muster the necessary motivation to ensure that the right kind of behavior actually occurs. One must have an "affection" toward that behavior in order for rational decisions to be carried out in a proper manner. Prejudice represents this predisposition toward a particular kind of behavior. Or, one might say, prejudice helps to bring one's will into conformity with one's reason.

A related observation that Burke makes in the above passage is that prejudice "is of ready application in an emergency." One can act quickly because, in a sense, one already knows what to do; one does not have to think much because certain responses and behaviors come almost automatically. Because prejudice "previously engages the mind in a steady course of wisdom and virtue," we become equipped to respond appropriately to various circumstances; we are not lost in unfamiliar territory, struggling to determine how best to apply abstract concepts to concrete situations. We develop the kind of internal resources necessary to act with confidence. Perhaps more important, Burke finds that "prejudice renders a man's virtue his habit, and not a series of unconnected acts. Through just prejudice, his duty becomes a part of his nature." Prejudice provides a kind of framework that links together the events of one's life and lends meaning to them. Because of prejudice we do not engage in "random acts of kindness" but develop consistent patterns of behavior, preferably of a virtuous type. We internalize a particular morality. This morality does not simply take the form of a general, abstract desire to do good, or a general feeling of benevolence toward humankind. It is the kind of morality that is expressed in concrete actions that, ideally, actually yield moral results. It is, likewise, the kind of morality that is expressed in the form of restraint from taking harmful action. This role for prejudice can be seen as essentially the same kind of shaping of the will to which Burke alludes when he says that prejudice lends an "affection" that gives a kind of "permanence" that reason alone does not provide. Thus prejudice for Burke plays an important part in what is often referred to today as "moral education" and "political education"; it is how we learn right (or wrong) behaviors, and it guides our judgment. It also helps constitute the horizon that provides meaning and supports political and social order.

Burke's interest in prejudice did not begin late in his career with the *Reflections;* it appeared very early and was a constant throughout his life. In an extremely informal letter to a friend, a 16-year-old Burke wrote:

What multitudes of things conspire to deceive, and Blindfold a Person in the pursuit of truth! He imbibes prejudice with his milk those he converses with impose on him, his Parents, and the very Books he reads . . . all join to hoodwink his reason and make him see with his eyes not his own, but above all himself he has in that respect no greater Enemy than his own person, how fond are we of our own opinions of our own reasonings, purely because they are ours. . . . How often do we invent false reasonings and Arguments to uphold em, and who to deceive but ourselves.[35]

Here Burke is attacking prejudice rather than defending it. The teenage Burke's remarks are much more reflective of the conventional Western view of prejudice than his later views would be; still, they foreshadow his later understanding of prejudice, reason, and more broadly, human thought and action. The young Burke makes the common complaint that prejudice serves as a barrier to truth and to the proper working of reason. We absorb various opinions and ways of thinking, often without reflection; once they become ours, we become attached to them and are very reluctant to relinquish them. Instead, then, of using our reason to find truth, we end up employing reason—or "false reasonings"—to justify opinions and understandings that we have already acquired through nonrational means, and that might not withstand impartial rational scrutiny. Burke here sees reason as being placed at the service of the irrational.

If the young Burke is correct about the dangers of prejudice, why does he later jump to prejudice's defense in the *Reflections?* If one considers only the *Reflections,* one might be tempted to attribute the shift simply to a difference in attitude between a youth and an older man. However, Burke was only 28 when he wrote in the *English History* of the wisdom of sparing the prejudices of the ancient pagans from rude shocks. Burke's youthful interest in prejudice and in its relationship to reason actually lays the groundwork for his later political-philosophical perspective. At age 16 he has already decided that we come to many of our opinions in some manner other than the simple use of reason. Indeed, he has observed that we seem just to absorb many of our views without much reflection. Eleven years later he writes that "it is by imitation far more than by precept that we learn every thing; and what we learn thus we acquire not only more effectually, but more pleasantly. This forms our manners, our opinions, our lives."[36] The bulk of our knowledge and our opinions are not acquired through deliberate tutelage or through conscious rational effort, but through a natural process of observation and imitation.

As a youth Burke focuses on the negative side of such nonrational learning, and speaks of how it encumbers reason. However, he also sees that we absorb such prejudices from everywhere, not only from our parents but from our very books. How, therefore, can prejudice be avoided? What Burke comes to realize later is that the absorption of prejudices simply cannot be prevented. Indeed—and this is critically important—he realizes that there is something fundamentally wrong with the manner in which "reason" and "prejudice" are typically contrasted. Implied in this contrast is a belief that judgments can be made on the basis of "reason" devoid of content, or that judgment may be employed on the basis of a very narrow set of specified content and does not incorporate the range of knowledge, opinions, and perspectives we have absorbed over the course of our lives. For example, in attempting to decide which of two automobiles to purchase, one may make a list of the costs and attributes of each in order to ensure a rational decision. But it is impossible to make the decision simply on the basis of the information listed. All sorts of background knowledge must come into play if one is to evaluate, prioritize, and, in fact, give real meaning to the enumerated data. (Most of this knowledge has nothing directly to do with technical aspects of automobiles, but is general life knowledge and an array of unspoken assumptions associated with it.) Indeed, all sorts of background knowledge come into play when one is framing the question about which car to purchase and creating the list of relevant data in the first place.

The contemporary philosopher Michael Oakeshott criticizes typical "conceptions of 'reason' or 'rational conduct'" that involve "the supposition that a man's mind can be separated from its contents and its activities. What needs to be assumed is the mind as a neutral instrument, as a piece of apparatus."[37] Likewise, Burke appears to recognize that we must always operate within some sort of framework, some way of understanding the world. And he seems to believe that for most purposes there is no really meaningful distinction between prejudice and other forms of knowledge. Burke may again be compared to Oakeshott, who criticizes the mistaken "rational" viewpoint that "childhood is, unfortunately, a period during which, from the lack of a trained mind, we give admittance to a whole miscellany of beliefs, dispositions, knowledge not in the form of propositions; the first business of the adult is to disencumber his mental apparatus of these prejudices."[38] This view is mistaken because it reflects a belief that one's mind has an existence independent of all of this material, which Oakeshott argues is not the case.

As will become increasingly evident, for Burke those who claim to operate free of prejudices are deluding themselves. They may have rejected certain ways of looking at things, but out of necessity they have adopted others, and their judgment will be shaped by those perspectives. Indeed, they may simply be following new prejudices that they fail to recognize as such. Oakeshott's view again parallels that of Burke:

> The doctrinaire in politics is not a man, the spring of whose activity is independent propositional knowledge about an end to be pursued, but a man who fails to recognize what the true spring is. Usually he is a man who, having rejected as worthless the current knowledge of how to behave in politics, falls back upon his knowledge of how to behave in other activities (which is not always a good guide) while erroneously supposing that he has fallen back upon knowledge independent of any activity and provided by some potentially infallible "intelligence."[39]

This is one reason why Burke comes to defend old prejudices so passionately against those who claim to discard them in the name of "reason." Such persons may not actually be following reason at all, but an idiosyncratic selfish will and various prejudices and scraps of knowledge—perhaps of a dubious sort—that align with that will. The old prejudices, in Burke's view, can serve as an antidote to this sort of willfulness; they are more likely to provide sound guidance to reason than any new perspectives, which falsely claim to be free of prejudice.

Preserving Humanity

In one of his last works Burke offered a portrait of the kind of person who rejects old prejudices and the traditional elements associated with a moral imagination. Although this well-known passage, discussing revolutionary ideological political thinkers and actors, is somewhat lengthy, it is very important and is worth quoting:

> Nothing can be conceived more hard than the heart of a thorough-bred metaphysician. It comes nearer to the cold malignity of a wicked spirit than to the frailty and passion of a man. It is like that of the Principle of Evil himself, incorporeal, pure, unmixed, dephlegmated, defecated evil. It is no easy operation to eradicate humanity from the human breast. What Shakespeare

calls the "compunctious visitings of Nature" will sometimes knock at their hearts, and protest against their murderous speculations. But they have a means of compounding with their nature. Their humanity is not dissolved; they only give it a long prorogation. They are ready to declare that they do not think two thousand years too long a period for the good that they pursue. It is remarkable, that they never see any way to their projected good but by the road of some evil. Their imagination is not fatigued, with the contemplation of human suffering thro' the wild waste of centuries added to centuries of misery and desolation. Their humanity is at their horizon,—and, like the horizon, it always flies before them. The geometricians and the chemists bring, the one from the dry bones of their diagrams, and the other from the soot of their furnaces, dispositions that make them worse than indifferent about those feelings and habitudes which are the supports of the moral world. Ambition is come upon them suddenly; they are intoxicated with it, and it has rendered them fearless of the danger which may from thence arise to others or to themselves. These philosophers, consider men in their experiments, no more than they do mice in an air pump, or in a recipient of mephitick gas.[40]

This portrait of what we can call a "monster metaphysician" has obvious relevance to the various totalitarian, revolutionary ideological political movements of the twentieth and twenty-first centuries. Indeed, the burst of new interest in Burke in mid-twentieth-century America might be attributed in part to this passage's new resonance in a world wracked by communism and fascism. Some more recent commentators have in fact disparaged the mid-century American conservatives' Burke as the "Cold War Burke," although any usefulness that Burke's writings may have had in supporting anticommunist containment strategies is highly unlikely to have constituted more than a very minor part of his appeal.[41] Burke's real significance is by no means so shallow. In observing the early stages of the French Revolution Burke became one of the first thinkers to grasp the uniquely modern phenomenon of such movements, before terms such as "ideological" and "totalitarian" came into use to describe them, and long before there was talk of a "modern crisis" or "existential crisis" that might support such phenomena.

It should perhaps be noted that Burke's use of the term "metaphysician" is sometimes misunderstood today to indicate a condemnation of philosophers or practitioners of metaphysics. This is of course not the case. In the England of Burke's time, especially in parliamentary debate, it was not unusual to see the terms "metaphysician" and "metaphysics" used in a manner similar to Burke's here. They referred to a particularly narrow and simplistic sort of abstractly based political thinking that Burke finds to be characteristic of the French *philosophes* and their English equivalents, not to true philosophy or metaphysics in the hands of sophisticated practitioners. In fact, Burke states that "they might learn from the catechism of metaphysics."[42] The sarcastic usage of "metaphysician" was partly the result of the lack of another readily available term. A substitute (but not completely synonymous) term, "ideologue," would not appear (first in French) until shortly after the *Reflections* was written. In a development that would not have surprised Burke, "ideology" was coined by French *philosophes* to refer to a new science of ideas, which would supposedly provide sound reason-based guidance for society, but within just a few years it became evident that the proponents of "ideology" had no new science or superior rationality at all, but simply their own biases and political agenda. Consequently the words "ideology," "ideological," and other forms quickly took on their contemporary, often disparaging meanings.[43]

In the extreme case that Burke describes above, the "metaphysician" is, much like Plato's tyrant, a kind of slave to a "master passion," in this case his ambition and his ideology, which is both a source of his ambition and a vehicle for it. Unbalanced, he has essentially lost his humanity and, as a consequence, has become an embodiment of evil. He is capable of doing tremendous harm in the name of some highly dubious hypothetical future good. In common parlance, we might say that such a person has "lost it." What has he lost? Again in common parlance, we might say that he has "lost his grip on reality" and that he needs to "get real."

The key function of the elements that make up the "wardrobe of a moral imagination" is to keep us anchored in reality. We do not, of course, perceive reality with our eyes and ears; these provide only raw sensory data, which our minds must interpret. In effect, we must build up a sense of reality for ourselves imaginatively.[44] Our "perception" of reality is, in a sense, our construction of the reality within which we function. We create a coherent, meaningful whole from the sensory data we receive. The kinds of touchstones, or moral anchors, that we possess can profoundly influence that imaginative construction. They help us make sense of things; they give meaning. Significantly, the metaphysicians, it will be recalled, are "worse than indifferent about those feelings and habitudes which are the supports of the moral world." In rejecting traditional moral and cultural frameworks and reference points, they lose the touchstones needed to provide that anchor in reality. Meanings have gone away. People, in fact, have ceased to be people; they are "mice in an air-pump"—objects subject to experimentation and manipulation, or tools for the monster metaphysician's use in pursuit of some greater end. For Burke our own humanity, and our perception of the humanity of others, is dependent upon a sound moral imagination.

Michael Oakeshott has observed that the absence of tradition is filled with ideology.[45] Reflecting on Burke's remarks we can observe that reason cannot function in a vacuum; it must have a conception of reality within which, or upon which, to operate. Something has to fill the void left by the loss of traditional touchstones, and adherence to an ideology becomes a convenient substitute way of providing an ordered reality. Whether or not the "metaphysician" adopts an established ideology, Burke maintains that he is a slave to ambition. Linked to his ambition is a deformed reality. One's understanding of reality is, in some ways, an individual's own creation. This is true of the metaphysician's reality, and it is also true of an understanding of reality built up with the aid of a more traditional "wardrobe of a moral imagination." However, in the latter case the dominant role played by traditional cultural elements contributes to a strong sense of an existing order in which the individual has but a humble place. Much about morality, about human beings, and about how the world works, is taken as a given. Of course, excessive traditionalism or excessive prejudice runs the risk of blocking the consideration of needed changes; we may take things as given that could in fact be made better. However, while much attention is given to this concern in the contemporary era, much less attention is given to the fact that a radical rejection of one's cultural inheritance poses an even greater danger.

A reality ordered without respect for traditional elements is one in which the individual can essentially assume the place of God. Since there are no longer believed to be a great many "givens" that largely define one's conception of reality, the individual becomes the unbounded creator of his own reality. In the situation Burke describes, no established points of reference exist to check the "metaphysician's" ambition, or to correct the corresponding distorted picture of the world that he holds. The metaphysician may, for example, come to believe that the imposition of a particular regime type or set of laws specified in the ideological vision may be all that is needed to yield a radical transformation of human life, and set about brutally stamping out those dissenters who are seen to constitute the only barriers to the realization of an earthly paradise. In contrast, one who is steeped in traditional sources of order and meaning may, first, have absorbed a more subtle and sophisticated—even if more compact—understanding of human nature and society from those sources, and, second, may have a greater sense of the difficulty of bringing about dramatic changes in the human condition. Information about reality available from his "wardrobe" of moral touchstones may help prevent his ambitions from spiraling out of control.

The actions of the "thorough-bred metaphysician" described by Burke are deficient on both an ethical and a practical level. Ethically, the metaphysician suffers from unchecked ambition and does not see other people as fully human. Consequently he inflicts tremendous harm on individuals and society. His schemes, however, usually do not even accomplish good results through bad means; they are usually ineffective in producing good results. This is partly because, in rejecting the "wardrobe of a moral imagination" in favor of what he believes to be superior abstract conceptual knowledge, the metaphysician actually moves to a less accurate, and more incomplete, understanding of reality. As was shown above, when writing favorably on prejudice Burke clearly indicates that he considers it to be, among other things, a form of knowledge. This type of nonrational or nonconceptual knowledge is seen by Burke as extremely important; it may be supplemented by abstract conceptual knowledge, but not replaced by it.

A roughly similar contrast between two sorts of knowledge has been discussed by numerous contemporary philosophical writers, including Oakeshott. Oakeshott applies the labels "technical" and "practical" to two basic categories of knowledge. Technical knowledge consists of "formulated rules which are, or may be, deliberately learned," while practical knowledge "exists only in use, is not reflective and . . . cannot be formulated into rules." Practical knowledge is a form of "traditional knowledge" and "the mastery of any skill, the pursuit of any concrete activity is impossible without it."[46] While Burke's "prejudice" is not precisely identical with Oakeshott's "practical knowledge," a close affinity is evident between the two concepts. Oakeshott associates "technical knowledge" with a "preoccupation with certainty," and he states that "rationalism" recognizes only this technical knowledge.[47] When Burke attacks "philosophers" and "metaphysicians" with their "naked reason," he is fighting this same rationalism, which ignores the vital role played by intuitive, internalized traditional knowledge.

Just as Oakeshott identifies two basic kinds of knowledge, he identifies two forms of moral life. One takes the form of "habit of affection and behaviour" and is unreflective in nature. The other takes the form of "the reflective application of a moral criterion"; this can appear as either the "observance of rules" or the "pursuit of ideals." For Oakeshott, while the second form of moral life can be very helpful in keeping individuals and societies on track, it is the first form of moral life that is a necessity. Moral rules and ideals are not sufficient, because their application to real-world situations is not automatic. Without proper "habit of affection and behaviour" one lacks the guidance necessary to make the rules and ideals work. And, unlike rules and ideals, "custom is always adaptable and susceptible to the *nuance* of the situation."[48] As Burke's discourse on prejudice shows, he, like Oakeshott, knows that one who lacks the right sort of unreflective predispositions is unlikely to be a moral actor. Prejudice, broadly understood, helps constitute character. Good prejudices make for good character, and without reasonably sound character the best ideals, rules, and abstract concepts have little value. In fact, they may lead to horrific results.

Oakeshott's observations that there are two forms of knowledge and two forms of moral life point toward an important element in Burke's thinking on prejudice and on the moral imagination. Prejudice is an important form of knowledge, but it represents more than knowledge. As was indicated earlier, it also represents a particular kind of willing. In Burke's terminology, prejudice supplies "motive." We are inclined in a particular direction. Similarly, the elements that make up the wardrobe of a moral imagination shape not just one's knowledge and one's reason but also one's will. While they play a vital cognitive role in helping supply an understanding of reality, they are also, as Burke says, ideas "which the heart owns," and they influence how we act through this affection. For example, chivalry and the idea of a gentleman do not just help provide a framework for developing an understanding of the world and of one's place in it. The appeal of such ideas and of the self-image they foster also provides encouragement to behave in certain ways that are consonant with those understandings of the world.

The "thorough-bred metaphysicians" who reject "those feelings and habitudes which are the supports of the moral world" suffer impairments in both reason and will. Their reason is defective because it is trying to function without the kind of imaginative framework and touchstones necessary to maintain an anchor in reality. Their will is defective due to a loss of proper standards to constrain behavior, and due to the loss of incentives and inclinations to adhere to those standards. Consequently, "ambition," or the will, runs rampant, unchecked. Burke does not make clear in this passage to what extent a warped perception of the world contributes to out-of-control ambition, and to what extent the metaphysicians' ambition contributes to their warped perception of the world, as they discard old prejudices in favor of their preferred models. Presumably, the metaphysicians' unchecked wills and deformed imaginations feed off each other in a vicious circle, making their understandings of reality more and more distorted. In the particular case described by Burke, one result is that the metaphysicians not only rationalize away any moral objections to their actions, but fail to perceive fully the dangers that their actions may pose to themselves or to others. They turn a blind eye to that which they do not wish to see.

The moral imagination is of fundamental importance in combating unchecked willfulness and arbitrariness, or, to use Burke's usual term, caprice. Consequently, it is of fundamental importance in promoting the kind of behavior that makes possible the stable and largely liberal political society to which Britain had become accustomed. Burke's conservatism, then, can be seen primarily as a desire to conserve a moral imagination in the citizenry and leadership of Britain, its colonies, and European society as a whole. This is not identical with simple political conservatism as it is usually understood, but it does have some relationship to it, since old prejudices, customs, traditions, ideas, and so on must, to a degree, be preserved in order to maintain a sense of a moral order. As will be shown, Burke does not see a moral imagination as simply the product of traditional elements, and a politics that reflects a concern for the moral imagination is not necessarily a conservative politics in the usual sense. Sometimes the preservation and fostering of a proper moral imagination may require changes—perhaps quite radical changes—in public policy. It is, still, critically important to Burke to conserve and to foster the cultural bases of sound moral and political norms. Otherwise, an unanchored imagination is likely to drift farther and farther from reality. Decades before writing about metaphysicians, Burke remarked in the *Sublime and Beautiful* that "when men have suffered their imaginations to be long affected with any idea, it so wholly engrosses them as to shut out by degrees almost every other, and to break down every partition of the mind which would confine it."[49] Once again we are reminded of Plato's tyrant, slave to a controlling master passion. It is easy to see Burke's ideological "thorough-bred metaphysicians" as examples of this condition.

Since Burke sees that old prejudices can be both good and bad, and does not assume a strictly conservative position politically, an important question is raised. How does one determine whether an old prejudice, or practice, or custom, or idea, or symbol, is desirable or not? This question is akin to Mansfield's question about how one can be "sure of the morality of prudence." Burke appears to recognize that one can never really be "sure" of anything; the simplistic quest for absolute certainty, and the belief that one has acquired it, is part of the metaphysicians' error of hubris. Burke's response to this epistemological problem is not one of radical skepticism but of humility, of caution, and of great care and concern regarding how people think. For him, actions that are moral and exhibit the proper kind of prudence require actors who are reasonably moral and prudent. No simple, self-applying formulas exist that can make one sure of anything. One has to develop into the right sort of person, which is a complex and muddy process.

People with good moral and practical judgment are, generally speaking, people with a well-developed moral imagination. Such a moral imagination is largely a product of the various cultural elements to which one is exposed. Decisions regarding whether to embrace or combat particular old prejudices, customs, ideas, and such are themselves matters of judgment, which people may be more or less equipped to make effectively. How well one is equipped to make such judgments is in part a function of one's moral imagination, and one's moral imagination is influenced by the elements to which one exposes oneself. Therefore a somewhat circular relationship exists, in that past judgments about how we live our lives influence our ability to make good judgments in the future. As will be seen, Burke is well aware of this circularity and of the potential for a downward spiral. In the case of the French Revolution he fears that in destroying, rejecting, and perverting the elements that support a moral imagination, the nation may have lost its capacity to recover. He contrasts the present situation in France with turbulent times of the past from which France recovered quickly: "Why? Because among all their massacres they had not slain the *mind* of their country. A conscious dignity, a noble pride, a generous sense of glory and emulation was not extinguished. . . . All the prizes of honor and virtue, all the rewards, all the distinctions remained. But your present confusion, like a palsy, has attacked the fountain of life itself."[50] Indeed, although France would ultimately regain stability, in the short term a downward spiral would in fact occur, as the Revolution became the Terror, to be resolved via the dictatorship of Napoleon.

Burke's politics of the moral imagination is at heart a fight against caprice or arbitrariness, and a fight for the kind of political morality and personal ethics necessary to sustain a stable, humane, and perhaps, liberal political order. As has been hinted, Burke's politics can be grounded in a sophisticated and insightful understanding of human cognition, ethics, and society. This understanding, and the politics that flows from it, will be explored in greater detail in the succeeding chapters. This exploration will begin with some attention to Burke's aesthetics, which is intimately tied to his moral, epistemological, and political thought.

2 Aesthetics, Ethics, and Politics

IN A BOOK ADDRESSING QUESTIONS of political and moral thought a discussion of aesthetics may seem to some a digression. Others know that aesthetics, ethics, and politics are intimately related. Burke's sense of the inseparability of these aspects of human experience is evident from the body of his work. Today, it is quite commonplace for postmodern thinkers to emphasize the importance of language, narratives, and art. Burke's understanding of their social and moral significance, though more compact, may be in some ways more insightful and useful than that of many contemporary thinkers, despite the fact that he operated without the benefit of a large, established body of philosophic thought in this area.

Burke's explicit aesthetic theory, set down in *A Philosophical Enquiry into the Origin of Our Ideas of the Sublime and Beautiful,* provides important insights into his thinking about the workings of human knowledge, judgment, and ethics; this thinking in turn shapes his political and social thought. Indeed, it can be argued that study of the *Enquiry* is critical to developing a good understanding of Burke. For one thing, with the possible exception of *A Vindication of Natural Society,* a satire on the works of Bolingbroke that attempts to repudiate his rationalism and "natural religion," the *Enquiry* is Burke's only explicitly philosophical work. Although even this work cannot be considered to be philosophically rigorous, it is Burke's only non-satirical work laid out in the form of a philosophical treatise, and it is about the only place in which Burke turns from political, rhetorical, and historical writing and openly explores philosophical questions from a relatively disinterested, scholarly standpoint. Despite its aesthetic focus, the *Enquiry's* explicit treatment of philosophical questions offers important insights into the thinking behind Burke's more philosophically compact political writings and speeches. Because it is a very early work, his thought is not fully developed in the *Enquiry* on the various themes addressed in this study; one cannot simply pick it up and find his mature epistemological and ethical views explicitly expounded. However, clearly evident in the work are certain directions of his thought, as well as certain philosophical concepts and areas of interest, which will help provide a grounding for his approach to morality and politics.

Burke's aesthetic thought is also a good place to begin because this is essentially where Burke himself began. The first edition of the *Enquiry* was published in 1757. While it was not Burke's first published work, it is widely believed to be the work he started on first, when he was a student at Trinity College in Dublin in the late 1740s. Literary matters were the young Burke's great love, and he had a keen interest in aesthetics and in rhetoric. Sent by his father to law school in England, Burke enjoyed the historical aspects of law but soon gave up on his studies to pursue a career as a writer. His later movement into political service appears to have been sparked at least in part by the fact that, for one without independent means, writing was hardly a practical career; this was especially true for Burke once he had a wife and child to support. For a while he attempted to pursue his government and writing careers simultaneously, but this caused frustration for both Burke and his employers. He soon gave up on nonpolitical writing, with the exception of paid writing and editorial work for the *Annual Register,* which he continued for several more years.

Burke's first publishing venture actually came very early, in his days at Trinity College, when with several friends he launched *The Reformer,* a citywide weekly devoted primarily to matters concerning the Dublin theater. This venture lasted several months, and the publication appears to have been popular, at least initially. The premier issue, 28 January 1748, addresses the question of why the periodical is devoted to the arts, rather than to weightier matters. It is explained to the reader that "the Morals of a Nation have so great Dependance [*sic*] on their Taste and Writings, that the fixing the latter, seems the first and surest Method of establishing the former."[1] From a young age Burke considered the realm of aesthetics to be intimately linked with that of morality and politics, and this nexus is a vital dimension of his perspective on the world.

A Philosophical Enquiry into the Origin of our Ideas of the Sublime and Beautiful is sometimes seen as the "odd man out" among Burke's major works, because its subject matter seems on the surface to be so different from his typical fare of political, social, and historical material. In Burke's own day, however, this was probably the work that most established his reputation as a man of letters. The work was very widely read at the time it first appeared and for at least a century thereafter. It was highly influential in Britain, especially with the emerging Romantic movement.[2] It was translated into French and made a mark on the Continent as well, including with the young Kant, who then published his own work on the subject.[3] While the *Enquiry's* fame and direct influence may have peaked in the eighteenth century, it never passed into obscurity; Tolstoy, for example, read and commented on it in 1895,[4] and it has remained a work of significant interest to literary scholars to the present day. However, traditionally, many of those who write on Burke from a political-philosophical perspective have ignored the *Enquiry*, openly dismissed it, or at best, seized upon one or two brief passages that are best described as asides not directly addressing the aesthetic problems at hand. Among those who do address the *Enquiry*, no consensus exists regarding the relationship of Burke's aesthetics to his political and ethical thought.

The *Enquiry* tends to become problematic and to suffer under close analysis because, as has been mentioned, it is really not an especially rigorous or highly systematic philosophical work, although it was well regarded in its day. Burke's *Enquiry* takes up a subject that had become very popular in British thought since the early eighteenth century, most famously with the works of Shaftesbury (from 1711), Joseph Addison (from 1712), and Francis Hutcheson (from 1725).[5] As was common at the time, Burke rarely identifies his sources, but he certainly possessed some familiarity with this thought. In fact, Burke had read a great deal of philosophical material of all sorts, ranging from works of the ancients to the most recent books available, and various competing influences are evident in the work. Besides the appearance of some of the same phases and terms that were utilized by the above predecessors, a number of elements in the *Enquiry* reflect the influence of Locke, some reflect Berkeley, and some reflect Hume and, more broadly, Scottish Enlightenment thought, which was then current. For example, Burke begins with a discussion of various basic human "passions," a common approach in his day. It is a mistake, however, to seize upon a particular phrase or familiar approach that is evident in the *Enquiry* and jump to the conclusion that Burke has simply adopted the complete philosophical framework of a particular thinker or school. Typically the influences are rather superficial and have not shaped Burke's thought in a wholesale way. In fact, the influences sometimes seem to contribute to confusion, not just on the part of the reader but on the part of the young Burke himself, since he sometimes adopts language or approaches he has seen elsewhere even when his own thoughts seem to be pulling him in a somewhat different direction. Often, it is evident that he is struggling with the material; he struggles partly because he feels strongly about the subject matter and recognizes its depth and complexity, and does not want to produce a pedantic work. The relatively unique nature of much of his thought, which does not closely align with that of any single established thinker, also makes the work somewhat challenging, to Burke and to us.

At any rate, a study of the *Enquiry* conducted as if it were in fact highly rigorous or highly systematic is likely to end either in frustration or in mischaracterizations of Burke's thought. Instead, a more productive approach may be to focus on those elements in the essay that Burke himself seems to regard as most important, and, in particular, on those elements of most interest to us in addressing problems of political modernity. There are three main treatments in the *Enquiry:* of the sublime, of the beautiful, and, in an introductory essay added in 1759, of taste. In each of these discussions Burke appears to be motivated by a desire to make certain key points, and it is these points that will be addressed here.

Burke on Beauty

The *Enquiry* reflected emerging trends in aesthetics that may be broadly grouped under the term "romantic," even though this label would not emerge until later. Indeed, given its known influence on writers and artists, Burke's essay may have helped to accelerate those trends; it has certainly earned him a reputation as one of the early articulators of romanticism. This is somewhat paradoxical; Harold Laski maintains that "no man was more deeply hostile to the early politics of the romantic movement . . . than was Burke; yet, on the whole, it is with the romantics that Burke's fundamental influence remains."[6] In applying the term "romantic" to Burke, care should be taken to recognize that this term has various meanings, and that romanticism exists to varying degrees and in varying forms. Here the term is used in a rather general sense, and Burke is seen as romantic largely to the extent to which he departs from classical aesthetics as they are typically understood. His romanticism is very important, however. Burke shows great concern for the affective dimension of the beautiful and the sublime. He sets up a sharp contrast—perhaps too sharp a contrast—between an experience of the beautiful and an experience of the sublime, relating those experiences to human passions. In the case of beauty, Burke explains that it is that quality in bodies "by which they cause love, or some passion similar to it."[7]

Burke's treatment of the beautiful is generally viewed as less controversial and less interesting than his treatment of the sublime. Nevertheless, it is noteworthy. Burke engages in a rather lengthy, sometimes problematic, and sometimes almost embarrassingly amateurish discussion of beauty and the qualities we associate with it; nevertheless the point that he most emphasizes is a very important one. This is that beauty is *not* "at all an idea belonging to proportion."[8] This rejection of proportion, along with similar rejections of "fitness" and "perfection" as other determinants of beauty, represents a direct repudiation of the standard classical and neoclassical views that dominated academic treatments of beauty in Burke's time. Burke had been steeped in classical writings, including those on aesthetics and including those of Aristotle; he was very respectful of those writings, and this apparent break is not something he would have made lightly. This is just one of the elements of Burke's thought that makes him classifiable as a romantic.

In the case of proportion, Burke explains that the problem is that "proportion relates almost wholly to convenience, as every idea of order seems to do; and it must therefore be considered as a creature of the understanding, rather than a primary cause acting on the senses and imagination."[9] Aesthetic experience has an immediacy to which Burke is very sensitive. Here Burke anticipates contemporary aesthetics.[10] Proportion is associated by him with "the measure of relative quantity,"[11] which is a matter for our reason, and we need not bring our reason to bear when deciding whether an object is beautiful. Instead, "the senses and imagination" are directly engaged without the intervention of reason. Leo Strauss maintains that the "most important thesis" of the *Sublime and Beautiful* is this refusal "to understand visible or sensible beauty in the light of intellectual beauty."[12]

For Francis Canavan, one of the most important mid-twentieth-century Burke scholars and a leader of the "natural law school" of Burke interpretation, which emerged in that period, Burke's rejection of proportion as the key criterion of beauty is tantamount to an exclusion of order from his aesthetic theory. Therefore, in Canavan's view, Burke's aesthetic theory cannot be tied to his political thought. This is the case because his general philosophical perspective, Canavan argues, fits rather neatly into the natural law tradition. In its most common form this tradition emphasizes God's reason, the resulting order in the world, and the ability of humans to know that order through the exercise of their own reason. Because Burke appears to reject any emphasis on order and reason in the appreciation of beauty, Canavan concludes that "it is doubtful that Burke's epistemology, as it appears in his early writings, was compatible with the metaphysic implied in his moral and political theory."[13] Unlike his aesthetics, "Burke's presuppositions about the nature of the universe and the moral law were intellectualist in quality, because he took for granted a metaphysical order intelligible to the human mind."[14] Burke does in fact take for granted a metaphysical order we can, to a degree, perceive, but one may question Canavan's assumption that his moral-political outlook is therefore "intellectualist" and that it contrasts sharply with his aesthetics. In support of his position, he cites Burke's own statement about the limits to the applicability of "the idea of beauty" to virtue. Burke states that we must not "remove the science of our duties from their proper basis (our reason, our relations, and our necessities,) [*sic*] to rest it upon foundations altogether visionary and unsubstantial."[15] Here, however, Burke's concern is with refuting those thinkers like Hutcheson whose systems implied that traditional, theocentric foundations of ethics could be replaced by one grounded in nothing but the aesthetic appeal of virtue.[16] This does not imply the absence of any relationships between Burke's aesthetics and his ethical and political thought. The actual connections are more subtle and sophisticated than this.

Burke's rejection of classical and neoclassical approaches to beauty is significant from our perspective. It was also highly controversial in Burke's day.[17] There are two basic thrusts to Burke's rejection of such approaches as a theory of proportion, and both of these thrusts are connected to Burke's politics. First, he argues that our experience gives us empirical evidence that proportion does not work as a formula for beauty, at least not in a particularly useful way. We may, for example, attempt to determine through exhaustive measurement the many different proportions that make a horse beautiful, but these will not be the proportions that make a dog beautiful. Burke's basic observation here of the inadequacy of an abstract theoretical formulation in the face of the complexity of reality may be compared to his later rejection of any emphasis on simplistic "metaphysical" schemes as a means of addressing subtle and complex political and moral issues. Second, Burke's rejection of proportion is based on his view, already mentioned, that the assessment of proportion has an intellectual quality, while beauty has an immediacy that affects us directly, without the intervention of our reason.

Burke's downplaying of the role of "reason" or "understanding" in aesthetics may be compared to his famous (or, to some, infamous) later disparagement of "reason" in politics. Strauss picks up on this connection. He finds that Burke's treatment of beauty represents "a certain emancipation of sentiment and instinct from reason, or a certain depreciation of reason. It is this novel attitude toward reason that accounts for the nonclassical overtones in Burke's remarks on the difference between theory and practice" and for his opposition to "rationalism."[18] Although the general thrust of Strauss's statement is, in some ways, correct, taken more precisely it is quite incorrect and requires important qualifications. For one thing, Burke's attitude toward reason, though certainly unique on a sophisticated level, is not entirely novel in the basic way that Strauss implies. An emphasis on sentiment, as opposed to reason, was very much in the air; for example, it appears in the works of David Hume and would very soon be evident in those of Adam Smith. Much more important, Strauss's reference to "instinct" is highly problematic. Burke is decidedly not a champion of "instinct," if one uses this term in the precise sense of designating innate, as opposed to learned, behaviors; this subject will be addressed shortly. Most important, what Burke is ultimately trying to achieve is not a simple "emancipation of sentiment . . . from reason." Burke does not seek to emancipate sentiment; he is thinking about both sentiment and reason in new ways, which render the idea of "emancipating" sentiment moot. Strauss thinks about "reason" and "sentiment" in ways very different from Burke, and a failure to grasp the precise differences severely compromises Strauss's analysis. He is certainly correct that there are "nonclassical overtones" present, but Burke is not a simple romantic either. His actual approach is more complex and requires further discussion and explication.

Taste and Judgment

In 1759, two years after the *Enquiry* came out, Burke published a revised edition. While there were numerous minor changes and additions, he did not significantly alter any of the positions he took throughout his study. However, one major change was the addition of an "Essay on Taste" as a preface to the work. Burke's motivation to add this preface may have stemmed in part from his acquaintance with Hume's 1757 essay *Of the Standard of Taste.*[19] He does not make reference to Hume, however, and, to the extent that Burke's essay may be seen as a response, it is less a direct attack on Hume's essay than an attempt to provide a clearer discussion of a subject that is sometimes handled by Hume in a confused and imprecise manner. It is possible that Burke may also have wished to respond to another piece, *Letters concerning Taste,* which was published in 1755 by John Gilbert Cooper.[20] Burke's primary motivation for the addition, however, may actually not have been a desire to respond to any particular work, but simply an interest in further developing and clarifying his own views on aesthetics.

In the new preface Burke observes that "there is rather less difference upon matters of Taste among mankind, than upon most of those which depend upon the naked reason."[21] Already a contrast with Hume is evident, since Hume instead emphasizes the "great variety in taste" among individuals, which he suggests is much greater than the variety of opinion regarding matters of "science."[22] Significantly, Burke's directly opposing suggestion that the exercise of taste yields more uniform results than the exercise of reason could be seen as an implicit challenge to the typical Enlightenment assumption (and, indeed, the broadly Western assumption) that "reason" yields truth in the form of "objective" scientific results while taste and feeling are subjective and do not really point toward truth, or do so in a manner much inferior to reason.

At any rate, it must be noted that Burke does not attribute similarity in taste to the fact that taste is a more "instinctive" or "natural" faculty than reason. In fact, a primary thrust of Burke's essay on taste is an explicit *rejection* of the view that taste is a "species of instinct by which we are struck naturally" or that it is "a separate faculty of the mind, as distinct from the judgment and imagination."[23] Here Burke is certainly much clearer than Hume, who fails to address this question directly but tends to speak of taste as if it were indeed a separate faculty, and who maintains that "many and frequent are the defects in the internal organs which prevent or weaken the influence of those general principles on which depends our sentiment of beauty or deformity."[24]

Burke's characterization of taste as essentially a matter of judgment and imagination is very important. Taste is a preference for one thing or another based largely upon whether that thing pleases us aesthetically. This preference is primarily not intellectual in nature. In most cases, it is essentially an immediate response, uncolored by much conscious consideration. Yet Burke explains that differences in taste generally "proceed from differences in knowledge." Taste involves a form of knowledge that is held and employed without the use of conscious reasoning. For him "the cause of a wrong Taste is a defect of judgment. And this may arise from a natural weakness of understanding . . . or, which is much more commonly the case, it may arise from a want of a proper and well-directed exercise, which alone can make it strong and ready."[25] Therefore, although Burke's discussion of beauty and of the sublime is to a great degree devoted to the rejection of an "intellectualist" approach to aesthetic response, he devotes his preface on taste to what might appear to be a contradictory project, the connection of aesthetic response to judgment and to knowledge.

For Burke, taste is primarily nonrational (or, at least, nonintellectualist) in nature but is nevertheless something we can cultivate and develop. We learn to like, to appreciate, to respond positively on an aesthetic level to some things, and to respond negatively to others. Burke maintains:

> It is known that the Taste (whatever it is) is improved exactly as we improve our judgment, by extending our knowledge, by a steady attention to our object, and by frequent exercise. They who have not taken these methods, if their Taste decides quickly, it is always uncertainly; and their quickness is owing to their presumption and rashness, and not to any sudden irradiation that in a moment dispels all darkness from their minds. But they who have cultivated that species of knowledge which makes the object of Taste, by degrees and habitually attain not only a soundness, but a readiness of judgment, as men do by the same methods on all other occasions.[26]

Taste is portrayed as virtually indistinguishable in operation from other forms of judgment. If one's taste has not been properly developed, a sudden or unreflective decision of taste will simply be a rash and uncertain one. For those who have developed their taste properly, however, good decisions come readily. Burke indicates that taste is to a great degree the product of experience, and of knowledge derived from both experience and study; that is, it is largely based upon our social, historical existence in human civilization. It is not a form of instinct that will provide the benefit of any "sudden irradiation" without cultivation. This discussion of taste brings to mind Burke's later treatment of political and moral judgment. In particular, it bears some similarity to his discussion of prejudice decades later. As discussed in the previous chapter, Burke finds that prejudice "does not leave the man hesitating in the moment of decision skeptical, puzzled, and unresolved."[27] The cultivation of what Burke calls "just prejudice," and its role in good moral and political judgment, would seem to parallel closely the cultivation of good taste, and the role of this cultivation in aesthetic judgment.

Burke and Hume are actually in agreement that practice and study are important in developing good taste. Hume, however, does not seem to have quite the same sense of why it is important as does Burke. As has been mentioned, Hume attributes poor taste to "defects in . . . internal organs," but he never specifies what these organs are, how they work, or the precise nature of the defects. When he speaks of the benefits of practice, what he seems to have in mind is the fact that one cannot give a proper critique of a fine work of art if one has not devoted proper study to that particular form of art, so that one can analyze the "relation of the parts," compare the work in question to noteworthy examples, and so forth.[28] While Burke's essay is not really in sharp disagreement with Hume's here, Burke's discussion of taste has a much less intellectualistic and elitist coloring, and addresses the subject more comprehensively. Rather than contrasting the cultivated tastes of an elite with the unsophisticated tastes of the masses, Burke explains how *all* taste works. Taste is *always* shaped by knowledge and practice, because taste is always a matter of judgment and imagination.

It should be made clear that an important point emerges from the pulling together of Burke's discussions of beauty and of taste. When discussing beauty, Burke argued that an aesthetic response is generally immediate and is uncolored by much rational thought. Indeed, we are told that the determination of beauty does not result from the application of formulas. When Burke turns to taste, he holds that aesthetic response is a function of judgment and imagination, and that it can essentially be equated with other forms of judgment, and developed in the same way. The conclusion one may draw is that judgment is itself often, and perhaps usually, not "intellectualist" in quality, and that judgment and "sentiment" are not distinctly different things. The feelings we get about things are expressions of intuitive judgments, and our ability to make good judgments—whether expressed through sentiment or through rational deliberation—is a function of much more than an ability to apply formulas.

Burke appears to remove any sharp categorical distinction between aesthetic response, or at least, decision-making tied to aesthetic response, and other forms of judgment. This may be seen as one repudiation of the "Enlightenment project," which, among other things, sharpened distinctions between morality and aesthetics.[29] For Burke, our responses to political and moral situations are akin to our aesthetic responses to beauty or ugliness. This should not be misunderstood to mean that Burke agrees with writers like Hutcheson who find that morality may simply be grounded in the appeal of its beauty. What it means is that, for Burke, both in aesthetic matters and in political and moral situations, a big part of our response occurs on a nonrational level, with "nonrational" understood to mean that we are not consciously thinking things through.

As will be demonstrated more fully in the next chapter, Burke believes that we can assess a political or moral situation intuitively, just as we can intuitively sense whether something is beautiful. Such an assessment, or judgment, may be nonintellectual in character, and may be expressed in the form of "sentiment." In the case of aesthetic taste, it is clear that for Burke judgment and knowledge are involved even if "reason" or the "intellect," narrowly conceived as conscious rational thought, may not be operative. Judgment and knowledge are at work on an intuitive, unarticulated, or subconscious level, but this fact in no way diminishes the importance of learning and experience in developing good taste. Through proper cultivation, the right responses can become a kind of second nature to us, even in those cases in which our responses are experienced in the form of sentiment. Strauss, in emphasizing the "nonclassical" main point of Burke's discussion of beauty, misses the main point of Burke's discussion of taste. For, as will be recalled, Strauss speaks of Burke's aesthetics involving the "emancipation of sentiment and instinct from reason." Burke, however, goes out of his way to argue explicitly that even though taste involves sentiment, it is *not* a "species of instinct." The operation of sentiment need not imply some sort of animal instinct. Taste is in fact developed in the same manner as other forms of judgment. The "depreciation of reason" that Strauss sees beginning in the *Enquiry* and continuing through Burke's political writings does not constitute a dismissal of judgment, and of course does not constitute a belief that knowledge, study, and practice are somehow unimportant. Rather, it represents a broader and deeper understanding on Burke's part of how people think and make decisions, emphasizing the unarticulated or intuitive (but not "instinctive") dimensions of judgment, or of "reason" broadly conceived.

It was observed that while Canavan is in basic agreement with Strauss regarding Burke's aesthetics, he sharply disagrees with Strauss's interpretation of Burke's politics and ethics. For Strauss, Burke's aesthetic thought dovetails with his approach to morality and politics; for Canavan, the epistemology implied in Burke's aesthetic thought contradicts the metaphysic implied in his moral and political thought. This perspective represents subtle but significant misreadings both of Burke's aesthetics and of his moral-political thought. In the case of Burke's aesthetics, Canavan concludes that reason has little or no place in Burke's aesthetic thought, a conclusion that disregards Burke's association of taste with judgment and knowledge. On the political and moral side, Canavan concludes that Burke falls within the natural law tradition. For Strauss, while much of Burke's thought does have a vague relationship to the natural law tradition, philosophically Burke ends up negating that tradition, perhaps without realizing it, because his political arguments ultimately point toward a rejection of reason. Canavan does not see such a rejection of reason in Burke's political thought, and, since he places Burke within the natural law tradition, he concludes that Burke's political thought must be "intellectualist" in nature and in sharp contradiction to his nonintellectualist aesthetics. Canavan is correct to reject Strauss's interpretation of Burke. But it is difficult to see how Burke's political writings, with their disparagement of "naked reason" and of "metaphysics," can be viewed as particularly "intellectualist" in character. So, in these interpretations, both Burke's political writings and his aesthetic writings are forced into philosophical categories (in the case of Canavan, polar opposite categories) that are based on extrapolations from elements present in his thought but that do not precisely capture his overall outlook.

Canavan's and Strauss's interpretations of Burke reflect a common characteristic of much of the secondary literature. Generally, it is presumed that belief in a moral order that humans can to some degree perceive must be linked to an emphasis on the power of human "reason," with the term "reason" usually narrowly understood in a particular "intellectualist" way. Because Burke seems *both* to recognize a moral order (at least, at times) *and* to disparage reason (at least, at times), he presents a problem for interpreters in this tradition. Consequently, either sharp tensions and contradictions are found within his thought, or philosophical unity is achieved by dismissing or downplaying much that Burke has to say. In contrast, sympathetic attention to Burke's discussion of taste, and to its relationship to his views on other matters of judgment, points toward another understanding of his thought. This is a perspective in which people can develop some understanding of reality, and in which the quality of that understanding can improve or decline as a result of learning, practice, and social influences, but in which that understanding may not be fully subject to articulation, and is not limited to the realm of conscious rational thought.

It is noteworthy that while Burke began his original *Enquiry* with a discussion of passions and emotions, he turned in a more epistemological direction when he added the preface on taste. After a few introductory paragraphs, he launches his discussion of taste by stating that "all the natural powers in man, which I know, that are conversant about external objects, are the Senses; the Imagination; and the Judgment."[30] Taste, Burke would conclude, "is partly made up of a perception of the primary pleasures of sense, of the secondary pleasures of the imagination, and of the conclusions of the reasoning faculty."[31] He describes each of these three components in turn. By "the senses," Burke at first seems to mean not just raw sensory data but perception itself, or the ideas formed using sensory data. This is somewhat problematic, but it does not significantly undermine his discussion. Burke views the senses as operating in a roughly similar manner in all people, although habit is a factor in determining how we respond to them. He then turns to the imagination by explaining that "besides the ideas, with their annexed pains and pleasures, which are presented by the sense; the mind of man possesses a sort of creative power of its own." He adds that "the imagination is the most extensive province of pleasure and pain, as it is the region of our fears and our hopes, and of all our passions that are connected with them."[32] Burke's emphasis on the imagination and its creative power again shows us the "romantic" Burke, in that he departs from the classical tradition, still dominant, which typically either ignored the imagination or emphasized its mimetic rather than its creative quality. Thomas Hobbes stated that "*Imagination* and *Memory*, are but one thing."[33] Such views remained the norm up to Burke's own day. For example, while Burke very likely draws the "pleasures of the imagination" phrase from Addison, in Addison's usage "imagination" remains something akin to memory.[34]

Burke explains that the imagination works by reproducing and reorganizing material originally presented by the senses.[35] Because the imagination is based on sensory material, Burke initially maintains that "there must be just as close an agreement in the imaginations as in the senses of men."[36] Although he first claims that the functioning of the imagination is basically the same in everyone, he then qualifies this claim with the statement that people have similar imaginations "as far as their knowledge of the things represented or compared extends." Burke seems to be indicating that because our experiences differ we build up different knowledge bases from which our imaginations can draw. As a result of such differences in knowledge our imaginations do in fact differ, and lead to differences in taste. To the extent that tastes tend to be broadly similar, this is partly attributable to the extent that our experiences tend to be broadly similar. Citing Locke, Burke explains that the great power of the imagination lies largely in finding resemblances, in contrast to judgment, which is chiefly concerned with finding differences. It is the finding of similarities and connections that most pleases us, and these similarities are found in reference to the material we have to draw upon. Because of the important role played by knowledge, our responses to the things we encounter will be impacted by the past experiences, which provide the fuel for our imaginations. According to Burke, "the mind of man has naturally a far greater alacrity and satisfaction in tracing resemblances than in searching for differences; because by making resemblances we produce *new images,* we unite, we create, we enlarge our stock; but in making distinctions we offer no food at all to the imagination." While in the main part of the *Enquiry* Burke discusses the appeal of novelty, here he goes on to suggest that we have a particularly strong affinity for things that are different from those we already know but that also connect powerfully with those images and ideas that our imaginations already have available. He adds that "it is upon this principle [of the imagination finding and delighting in resemblances], that the most ignorant and barbarous nations have frequently excelled in similitudes, comparisons, metaphors, and allegories, who have been weak and backward in distinguishing and sorting their ideas."[37] This may be taken as an indication that for Burke the imagination plays a powerful role in our grasp of reality, including, presumably, moral reality. Even if we are incapable of formulating and articulating certain ideas in an explicit conceptual way, we can still make use of those ideas, or their underlying truths, intuitively through the aid of the imagination.

Burke devotes more space to the imagination than to any other single topic in his preface on taste. He lays out a broad role for it, sometimes using "wit" as a synonym. His references to the creative power of the imagination and to the making of "new images" through "making resemblances" suggest that Burke sees in the imagination a complex interplay at work between new sensory data and the knowledge built up from past experience. This interplay not only helps determine our response to the new information, but builds up our imaginative base for future use. Much of his discussion is confusing, however. While we get the strong impression that Burke views the imagination as very powerful and very important, his precise understanding of its role and its workings is never made entirely clear. Burke may not in fact have a precise understanding, since his ground seems to be continually shifting throughout the preface on taste and the *Enquiry* in general. It should be remembered that Burke was still a fairly young man when even the revised *Enquiry* was published, and that he was trying to work through his ideas and respond to a wide variety of conflicting philosophical influences.

Burke states quite plainly that judgment is, along with imagination and the senses, one of the aspects of taste, or one of the faculties that make up taste. However, Burke also equates judgment with taste. More precisely, he identifies taste as the special case of "judgment in the arts."[38] If "judgment" is a more general name for taste, and if "judgment" is one component of taste, the seemingly illogical implication is that "judgment" is just one component of "judgment." Similarly, as was observed early in this examination of Burke's views on taste, he concludes that "the Taste . . . is improved exactly as we improve our judgment, by extending our knowledge, by a steady attention to our object, and by frequent exercise." In his earlier treatment of the three faculties making up taste, however, he refers only to "attention" and "exercise" in connection with judgment; "knowledge" is discussed in connection with the imagination. "Judgment" clearly has at least two different meanings in this essay, which can be labeled "judgment (1)" and "judgment (2)." Judgment (1), or a narrow conception of judgment, is a simple faculty that interacts with the imagination and is a component of taste. Since at one point early in his discussion on taste Burke referred to its components not as the senses, imagination, and judgment, but as senses, imagination, and "the reasoning faculty," it appears that judgment (1) is a synonym for "the reasoning faculty," or instrumental reason narrowly understood. There is also judgment (2), or a broader conception of judgment, of which we are told that taste is one form. Judgment (2), or judgment broadly conceived, is a complex faculty that is made up of several components, one of which is the senses, one of which is the imagination, and one of which is "the reasoning faculty" (or judgment (1)). When we sort through the muddle, the important idea that emerges from Burke's struggle is that human judgment broadly understood—or, one could say, cognition—involves the interplay of reason and the imagination.

Burke's confusion and lack of consistency in terminology confirms the general observation made at the beginning of this chapter, which is that the *Enquiry* does not hold up well under close philosophical scrutiny. At the same time, there is a depth and originality in Burke's thought that contributes to the muddle. More conventional and prosaic thinkers would have found it easier to express themselves with clarity and consistency, but at the outset of the preface on taste Burke indicates that he is not going to worry about establishing precise definitions,

> for when we define, we seem in danger of circumscribing nature within the bounds of our own notions, which we often take up by hazard, or embrace on trust, or form out of a limited and partial consideration of the object before us, instead of extending our ideas to take in all that nature comprehends, according to her manner of combining. We are limited in our enquiry by the strict laws to which we have submitted at our setting out. . . . A definition may be very exact, and yet go but a very little way towards informing us of the

nature of the thing defined.[39]

This passage says a lot about Burke's approach to philosophical matters in general, and ties closely to the contempt he would later express for those who would solve profound and complex questions with neat little formulas derived from "the metaphysics of an undergraduate." In the specific context of the *Enquiry* Burke's remarks suggest that the imprecise and somewhat inconsistent nature of the work is not the result of incompetence but of a deliberate attempt to maintain the maximum possible openness toward the subject matter. Burke does not want his thinking to become trapped in a particular philosophical box that would end up distorting or oversimplifying his analysis through a false precision or coherence.

It can be argued that Burke's reluctance to lock himself into a rigid philosophical framework springs in part from his recognition that there is no well-established school of thought available that will properly convey his ideas. By traditional standards Burke's thought appears to be pulled in several different directions. There are both "classical" and "romantic" sides to Burke, if those terms are applied in a broad and general way. As has been observed here, he is a romantic in that he emphasizes powerful roles for the imagination and for human emotions and passions, and rejects highly intellectualistic models. Burke, however, took a very dim view of Rousseau—who would later come to be one of the chief figures associated with romanticism. Burke also emphatically rejected some of the tendencies that would come to be associated with romanticism—tendencies to exalt instinct, or innate unreflective qualities, or an expansive, capricious will, at the expense of self-restraint and the benefits of civilization. Burke was steeped in classical writers and he took to heart the classical emphasis on such concepts as virtue, prudence, and the cultivation of a well-ordered soul in the context of civilized social life. He absorbed the classical belief that reason must be the dominant element in one's psyche, although his conception of "reason" grew in depth and complexity beyond typical formulations. He also conceived of humanity and society in a generally teleological manner. Some of the confusion and apparent contradiction in the *Enquiry* arises from the tension between these strongly classical and strongly romantic elements in Burke's perspective. What Burke is really trying to do can be characterized in part as a kind of synthesis of romantic and classical strains of thought that contains elements of both but is really something new. While he does not quite possess the resources to develop or explicate fully this synthesis in philosophic terms, ultimately he does succeed on a more compact level. That is, Burke does develop an effective and sophisticated, if diffuse and unfinished, philosophical framework, which informs and is communicated by the body of his work.

As has been noted, connections between Burke's aesthetic thought and his moral and political thought are always controversial. The contemporary biographer Lock has been critical of efforts to link aspects of the *Enquiry* to aspects of the *Reflections on the Revolution in France*. He is certainly correct to criticize those who connect these two writings in simplistic ways that are not informed by Burke's many other works. But, some of Lock's objections are puzzling and highly problematic. He complains that, while the essay on taste in Burke's *Enquiry* devotes much attention to the imagination, "the *Reflections* is addressed primarily to the understanding or judgment, only secondarily to the imagination."[40] Here Lock misses (or implicitly rejects) the fact, explicated above, that for Burke the imagination is a key component of judgment. To emphasize the separateness of the two, Lock maintains that Burke expresses in the essay the "commonplace" view that "Imagination may be strongest early in life; judgment matures with age and experience."[41] The problem is that Burke does not say this. Burke's actual statement is that "sensations" are strongest in the young, not "imagination."[42] Lock appears to be determined to attribute to Burke "commonplace" views that Burke does not possess. Similarly, Lock maintains that Burke was "writing in a rhetorical tradition which accorded primacy to the rational appeal," and that "for Burke, as for Aristotle" emotional appeals had a distinct secondary role.[43] He does not consider the possibility that Burke may be informed by a different way of thinking about the "rational" and "emotional," as well as a different conception of the imagination and its role, than the "commonplace" views; hence he misses much of Burke's significance.

The Sublime

The sublime has been left for last in this discussion, even though it is the subject that Burke treats first. In the *Enquiry* Burke's discussion of the sublime precedes his discussion of the beautiful, and it was of course written before the essay on taste, which would be added later as a preface. Of the subjects discussed in the *Enquiry* the sublime is clearly the one that most captures Burke's imagination, and it is the one that receives the most attention from scholars. Burke's consideration of the sublime highlights aspects of his aesthetic thought that are only hinted at in his treatment of the beautiful and of taste, but which have significant bearing on his politics. Central to Burke's approach to the sublime is his identification of terror as its "ruling principle." This is contrasted in the *Enquiry* with beauty's core passion, love. While there was a history of writing on the "sublime and beautiful" going back to Shaftesbury, Burke's sharp cleavage of aesthetic experience into these two highly distinct categories, his emphasis on the importance of the sublime, and his emphasis on "terror" all constituted significant departures from other eighteenth-century English aesthetics.

For Burke the terrible "is a source of the sublime; that is, it is productive of the strongest emotion which the mind is capable of feeling." He explains that danger and pain, "at certain distances, and with certain modifications . . . are delightful."[44] Consequently, he finds that, for example, large, ferocious animals, powerful people, and other things that strike fear in us can be sublime. This argument generated some ridicule when the *Enquiry* was published, but when Burke issued the second edition he did not take advantage of the opportunity to modify or qualify it. Instead, he beefed it up and made a point of defiantly reiterating his commitment to all the controversial positions he took throughout the work.

Burke essentially treats the sublime and the beautiful as opposites; an experience of the sublime is for him dramatically different from one of the beautiful. The sublime evokes particularly powerful and unique emotional responses, which are a key to its appeal:

> The passion caused by the great and sublime in *nature,* when those causes operate most powerfully, is Astonishment; and astonishment is that state of the soul, in which all its motions are suspended, with some degree of horror. In this case the mind is so entirely filled with its object, that it cannot entertain any other, nor by consequence reason on that object which employs it. Hence arises the great power of the sublime, that far from being produced by them, it anticipates our reasonings, and hurries us on by an irresistible force. Astonishment, as I have said, is the effect of the sublime in its highest degree; the inferior effects are admiration, reverence and respect.[45]

In extreme cases, at least, one's reasoning is suspended when one is under the influence of the sublime; one is powerfully compelled on a subrational or super-rational level. This description of the sublime and its effects bears some resemblance to Nietzsche's concept of the "Dionysian." Nietzsche associates the "Dionysian" with the experience of certain types of art—especially, but not exclusively, tragedy and music—and explains that "so stirred, the individual forgets himself completely."[46] Burke's anticipation of Nietzsche is particularly evident when he speaks of the "acknowledged and powerful effect of instrumental music" versus that of clear imagery.[47] Nietzsche similarly contrasts the ecstatic and "Dionysian" element with what he calls the "Apollonian," representing visual imagery, symbols, order: "Apollo himself may be regarded as the marvelous divine image of the *principium individuationis*, whose looks and gestures radiate the full delight, wisdom, and beauty of 'illusion.'"[48] The "Apollonian" element brings with it not just beauty but reason and differentiation, but it lacks something present in the inarticulate "Dionysian" element, which connects with us powerfully and viscerally.

Of course, Burke's sublime should not be associated too closely with Nietzsche's "Dionysian"; Burke was certainly not Nietzsche. And Burke's contrast between the sublime and the beautiful is not identical with that between Nietzsche's "Dionysian" and "Apollonian." Similarities are evident, but Nietzsche's contrast is represented in Burke partly by the contrast between the sublime and beautiful, but to an even greater extent by the contrast evident in Burke between aesthetic experience in general and the mere workings of "the reasoning faculty," which excels in making distinctions but not in making connections, and which lacks the force or vitality of nonrational aesthetic experience. At any rate, the role of terror that Burke sees in the sublime is to a degree mirrored in Nietzsche's view that the "Dionysian" involves an embrace of all of life, including violence and death. According to one commentator, Nietzsche's "Dionysian" is identified "with knowledge . . . of the chaos and of the artifice of human life and importance," and it "sees through the illusion that provides form and definition of the culture."[49] Although Burke believes in an ordered universe and not in chaos, through a confrontation with what one might refer to as ultimate things Burke's sublime also helps one to see through "the artifice of human life and importance," and yields a new perspective on it.

An important part of Burke's treatment of the sublime is his extended discussion of "obscurity."[50] Burke maintains that to make a thing "terrible" in a way that is sublime, "obscurity seems in general to be necessary."[51] This obscurity may take different forms, such as darkness, blinding brightness, or poetic language. In part, obscurity helps to make things sublime because of our fear of the unknown. However, it is hard to see terror or danger at play in all of the examples Burke discusses. In fact, Burke suggests that "obscurity" contributes to almost any sort of emotional response. He finds that "in reality, a great clearness helps but little towards affecting the passions, as it is in some sort an enemy to all enthusiasms whatsoever."[52] It is in part because of its "obscurity" that Burke attributes great power to poetry, which is in his view usually more effective than simple prose or a clear visual image in evoking an emotional response; along these lines, he believes that dark temples, dark woods, and the like have a stronger effect on us than well-lit places and images.

One may make an argument that "obscurity" has a more powerful effect than clarity because it provides greater stimulation to the imagination. Clarity tends instead to stimulate one's reason, and this may have the effect of suppressing the imagination or reducing its role. Burke hints at such an argument in several places, such as when he discusses how poetic language may affect us, but he fails to develop it explicitly here. However, this line of thought is suggested by Burke's discussion of the imagination in the preface on taste, when he emphasizes the imagination's delight in finding resemblances, and its creation of new images in the process. Clarity would facilitate the judgment's finding of distinctions, and all of these distinctions would presumably dampen the finding of resemblances and the creation of connections. Obscurity would allow much more free play for the imagination to exercise its creative power, and, since for Burke the imagination offers an experiential immediacy and a connection to passions that reason lacks, the likely result is the evocation of strong personal responses.

The explicit argument that Burke does offer for the power of obscurity is at first blush rather surprising. He states that "there are reasons in nature why the obscure idea, when properly conveyed, should be more affecting than the clear. It is our ignorance of things that causes all our admiration, and chiefly excites our passions."[53] Burke's pairing of "ignorance" with "admiration" may seem a bit odd, but he is getting at the fact that we admire that which is, in some way, above or beyond us. To admire something is to look up to it, and it is difficult to look up to something that we fully understand, since if we fully understand something it is presumably on our level, at least in some sense. Burke's interest in "obscurity" is therefore closely tied to his less surprising identification of "vastness" and "infinity," or suggestions of infinity, as important sources of the sublime. A kind of humbling is associated with sublime experience, which gives us a new perspective on ourselves and on our lives. It may also be argued that what infinity and the sublime in general give us is a sense, not of chaos as in the case of Nietzsche, but of a greater order in which humanity participates. This order, being greater than humanity, is an order that humanity can only partly understand. Burke's sublime is therefore tied to an experience of mystery.

In discussing the role of obscurity in the sublime, Burke defends his position with this argument: "But let it be considered that hardly any thing can strike the mind with its greatness, which does not make some sort of approach towards infinity; which nothing can do whilst we are able to perceive its bounds; but to see an object distinctly, and to perceive its bounds, is one and the same thing."[54] Obscurity, then, is sublime in part because it suggests the infinite. As an example Burke cites an "amazingly sublime" passage in the book of Job, recounting a terrifying night vision in which an indiscernible form appears and a voice is heard saying "Shall mortal man be more just than God?"[55] No clear painting of this or any other vision, Burke argues, could approach the sublimity of the poetic text. Significantly, this example pulls together many of the different elements of the sublime that Burke discusses. One element is "obscurity" in the form of the text, the darkness, and the vision itself. Another is the experience of terror arising in part from this obscurity. Finally, there is the humbling sense of the awesome power and ultimate unfathomability of God, and of man's inadequacy in the face of it.

Burke ends the preceding passage on obscurity and infinity with the striking conclusion that "a clear idea is therefore another name for a little idea."[56] This remark may be taken in part as a case of youthful hyperbole. Burke's own political writings and speeches certainly contain many "clear ideas," and many of these ideas are by no means little. While his works are known for their rhetorical strength and poetic elements, he does not hesitate to muster impressive arrays of precise facts and figures where appropriate. Burke never seems to be out to confuse his listeners or readers, but to convey ideas to them as clearly as possible. At the same time, one may see great wisdom in Burke's observation; it can certainly be connected with his remark in the *Enquiry's* preface about precise definitions. It can also be seen as a foreshadowing of his later adamant denunciation of attempts to address complex moral and political questions with maxims and simplistic "metaphysical" formulas that barely scratch the surface of reality. If we think we can solve great problems with simple formulas, this means that we do not know enough even to realize how much we do not know. Ultimately, life is shrouded in mystery, and ideas about important questions must necessarily be complex and somewhat fuzzy, and will be difficult to formulate or express clearly. Our response to mystery need not, and should not, be a sense of futility, but must include a profound humility. Burke expresses some of this humility quite explicitly in the *Enquiry*. When he discusses the cause of the sublime and beautiful, he is careful to specify that he is enquiring into the efficient cause only, since "that great chain of causes, which linking one to another even to the throne of God himself, can never be unraveled by any industry of ours. When we go but one step beyond the immediately sensible qualities of things, we go out of our depth."[57] While this statement may have been influenced by Humean skepticism or Lockean empiricism, in Burke it conveys neither skepticism as it is found in Hume nor empiricism as it is found in Locke, but a strong sense of mystery.

The "humble" perspective on the world, which Burke associates with the sublime, is highlighted and given additional depth by his discussion of how and why power can be sublime. He uses the example of a horse, an animal with many useful qualities, which Burke briefly lists. To illustrate how such an animal may be sublime Burke turns again to the book of Job, this time to God's first speech recounting the greatness and mystery of His creation. The poetic portrayal there of the horse, "who swalloweth the ground in fierceness and rage,"[58] is in Burke's view highly sublime, and stands in sharp contrast to a portrayal of the useful aspects of a horse, which is not sublime at all. Burke explains that "whenever strength is only useful, and employed for our benefit or our pleasure, then it is never sublime; for nothing can act agreeably to us, that does not act in conformity to our will; but to act agreeably to our will, it must be subject to us; and therefore can never be the cause of a grand and commanding conception."[59] That which acts simply in conformity to our will, or that which is simply useful, cannot be sublime. This observation anticipates Heidegger's concept of *Zuhandenheit*—"to hand-ness" or "at hand-ness," or the quality of things fitting our existence well. These are things that are useful, and that, to the extent that they are given much thought at all, are thought of in terms of their usefulness. The problem with *Zuhandenheit* for Heidegger is that experiences that occur in this context, fully in conformity to one's will, do not raise the central problem of Being. As such they contribute to an inauthentic existence, which is characterized by an insignificance of everything, in contrast with an authentic existence, which is characterized by wonder and by appreciation of everything.[60] Wonder and appreciation—and, ultimately, meaning—are therefore linked to a sense not only of the limitations of human understanding, but of limitations to human will.

For Heidegger a key characteristic of the modern world is that "man sets up the world toward himself, and delivers Nature over to himself." Burke's contrast between the sublime horse of God's creation and the non-sublime, useful horse of our everyday thought likewise can be seen as reflecting a concern on Burke's part regarding the modern mentality and the dangers that can result from that mentality. Heidegger describes modern man as "the one who wills." In this modern context there is a great loss; a sort of closure occurs, and everything "turns irresistibly into material for self-assertive production. The earth and its atmosphere become raw material. Man becomes human material, which is disposed of with a view to proposed goals." This sort of willing, and this sort of relationship to the world, emerges in part in an excessive emphasis on science, and leads to the appearance of the "total state."[61]

Burke's interest in the sublime and his contrast of the sublime with the useful, therefore, can be seen to have a connection to his later visceral reaction to the "thorough-bred metaphysicians" who would treat human beings as "mice in an air-pump," as well as his strong aversion to "caprice" or uncontrolled willfulness in various forms. For Burke a particular response to the world, characterized by awe, openness, and a sense of humility, and seen aesthetically in the experience of the sublime, is a necessary element of political morality. The idea that power can be, and in fact usually is, sublime—as in the example of the horse—also has political implications. For Burke, this sense of the sublime, which tends to surround power and its trappings, should be exploited, not to impose a tyrannical state, but to make a liberal state possible by engendering the sort of respect for, and deference toward, political institutions that is necessary in order to have rule of law and political stability without oppression. More attention will be given to this topic later.

In recent years a number of scholars have drawn attention to Burke's use of the sublime; a particularly strong connection between Burke's aesthetic interest in the sublime and his political thought is made by Stephen K. White. White argues that what most animated Burke's rejection of the French Revolution, and his response to "political modernity" in general, was a concern regarding the emergence of a "false sublime." (This term, it should be noted, does not appear in Burke.) In the true, or classical, sublime, one experiences human limitedness in the face of the limitless. In contrast, in the false sublime, "human beings themselves now *produce* a sort of *human infinite* that displaces what had before stood for the infinite, or God, or fate."[62] Common examples of such a humanized sublime identified by White include romantic genius and the shocking work of an avant-garde artist. To demonstrate Burke's awareness of this phenomenon, White points out that Burke expresses some of his greatest horror and detestation not for the violent acts of the French revolutionaries but for the revolutionary festivals and vast spectacles they put on for the public.[63] This "false sublime," which "annihilates the confrontation with finitude,"[64] produces the opposite effect of the authentic sublime. While traditionally an experience of the sublime encourages humility, a sense of the new humanized sublime "allows the familiar vice of 'vanity' to cathect itself to the unlimited horizons of rational imagination." Traditional constraints are thrown off, and the human will is empowered "to embrace limitlessness itself."[65] Because people, individually or collectively, now embody the infinite, they see no limits, either moral or practical, on their ability to remake the world and each other.

White's "false sublime" can be seen in part as an aesthetic manifestation of the phenomenon that Eric Voegelin labeled "Gnosticism." Gnosticism involves a "divinization" of the state or of society, and is for Voegelin a key characteristic of modernity. Eschatological expectations are transferred from the divine realm to the temporal realm, and political activity is undertaken with the aim of self-salvation. Put simply, "the Gnostic revolution has for its purpose a change in the nature of man and the establishment of a transfigured society."[66] Although the phenomenon is a very old one, Voegelin associates it particularly strongly with the twentieth century's revolutionary totalitarian mass movements. The "thorough-bred metaphysicians" who "are ready to declare that they do not think two thousand years too long a period for the good that they pursue" exemplify Voegelin's Gnosticism. Because humans essentially stand in the place of God, their wills become unbounded. Burke's observation that Jacobin morality "has no idea in it of restraint" reflects his own, more compact understanding of this phenomenon.[67] In the process of the divinization of human society there is an undermining of traditional Christianity and of traditional religious experience in general; a kind of closure occurs. This is not surprising if one considers the incompatibility of an unbounded "divinized" human will with the humbled will of one who has a sense of human limitation in the face of divine mystery.

In this context it makes sense that White finds that for Burke, the false sublime "rapidly depletes the natural sensibility for the authentic sublime."[68] White recounts Burke's mention of the fact that the space under the scaffold in Paris was hired out to a troupe of dancing dogs to entertain the crowds between executions.[69] The executions are horrible, but more horrible still is the loss of any sense of the gravity of the taking of a life, which is a consequence of the loss of any sense of the sanctity of human life and of the dignity of the human person. What may seem to be simply an aesthetic issue, a matter of bad taste, has a deep moral significance. A loss of a sense of the true sublime is linked to a loss of moral bearings in general, since it is a loss of the sense of anything more meaningful or important than a capricious human will.

The political and moral implications of Burke's perspective on the sublime serve as an illustration of the sort of romantic/classical synthesis that emerges from his aesthetic thought. While Burke's aesthetics emphasize the passions, the creative power of the imagination, and the nonrational experience of the sublime, this does not point to the sort of expansive, undisciplined willfulness that is commonly associated with some forms of romanticism. Instead, Burke's perspective points in the opposite direction: toward humility, toward reverence, toward a sense of order and of moral values, and toward an emphasis on the development of sound judgment in the context of civilized life.

From Burke's aesthetic thought, then, we can draw several points that are critical to developing a better understanding of the philosophic basis of his politics, and help illuminate the insights he offers on approaching questions of meaning and order in late modernity. There is the observation that aesthetics is intimately related to ethics, and that matters of taste impact greatly upon a nation's morals. There is a downplaying of intellectualistic or rationalistic thought in favor of the role of sentiment and, using contemporary language, intuition. Intuitive responses are however sharply distinguished from instinct; they are informed by knowledge and practice and are forms of judgment. In another departure from the traditional thought of his time, Burke emphasizes the importance of the imagination in human thought as a creative and linking power. Significantly, taste is understood to be a form of judgment, and taste/judgment is found to be the product of three faculties: the senses, the imagination, and the reasoning faculty. The impact of knowledge on judgment occurs largely through its influence on the imagination. Burke also remarks that there tends to be more agreement among people on matters involving taste—that is, involving intuitive judgments—than matters approached in an intellectualistic or rationalistic manner. This contradicts common Western thought that reason and science serve as unifiers; to Burke, highly intellectualistic approaches appear to present opportunities for greater divergence of thought, and perhaps, for error.

Finally, there is Burke's special emphasis on the sublime, which he understands to be linked to the passion of "terror" and to be associated with power, infinity, obscurity, and the like. An experience of the sublime gives us a new perspective on ourselves; some of the political implications of the sublime have been mentioned above, but more will come up. Broadly speaking, the philosophical issues raised here in the context of Burke's aesthetics reappear repeatedly in the context of his politics. It is within Burke's political works that a further understanding of these issues and their meaning must be pursued.

3 Reason, Emotion, Knowledge, and Morality

FROM THE PRECEDING DISCUSSION of Burke's aesthetics it should be evident that for him aesthetic response is not a category of human experience wholly distinct from other areas of human experience, such as ethical and political behavior. Taking Burke's writing on aesthetics together with his writings on political, social, and historical matters, it is possible to develop a partial model for human thought and action that illuminates questions of contemporary politics and life. The fundamental understanding of knowledge and morality offered by Burke, while according well with many of the "commonsense" notions typically drawn from life experience, represents a significant shift from the kinds of assumptions—sometimes explicit, more often not—that underpin most social and political thought, and that tend to drive approaches to basic problems of meaning and order in human life. Our understanding of *how* we think matters greatly, and it is in this area that some of Burke's most important contributions lie.

Imagination and Reason

As has been suggested in the preceding chapters, Burke is keenly aware that reason does not function in a vacuum. It operates under various influences and, most importantly, it operates within an imaginative context. In his early discussion of aesthetics it was clear that he considered the imagination to be very important, even if his articulation of its role was somewhat confused. Although Burke does not offer much explicit discussion of the imagination after the *Sublime and Beautiful*, his understanding and appreciation of it continued to grow and develop. Irving Babbitt, who helped draw American attention to Burke's wisdom in the early twentieth century, has written that "Burke is the exceptional Whig, in that he is not only splendidly imaginative, but admits the supreme role of the imagination rather more explicitly than is common among either Christians or Platonists with whom I have associated him."[1] What is the "supreme role" of the imagination? At a basic level, the imagination is important to cognition. According to Babbitt, imagination plays an important role in perception, because to perceive one must also conceive. Babbitt explains that "conceit, it should be remembered, was in older English usage . . . one of the synonyms of imagination. . . . Now to 'conceive' is, in an almost etymological sense, to gather things together, to see likenesses and analogies and in so far to unify what were else mere heterogeneity. The imagination, says Coleridge . . . is the 'esemplastic' power—the power, that is, that fashions things into one."[2] Burke's identification of the imagination as the mind's "creative power," his observation that the imagination's power lies chiefly in finding resemblances, and his suggestion of the epistemological and moral role of narratives in societies lacking in philosophical discourse, suggest a similar, albeit more compact, understanding on his part.

Building upon Babbitt, Claes Ryn explains that, through its creative power and its ability to find resemblances and make connections, the imagination constitutes wholes; without the function of the imagination, we would experience nothing but meaningless heterogeneity. For Ryn, "philosophical reason gives conceptual self-awareness to the categorical structure of experience, experience having been constituted into a pre-cognitive whole by the imagination."[3] Burke's concern regarding the moral imagination and the elements that support it reflects an awareness of this critically important "pre-cognitive" role for the imagination. In one sense, we each live in a world that is an imaginative construct; that is, we must perceive or "get at" reality with the aid of the imagination. It is the imagination that gives order and meaning to sensory data. Reason, narrowly understood as instrumental reason (or, in Burke's words, "the reasoning faculty"), must, in turn, operate on the basis of these imaginative wholes. The extent to which one's imagination succeeds or fails in getting at reality has a tremendous impact on the results of one's reasoning. For example, the Nazi death-camp system was, in its operation, a highly "rational" enterprise; it was well organized and efficient, it served its intended purpose, and so on. There was nothing wrong with the Nazis' "reason" per se, if "reason" is understood in a narrow, instrumental sense; the problem was in their imaginative construction of reality. As was mentioned in chapter 1, Burke finds that one reason why the monster metaphysicians' projects can do so much harm is that to them people are "mice in an air pump." Their imaginations have become warped to the point that they live in a reality in which there is no real concept of a person; a tremendous loss of meaning has occurred.

This understanding of the role of the imagination is compatible with Burke's suggestion in the *Sublime and Beautiful* that judgment is made up of three elements: the senses, the imagination, and "the reasoning faculty." The imagination finds resemblances, draws connections, and operates creatively to make wholes out of sensory data. Instrumental reason takes these imaginative wholes and finds differences. It draws distinctions and completes the process of judgment. Of course, one must be careful not to take such identifications of various faculties and processes too literally; the subject matter addressed here is the mysterious workings of the human mind, not the operation of a factory. What we are trying to do is develop, and express in a shorthand way, a model that conforms reasonably well to experience, and that aligns with what is indicated by Burke. The distinctions among various faculties or aspects of thought are hard to fix, and the labels applied to some of them may be somewhat arbitrary. This does not prevent such models from being useful, provided that they are taken in the right spirit. In this particular case, the identification of "reason" or, in perhaps better language, a "reasoning faculty" as one element of judgment is potentially confusing or problematic, in that the term "reason" can be used in many different ways. In Burke's writing it can be used, first, to refer either narrowly to instrumental reason, that is, to that particular faculty that is most manifest in the making of distinctions, or more broadly to the complex processes by which we think and judge. Second, whether the processes referred to are simple or complex, the term "reason" can be applied solely to those activities that occur in the realm of conscious rational thought, or it can be applied more broadly to processes that go on whether or not we are fully aware that they are occurring. Burke's particular term "reasoning faculty" would seem to refer narrowly to that power that makes distinctions, but would seem to apply whether or not we are consciously and deliberately exercising judgment.

It is noteworthy that the understanding of the role of the imagination, which is here found to be implicit in Burke, bears some similarity to that which has been found in both David Hume and Adam Smith. While interpretations of Hume and Smith vary greatly among scholars, contemporary philosopher Knud Haakonssen finds:

> For both Hume and Smith the imagination is a mental faculty by means of which people create a distinctly human sphere within the natural world. It is the imagination that enables us to make connections between the perceived elements of both the physical and the moral world, ranging from binary relations between particular events and things to complex systems such as the national or international economy, the idea of the cosmos or of humanity as a whole. The activity of the imagination is a spontaneous search for order, coherence and agreement in the world.[4]

Haakonssen labels one type of imagination discussed by Smith the "practical imagination" and states that for Smith "the practical imagination creates the moral world. This form of imagination Smith calls sympathy, using the word in a somewhat special sense that has led to much confusion both in his own time and subsequently."[5] The model described by Haakonssen is not set forth clearly and concisely in one place in Hume or Smith; Haakonssen draws upon numerous works, including relatively obscure and posthumously published material of Smith's to which Burke is very unlikely to have had access. However, Burke was in contact with both Hume and Smith at various times in his life, and he took interest in their writings. Burke reviewed the *Theory of Moral Sentiments* favorably in the 1759 issue of *The Annual Register,* a yearbook for which Burke was hired as the principal editor and writer.[6] It may be significant that the passage from Smith's work that Burke chose to excerpt in the review is on the subject of "sympathy." If Burke's understanding of Smith's "sympathy" resembled that of Haakonssen in even a vague way, this understanding may have supported and contributed to the moral-epistemological outlook that Burke was developing.

Many general similarities may be found between the moral and epistemological dimensions of Burke's thought and the writings of both Hume and Smith; among these are Burke's leanings toward (but not embrace of) skepticism and empiricism, his cautious attitude toward reason and toward heavy reliance on explicit moral principles, and his interest in imagination, sentiment, and custom. However, it would be wrong to ascribe to Burke any particular philosophical positions attributed to Hume or Smith, or to Locke or any other writer, without specific evidence that Burke accepts those positions. Although Burke was certainly influenced by these philosophers (and may have influenced Hume and, especially, Smith somewhat also), there is no evidence that Burke accepts any other philosopher's outlook wholesale; in fact, the evidence is to the contrary. For example, while Burke's review of Smith's *Theory* is generally favorable, he includes the remark that "there will, in a work of this kind, always be great deficiencies."[7] (Unfortunately, Burke does not spell out for his readers what those great deficiencies are.) Also, by 1784 Burke spoke of the *Theory of Moral Sentiments* negatively.[8] As for Hume, it is perhaps not surprising that those who portray Burke as a natural law thinker take pains to differentiate his thought very sharply from Hume's.[9] More important, even those scholars who see significant Humean influences in Burke are generally careful to note that he does not simply follow Hume. Of the major writers on Burke, James Conniff probably makes the strongest claim in associating him with Hume, maintaining that "Burke was, in a sense, a Humean philosopher in action."[10] But Conniff also observes that "Burke never became the relativist that Hume did," and states that Burke "developed a related but slightly different approach" from that of Hume.[11] A precise understanding of the relationship of Burke's thought to that of Hume or of Smith depends, of course, not just on one's interpretation of Burke but of Hume or Smith. At any rate, as a caution against drawing too close a connection, it is perhaps enough to note that in addition to finding "great deficiencies" in Smith, the record indicates that Burke eventually disassociated himself sharply from Hume both intellectually and personally, citing Hume's epistemological skepticism and his rejection of traditional religion.[12]

Sentiment and Judgment

The epistemological outlook that we can derive from Burke helps to make sense of his strong interest in "sentiment." When considering the operation of taste and of other forms of judgment, it becomes evident that judgments can occur on either a conscious or subconscious level, if by "subconscious" we mean simply that we are not fully aware that we are making a judgment at the time. Ryn points out that all perception involves a judgment, since in perceiving one decides that "this is something perceived, not imagined." In fact, Ryn observes that "categorizing thought" is almost always taking place, except in special cases such as that of "intense aesthetic experience."[13] This exception roughly corresponds to Burke's characterization of intense experiences of the sublime as involving the suspension of "reason." Under normal circumstances, we are always categorizing, always making judgments. We decide what things are, what they mean, how they relate to one another, whether they are important, etc. In whatever manner one may choose to divide this activity between the imagination itself and the reasoning faculty, which works with the imagination, it is clear that perception must by necessity be powerfully shaped by the imaginative wholes that precede it.

The word "subconscious" was not in Burke's vocabulary, and he rarely uses the term "emotion" either. However, he frequently employs the language of emotion in the form of his numerous references to "sentiment," "feelings," "passion," and related terms. Frequently these references are favorable. One of his more famous observations in this area is that "it is, I own, not uncommon to be wrong in theory and right in practice; and we are happy that it is so. Men often act right from their feelings, who afterwards reason but ill on them from principle."[14] Such remarks, combined with Burke's derogation of "naked reason" and "metaphysics," lead commentators such as Strauss to exaggerate Burke's disparagement of reason to the point that human agency has little or no power to do good in the world. Under such a model, humanity is placed in a highly deterministic context in which it is at the mercy of historical forces, instinct, and the like. Burke's interest in feelings, however, actually reflects a broadened and deepened understanding of cognition. Feelings, for Burke, contain information, often very valuable information. They are essentially expressions of judgments we have made on a subconscious level. They are not always more accurate than the sort of judgments that we more readily identify with the deliberate employment of "reason," but they often are. Burke's treatment of sentiment or feeling is actually similar to his treatment of prejudice. This is not surprising, since the distinction between a feeling and a prejudice is in fact not easily drawn. Burke recognizes this, referring in one place to "the moral sentiments, so nearly connected with early prejudice as to be almost one and the same thing."[15]

Burke, of course, is neither the first nor the last thinker to see value in feelings. One of many contemporary commentators on the value of emotions is Martha Nussbaum, who devotes a book to the argument that "emotions . . . involve judgments about important things."[16] While this idea may seem obvious to some, Nussbaum points out that a great deal of modern thought (especially, but not exclusively, academic philosophical thought) is premised, either explicitly or implicitly, on the idea that emotions convey little or no useful information about matters at hand. Consequently, emotions tend to be seen as obstacles to good judgment, rather than as reflections of (usually sound) judgments. Burke's position is clearly in line with Nussbaum's here in that he sees emotions as frequently valuable aids in decision making.

The popular misunderstanding of human emotions, springing from a narrow conception of reason as the sole guide to right action, contributes significantly both to broad errors in modern political thought and action and to some of the specific disagreement and confusion in interpreting Burke. For example, the assumption is sometimes made that any political-philosophical thinker who is concerned about feelings must be something like a Benthamite utilitarian, or must be a simple democrat or political pragmatist who just wants to make the greatest number of people feel happy; he cannot be seriously interested in "truth" or the "good" or any universals. The relationship of Burke's thought to universals will be addressed in some depth later, but it should be evident that if emotions do in fact "involve judgments about important things," Burke's interest in sentiment does not imply a lack of concern about truth, much less a rejection of a universal moral order.

One of Burke's most important discussions of sentiment comes in the *Reflections,* when he is confronting the British supporters of the French Revolution. (*Reflections* was written in 1790, when the Revolution was still widely celebrated in Britain and long before the Terror began.) Burke raises and answers the question of why the accounts of events in France move him to oppose the actions that have taken place there:

> For this plain reason—because it is *natural* I should; because we are so made as to be affected at such spectacles with melancholy sentiments upon the unstable condition of mortal prosperity and the tremendous uncertainty of human greatness; because in those natural feelings we learn great lessons; because in events like these our passions instruct our reason; because when kings are hurl'd from their thrones by the Supreme Director of this great drama, and become the objects of insult to the base, and of pity to the good, we behold such disasters in the moral as we should behold a miracle in the physical order of things. We are alarmed into reflexion; our minds (as it has long since been observed) are purified by terror and pity, our weak, unthinking pride is humbled under a mysterious wisdom.—Some tears might be drawn from me if such a spectacle were exhibited on the stage. I should be truly ashamed of finding in myself that superficial, theatric sense of painted distress whilst I could exult over it in real life.[17]

A great deal is going on in this passage; it is therefore worthwhile to devote some time to unpacking it. For one thing, Burke states that "in those natural feelings we learn great lessons." We should pay attention to our feelings because they are telling us something. They are reflective of judgments we have made about particular events or people on a subconscious level. These judgments may sometimes be better than the judgments we make through a more self-conscious or "detached" application of reason.

A brief digression may be appropriate here regarding Burke's use of the term "natural," since he is talking about "natural feelings" and emphasizes that it is "natural" that he should have them. The feelings are "natural," in one sense, because our capacity for various feelings is innate; it is clear that Burke recognizes this fact. However, it should be emphasized that by "natural feelings" Burke does not mean feelings that are wholly "instinctive" or that would exist in some sort of primitive "state of nature." Burke strongly opposed any "state of nature" talk. And he devoted a book, *A Vindication of Natural Society*, to ridiculing, among other things, advocacy of some sort of "natural society" that is opposed to our "artificial society."[18] In saying that it is "natural" to have certain feelings Burke is simply using the term in a conventional manner. That is, he means that certain feelings can be expected to arise in a normal, morally healthy person, who for Burke is not someone in a primitive "state of nature" but someone who has been properly raised in a morally healthy society. In this sense the term "natural" is perhaps more normative than descriptive. It is also somewhat teleological, as Joseph Pappin points out in his study of Burke.[19] An earlier commentator, Charles Parkin, similarly finds that for Burke "the 'natural' in man is not his rudimentary, least characteristic quality, but his most distinctive and complete form of expression."[20] The term is, however, also descriptive in the sense that Burke finds that these feelings occur "naturally," by which he means that they seemingly arise in us of their own accord, without the conscious employment of reason and without any deliberate efforts on our part. This does not mean that our specific feelings in specific contexts are not, to a degree, learned. Burke makes reference at one point to man "when made as he ought to be made."[21] What is "natural" to Burke is, generally speaking, what comes "naturally" not to some hypothetical primitive person, but to one who is "made as he ought to be."

In the above passage on the Revolution Burke finds that "in events like these our passions instruct our reason." Events like what? Burke does not explain precisely under what circumstances our passions instruct our reason. However, in this particular case he is almost certainly attempting to evoke the sublime. His immediate concern is with occasions "when kings are hurl'd from their thrones by the Supreme Director of this great drama."

A brief aside is called for noting that Burke sees the hand of God at work, even in an event he vehemently opposes such as the French Revolution. This subject will be addressed briefly later in this study. What matters here is that such evocations of mystery, terror, and great power conform to Burke's description of the sublime as discussed in chapter 2. The effect is that "we are alarmed into reflection; our minds . . . are purified by terror and pity, our weak, unthinking pride is humbled under a mysterious wisdom." Again, this closely matches Burke's decades-earlier description of the effects of the sublime. In the 1750s, Burke was primarily concerned with the sublime as it was manifested in literature, art, and music. Now his focus is on its presence not in the arts but in real life; that is, in political events of tremendous magnitude. In both his 1757 and 1790 descriptions of the effects of the sublime, normal rational thought processes are essentially suspended. Here, he states that terror and pity "purify" our minds. The implication is that our minds often tend to become cluttered with rationalizations, abstract theories, and so on, and that strong emotion pushes all this aside. We stop analyzing the Revolution according to theories of government and respond to its events viscerally.

In this particular case, at least, Burke believes that a direct emotional response represents a better understanding of reality than that which is gained through any conscious rational analysis performed in the context of abstract conceptual formulations. Our feelings sort of shock us into awareness; we receive what is today colloquially referred to as a "wake-up call," tearing us away from our abstract musings and forcing us to confront the real meaning and import in human terms of particular lines of reasoning or action. Burke's famous (or infamous) description in the *Reflections* of Marie Antoinette's radiant glory and then tragic plight, a passage much derided by Burke's critics, is an attempt to evoke a similar response from his reader:

> It is now sixteen or seventeen years since I saw the queen of France, then the dauphiness, at Versailles, and surely never lighted on this orb, which she hardly seemed to touch, a more delightful vision. I saw her just above the horizon, decorating and cheering the elevated sphere she just began to move in,—glittering like the morning-star, full of life and splendor and joy. Oh! what a revolution! and what a heart must I have to contemplate without emotion that elevation and that fall! Little did I dream when she added titles of veneration to those of enthusiastic, distant, respectful love, that she should ever be obliged to carry the sharp antidote against disgrace concealed in

that bosom; little did I dream that I should have lived to see such disasters fallen upon her in a nation of gallant men, in a nation of men of honor and of cavaliers. I thought ten thousand swords must have leaped from their scabbards to avenge even a look that threatened her with insult.—But the age of chivalry is gone.—That of sophisters, oeconomists, and calculators, has succeeded; and the glory of Europe is extinguished for ever.[22]

In using such romantic, affective language, dripping with nostalgia for a France that some might claim never really existed, one could say that Burke is attempting to move his readers on two levels. One level is sympathy for a person to whom terrible things are happening; such a response relies upon people's identification with Marie Antoinette as another human being. The other level is shock and horror at the Earth-shattering political event—the overturning of an ancient order. There are not really two levels, however. For Burke, the ancient order is embodied in Marie Antoinette and other individuals; each level essentially subsists in the other. Such persons represent not just a political structure but an entire way of life, taken at its best. We tend to respond to such embodiments and symbols much more powerfully than to any abstract terminology that attempts to express the same ideas.

One of the earliest and foremost critics of Burke's discussion of the Queen was Thomas Paine, who remarked that Burke "pities the plumage and forgets the dying bird."[23] For Burke, the plumage and the bird cannot really be separated. Burke is concerned about "plumage" because of its powerful effect on the imagination. For Burke, our response to anything is, in part, a kind of aesthetic response, just as the bad taste of interspersing executions with dancing dogs reflected deep moral issues.

In writing on the French Revolution it is natural that Burke would appeal to his readers on an aesthetic, emotional, and intuitive level. Our position on the Revolution, like our response to most things, is for Burke something we largely intuit. We make judgments subconsciously as we fit new sensory data into existing imaginative wholes, and get a particular "feeling" about a situation or person as a function of making those judgments. Symbols such as the King and Queen help to concretize a broad range of ideas and concepts—some of which may be difficult to express adequately in a verbal manner—and thereby help elicit a strong imaginative or intuitive response. Burke criticizes the "metaphysicians" who ignore this important dimension of human life: "On the principles of this mechanic philosophy [of the revolutionaries], our institutions can never be embodied, if I may use the expression, in persons, so as to create in us love, veneration, admiration, or attachment. But that sort of reason which banishes the affections is incapable of filling their place. These public affections, combined with manners, are required sometimes as supplements, sometimes as correctives, always as aids to law."[24]

Paine's dismissal of the Queen as "plumage" reflects the kind of reductionist thinking that Burke specifically denounces in the *Reflections*. Burke famously remarks that, for those "metaphysicians" who support the Revolution so enthusiastically, "a king is but a man, a queen is but a woman; a woman is but an animal, and an animal not of the highest order."[25] The idea of kingship involves more than a structure of government; it is the sort of "superadded idea" that Burke considers to be important to a moral imagination. In reducing a king to a mere man, important meaning is lost. For one thing, the king ceases to be sublime. The sense of participation in a greater order is lost. Once reductionism starts, there is no end to it. Just as there is nothing to distinguish a queen from an ordinary woman, there is nothing to distinguish a woman from an animal. The loss of meaning becomes a loss of all meaning, including that of humanity itself.

Burke is appalled that the British enthusiasts for the French Revolution can be so callous as to rejoice in actions that are uprooting an ancient order and causing so much human suffering. He points out that, should he see such actions dramatized on the stage, he (and, we presume, he hopes his readers also) would be moved to tears. There is, in his view, something very wrong with someone who can be moved by stage tragedy but unmoved by reports of tragedy in real life. This perspective of Burke's is of course in line with that which he expressed regarding "thorough-bred metaphysicians" in the passage in the *Letter to a Noble Lord* that was quoted in chapter 1. In embracing revolutionary ideology, the enthusiasts have sacrificed a part of their humanity, a part of their grip on reality. We could say that the imaginative wholes created by their imaginations, and the intuitive judgments that are based on those wholes, have been transformed. The usual reference points that help support our recognition of the humanity of others and our ability to empathize with them have been replaced by an ideological framework that does not admit such human sympathies if they challenge the supremacy of the revolution.

As was observed, Burke finds that in evaluating events such as those of the French Revolution, "our passions instruct our reason." Burke uses the word "passions" in various ways; in this context it appears to be a synonym for "feelings," a word used in the immediately preceding clause. It is noteworthy that Burke does not adopt the better-known language of his acquaintance Hume, who famously asserts that reason is a "slave of the passions."[26] In Burke's more measured approach, reason remains important to human agency and judgment. He does not actually exalt passion in place of reason. Burke can be seen to share the classical view that one must be one's own master, although for him it is not a narrowly construed "reasoning faculty" that must predominate, but a broad-based sense of judgment, which includes properly cultivated passions. Burke's recognition that "reason" narrowly understood is not the sole source of knowledge or good judgment does not lead him to adopt Hume's perspective on human agency, in which one is not quite one's own master but is subject to forces that, despite being internal, are nonetheless beyond one's control. Hume's view here actually fits much more closely with the traditional opposition of "reason" and "passion" than does Burke's, which reflects new ways of thinking about both.

Interestingly, Burke uses pedagogical metaphors twice in succession: we learn "great lessons" from our feelings, and our passions "instruct" our reason. Reason, or conscious rational thought, is not a slave to our feelings but is under their tutelage. Our feelings seem to possess information that intellectualistic thought does not, at least some of the time. This relationship, which, for want of better language, can be cast as one between the "rational" and the "intuitive," recalls Burke's boyhood remarks regarding the relationship of reason and prejudice. As was cited in chapter 1, the young Burke observed that we often invent "false reasonings" to uphold irrational opinions. This early formulation seems closer to Hume's, in that reason is cast less as the pupil of the nonrational than as its servant. In that particular case the sentiments that were driving reason were seen as the result of undesirable prejudices, not of healthy feelings. Similarly, it was shown that in Burke's characterization of monster metaphysicians, the metaphysicians do in fact become slaves to passion, in the form of ambition and ideological zeal. So, the relationship of reason to passion and sentiment can vary with individuals and circumstances, and Burke does not always exalt the nonrational.

It is clear that for Burke feelings, sentiment, passion, and the like can be both good and bad. They may provide sound direction for our reason or may lead it astray. Burke avoids both the formulations of those who assert that emotion serves merely to get in the way of "reason's" understanding the world, and the formulations of those like Rousseau who (sometimes) exalt unreflective emotional, instinctive, or impulsive responses as the best source of correct or virtuous action. Since sentiment is neither always good nor always bad, a problem may seem to arise of determining when to allow "passion" to instruct one's reason, and when to disregard or reject it. But this is not quite the correct formulation of the problem. As has been shown, Burke seems to realize that there is really no such thing as an independently functioning "reason," in the sense of a truly "naked reason" which can operate without material to inform it. One's reason must function in the imaginative context one creates, and it is influenced by the intuitive judgments that are made in the creation of those imaginative wholes and expressed (in part) in the form of feelings and sentiments. As in the case of the doctrinaire "thorough-bred metaphysicians," the more, in fact, that one attempts to employ a "naked reason" that rejects those elements that traditionally have helped to constitute a moral imagination, the more one's imaginative framework becomes compromised and deformed, and the more one is likely to become a slave to base passions such as the ambition to dominate all one surveys.

One might say, then, that instead of deciding when to follow one's feelings and when to reject them, the problem is one of determining which feelings and intuitions to obey, and which to reject. This formulation, however, is still wrong. It implies that there exists a "reason," or some other power, that can stand above all of these impulses and can evaluate and rule over them. As was pointed out in chapter 2, at one point in the *Sublime and Beautiful* the young Burke seems to hint at such a classical-type model. But if Burke actually rejects such an independently functioning "reason," this model would seem to collapse.

One way of dealing with the problem of determining right action is by seeing it in terms of willing. It was mentioned in chapter 1 that, although Burke does not really discuss the will, it nevertheless seems to loom large in the background of his ethical thought. One contemporary commentator, Stephen Browne, maintains that "virtue as Burke understood it was an expression of individual will."[27] One might in fact argue that an important role for the will is implied by Burke's refusal to exalt either an independent reason or "instinctive" sentiment as the source of ethical action. Burke scholar Peter Stanlis has noted that "Burke's Anglicanism prevented him from assuming any single, simple mainspring of human conduct, and enabled him to accept a philosophy of human nature in which the claims of passion, reason, and faith were synthesized," and that "through his strong belief in free will, Burke always held man morally responsible for his own destiny."[28] Separating will from judgment is, in fact, a problematic task. The early twentieth-century philosopher Benedetto Croce maintains that judgments follow assertions of will, rather than precede them, and are in fact "the expression of an act of willing." For Croce, "A good or useful action is a willed action: from the objective examination of things it will never be possible to distill a single drop of utility or goodness. We do not want things because we know them to be useful or good; rather we know them to be useful and good because we want them."[29]

In chapter 1's treatment of Burke's writings on prejudice it was observed that, for him, prejudice seems to represent in part a tendency toward a particular sort of willing. An emphasis on will is likewise implied in Burke's description of the "thorough-bred metaphysicians." As will be recalled, Burke remarked that

> it is no easy operation to eradicate humanity from the human breast. What Shakespeare calls the 'compunctious visitings of Nature' will sometimes knock at their hearts, and protest against their murderous speculations. But they have a means of compounding with their nature. Their humanity is not dissolved; they only give it a long prorogation. They are ready to declare that they do not think two thousand years too long a period for the good that they pursue.[30]

Although the metaphysicians' imaginative frameworks have become warped, and consequently they have lost some of their grasp of reality, their ethical perception is not completely gone. Something within them recoils at the harm they are inflicting. This something is most likely seen by Burke as conscience in the Christian conception, although, interestingly, Burke refrains from simply stating so, instead relying upon the quote from *Macbeth*. At any rate, the ideologically driven "thorough-bred metaphysicians" have to make an effort to silence or assuage this inner voice, by focusing upon all the good that they will bring about in the distant future. There is a willfulness to this eradication or suppression of their own "humanity"; Burke states that this is "no easy operation." The ideologues deliberately thwart their ethical intuition while allowing free play to their ambition.

Although Burke does not much discuss the will, Babbitt, whose political-ethical writings were much influenced by Burke, places a strong emphasis on will in his own ethical thought. Babbitt uses a kind of dualistic model in which people possess a "lower will" and a "higher will"; it is the higher will, or ethical will, that checks selfish, expansive, and otherwise undesirable impulses and allows desirable impulses to be translated into action. For Babbitt, what most determines whether an action will be ethical is not the theoretical framework followed by an actor, but the kind of will that that actor possesses.

One who lacks a well-developed higher will is likely to be governed by the kinds of sentiments and passions that undermine virtuous action, even if the individual espouses the most elevated ideals. While Burke does not appear to adopt quite the same model as Babbitt, its relationship to Burke's discussion of the metaphysicians is obvious. Babbitt maintains that "the unit to which all things must finally be referred is not the state or humanity or any other abstraction, but the man of character."[31] The exact nature and source of the "higher will" or ethical will is for Babbitt ultimately mysterious. However, it is developed in part through discipline and practice. This may be compared to Burke's observation that one of the benefits of prejudice is that it "renders a man's virtue his habit." Since the determination of which impulses to check and which to encourage involves a judgment, one may compare Babbitt's views on the development of an ethical will to Burke's discussion of the development of judgment and taste through practice. One essentially develops a "taste" for the sort of action that is truly ethical, and a distaste for its opposite. In one of his late writings, in fact, Burke makes reference to "a moral taste."[32]

Many writers on Burke, including Francis Canavan and Joseph Pappin, have spoken of Burke's emphasis on our "second nature."[33] Prejudice of course represents for Burke one way of developing a second nature. Using Babbitt's framework, Ryn finds that "in the person who, having followed Aristotle's admonition to develop sound habits, has acquired a taste for morality, the impulsive life tends to merge, without special effort, with the higher will."[34] This observation may be compared to a statement by Parkin that "Burke . . . adopts an Aristotelian position; the highest development in man lies in the most complete union between the spontaneous self-expression of the individual and his moral perception of his place in the community of his fellows."[35] In any of these models, there occurs over time a reduction in the tension between one's impulses or "passions" and one's sense of what is morally the right thing to do. One may argue that this harmonizing occurs because, as it is developed, the moral imagination not only increasingly supports the kind of judgment or will that allows one to check undesirable impulses, but also increasingly shapes one's impulses in particular ways. This occurs because our impulses or passions are, in part, reflective of judgments we have made intuitively as our imagination draws connections and creates wholes. We just "naturally" do the right thing, because this is what we have learned to do, and because this is what makes sense within the worldview that we have built up.

It should be noted that, although Parkin's above description of Burke's "Aristotelian position" is sound in itself, it is preceded by another description of this position that is highly problematic. Parkin states that "the idea of man's nature on which Burke's conception of nature rests is a harmonised state of instinctive feeling and acceptance of moral obligation; and his method of proving other conceptions of nature false is to show that their practical realisation would provoke the emergence of passion, that is, the loss of this harmony. Passion is not natural to man."[36] There are at least two problems with this statement. A minor issue is the reference, which occurs repeatedly in Parkin, to the "instinctive." As was noted when confronting Strauss in chapter 1, Burke does not endorse "instinct," if the term is understood in the technical sense of untaught, animal-type behaviors. He rarely uses the term, and when he does use it, it is more often than not to make the point that something is *not* "instinctive." Given Parkin's normative and rather teleological definition of the "natural," one may reasonably presume that he is not actually using "instinctive" in the sense of designating biologically programmed behavior, but in its more conventional sense, as a rough synonym for "spontaneous" in Parkin's other statement. The use of such terms as "instinctive" should be avoided, however, since they contribute to confusion regarding Burke's actual position.

A much more serious problem is Parkin's association of the emergence of passion with a loss of harmony, and his claim that for Burke "passion is not natural to man." Parkin reinforces these statements by adding that Burke sees the French Revolution as an "outburst of passion." Given Burke's frequent positive or neutral references to "passion" and tendency to criticize those who are "cold," and given his clear statement that, in some circumstances at least, we should allow "our passions" to "instruct our reason," it is very difficult to see how Parkin could attribute the above views to Burke. It may be that Parkin is using the term "passion" in a special negative way, as in the case of the metaphysicians who are overcome with passion in the form of ambition and attachment to an ideology. Parkin does not explain this, however, and that is certainly not how Burke uses the term. If anything, Burke tends to portray the "good guys" as moved by passion. He contrasts the French Jacobins with the nonrevolutionary people of England:

> In England we . . . still feel within us, and we cherish and cultivate, those inbred sentiments which are the faithful guardians, the active monitors of our duty, the true supporters of all liberal and manly morals. We have not been . . . filled, like stuffed birds in a museum, with . . . paltry blurred shreds of paper about the rights of men. We preserve the whole of our feelings still native and entire, unsophisticated by pedantry and infidelity. We have real hearts of flesh and blood beating in our bosoms.[37]

In characterizing Burke as an opponent of passion, Parkin seems to fall into a trap similar to that which Canavan falls into when he insists that Burke's aesthetic thought is incompatible with his ethical and political thought. In placing Burke with the natural law tradition, commentators have a tendency to make him too much into a Greek. As will be discussed in more detail later, Burke can in fact be placed within the natural law tradition in a broad and general way, and, as has been mentioned, he was well read in the classics and influenced by them. However, his thought also includes important departures from classical thought. One can find in Burke a sort of synthesis of classical, medieval Christian, and modern elements. Burke places much more emphasis on passion, sentiment, imagination, will, and such than do most classical writers. For him, everyone has passions; passion is certainly not something "that is not natural to man." A well-ordered soul for Burke is not one without passion, but one in which the right sort of passions predominate, and in which one maintains a solid imaginative foothold in reality, which no particular passion may dislodge. Again, emotions reflect judgments, and a properly developed person has the right emotional responses to various situations. Burke's basic outlook, it is argued here, is really best characterized as a moral-imaginative one, and when commentators attempt to utilize a neoclassically derived reason-based framework to understand it, problems develop and elements of his thought are ignored or distorted.

When explaining Irving Babbitt's thought, Ryn states that "the crux of the ethical life . . . is not acquiring definitive theoretical knowledge of the good, which is beyond man, but the ability to *act* on whatever ethical insight one does have. As man grows in character and performs new good actions, the light of reality streaming forth from these actions will brighten."[38] The right sort of will-action actually helps to develop one's understanding of reality. If one finds a similar sense in Burke, this serves as a partial reply to Harvey Mansfield's question, mentioned in chapter 1, about how one is to "be sure of the morality of prudence." One learns through one's actions and through the results that follow from them, and through one's observation of the actions and results of others. To say that the will contributes to one's grasp of reality is also to say that it contributes to the shaping of the imagination. Not only does the will help to shape the imagination, but the will is also powerfully shaped by the imagination; like reason, one's will must operate within the imaginative wholes that one builds. A circular relationship between imagination and will therefore exists. One may get on a track in which a moral imagination promotes an ethical will, which in turn further develops the imagination in a positive way. In persons such as Burke's metaphysicians, the opposite happens, and the imagination and will negatively reinforce each other, taking them further and further away from reality. For everyone, moral reality is primarily grasped intuitively, as a result of the imaginative wholes one builds through experience.

The imagination, then, helps to shape the feelings, intuitions, and other impulses with which we are bombarded; it is, in a sense, identified with them. The imagination also powerfully influences the reason and the will, which must either check those impulses or translate them into action. Consequently Babbitt maintains that "the imagination . . . holds the balance of power between the higher and the lower nature of man."[39] It holds this balance because of the vital cognitive or pre-cognitive role it plays. Whether one believes oneself to be following feelings and intuitions, or to be performing a dispassionate rational analysis, one has no choice but to operate within the imaginative frameworks one has constructed. Sharp distinctions, in fact, between judgments based on feelings or intuitions and those based on "reason" are difficult to maintain.

The Ethical and the Personal

Why does Burke place such stock in feelings and intuitions? Babbitt makes reference to "the universal experience of mankind which is that the truths on which the inner life depends are not clear in the logical or any other sense. These truths are rather a matter of elusive intuition."[40] This may be compared to Burke's claim that "a clear idea is . . . a little idea." Life is mysterious; its truths are not completely beyond humanity's grasp, but neither can they be boiled down in such a way that they can be clearly and fully articulated. Much of the power of mythology, fiction, poetry, drama, etc. lies it the ability of these art forms to convey truths through vicarious experience, which cannot be as easily or effectively conveyed through maxims or other more explicit and direct articulations. Burke, of course, was familiar with the great classical epics and myths and was keenly aware of the importance and power of such works, and of more modern works, in teaching great truths compactly. One of his more explicit references to this role of literature is found in his 1761 *Hints for an Essay on the Drama,* where he remarks:

> Without question the subject of all poetry was originally direct and personal. Fictitious character is a refinement, and comparatively modern; for abstraction

is in its nature slow, and always follows the progress of philosophy. Men had always friends and enemies before they knew the exact nature of vice and virtue; they naturally and with their best powers of eloquence, whether in prose or verse, magnified and set off the one; vilified and traduced the other.[41]

Notice the distinction Burke makes between "friends and enemies" and "vice and virtue." Vice and virtue are abstractions derived from our observation of real people. One may acquire intuitive knowledge of vice and virtue experientially, and put it to use practically, without having expressed this knowledge conceptually. Croce, in discussing the relationship between an "intuition" and a "concept" or "universal," finds that while intuition may operate without conceptual knowledge, "without intuitions, concepts are not possible, just as, without the material provided by impressions, intuition itself would not be possible."[42] Michael Oakeshott has observed that "moral ideals are not, in the first place, the products of reflective thought, the verbal expressions of unrealized ideas, which are then translated . . . into human behaviour; they are the products of human behaviour, of human practical activity, to which reflective thought gives subsequent, partial and abstract expression in words."[43] Burke likewise seems to believe that morality begins with how we act and how we feel about particular people and events. Joseph Pappin finds that for Burke "rational man acts without regard to abstractions and universals."[44] Verbal expressions of universal moral ideals and principles are derivative of how we act and feel about concrete particulars. Those derivative expressions are necessarily incomplete, and are sometimes erroneous. Remember Burke's observation cited early in this chapter: "it is, I own, not uncommon to be wrong in theory and right in practice; and we are happy that it is so. Men often act right from their feelings, who afterwards reason but ill on them from principle."

It is interesting that Burke emphasizes that poetry began with the "direct and personal." Intuitive knowledge, and the feelings that express it, seem to be most useful in matters involving one's personal response to other people. Nussbaum, in defending the idea of emotions as judgments of value, remarks on the highly personal nature of emotional responses. She points out that this personal quality has long been cited as a reason to reject emotions as cognitively useful. We are supposed to be disinterested, but emotional responses clearly are not. Nussbaum argues that there is value in the personal nature of emotions. She sees emotions as "*eudaimonistic,* that is, concerned with the person's flourishing."[45] It would seem that we have an intuitive sense of this "*eudaimonism*" that tends to surpass conceptual expressions. Consequently emotions are for her "richly particular," in contrast to "abstract judgment," which is not.[46] The fact that emotions have a *"eudaimonistic"* quality does not mean that they are always selfish. One of Babbitt's reasons for talking of a "higher will" is to emphasize the fact that we learn to check at least some of our selfish impulses. Our imaginations, in fact, allow us to put ourselves into the shoes of others and, to a degree, to respond to others' circumstances as if we, or someone important to us, were in the same situation. In the *Reflections,* Burke follows up his discussion of how the events in France would move us if presented on the stage with the remark that "indeed, the theatre is a better school of moral sentiments than churches, where the feelings of humanity are thus outraged."[47] We tend to respond to a play more than to a dry sermon, even if the people and events depicted are fictional. We may in fact learn more from the vicarious experience of the play, just as we can learn from poetry, epics, and other art forms. Here Burke anticipates those contemporary postmodern-leaning theorists like Rorty who emphasize that *"fiction . . . gives us the details of suffering being endured by people to whom we had previously not attended. Fiction . . . gives us the details about what sorts of cruelty we ourselves are capable of, and thereby lets us* redescribe ourselves. That is why the novel, the movie, and the TV program have . . . replaced the sermon and the treatise as the principal vehicles of moral change and progress."[48] Burke would of course maintain that fiction has *always* been an important vehicle of moral change.

Burke believes that our feelings and intuitions are most important and most reliable when we are responding to other people, rather than simply responding to events. In his writing on drama he maintains that "more observe the characters of men than the order of things; to the one we are formed by Nature and by that sympathy, from which we are so strongly led to take a part in the passions and manners of our fellow men. The other is as it were foreign and extrinsical."[49] Burke points out that most good plays have rather simple and conventional plots; it is the characters that are of primary importance. The fact that we identify closely with others means not only that we respond more strongly to people than to events, but that we "observe the characters of men" better than we analyze events. That is, we tend to make better judgments about people than about events disassociated from particular individuals.

Burke took this belief to heart and put it to practical political use. Stephen Browne discusses some of Burke's more famous speeches, and notes that his arguments on any subject usually will, sooner or later, take on a kind of "ad hominem" character. This is not a criticism on Browne's part. The most famous case of Burke's "ad hominem" approach is the impeachment of Warren Hastings, in which Burke uses the governor-general of Bengal to personify all that is wrong with Britain's India policy. This will be addressed in more detail later. The Hastings case, though the most obvious, is not exceptional. For example, in his *Speech on Conciliation with America* Burke discusses the history of Britain's relations with America in a rather unusual way. He identifies various past policies very closely with the specific historical political figures who promoted those policies. Burke describes the character of each of those individuals, showing those who promoted policies that Burke considers to have been desirable and successful to have been virtuous, while showing those supporting the opposing policies to have had significant character flaws. These individuals were of course known to most members of Parliament, in some cases personally but more often by reputation. Browne finds that throughout Burke's speeches "the character portraits provide a space for reflective judgment; and as they concern character—public character—they invite the reader into the text in a way that the more technical aspects of the narrative cannot." They serve as "interpretive keys," providing a way for listeners to make sense of a complex narrative.[50]

One may argue that Burke uses portraits of individuals in his speeches because, as human beings ourselves with our own interior lives, and with our extensive experience in dealing with other human beings and in hearing stories about them, they are what we know best. Our imaginations have equipped us relatively well to perceive and to respond to human characters of various types; we have a capacity to identify with other people and to develop at least an inarticulate understanding of them. Because of basic commonalities of life experience, people are presumably more likely to agree on whether certain traits in a particular individual are good or bad than on how the effects of particular government policies should be interpreted. We may not be experts on the subtleties of colonial or economic policy, but we all are, comparatively, experts on people. Burke also seems to believe that his listeners are very willing to connect various individuals' character traits to government policies and to use them as touchstones in evaluating those policies. Many people may in fact be willing to do so, because descriptions of individuals generally offer much better food for the imagination than do presentations of technical data, or even historical outlines of government policies. Information on other individuals is more appealing to us because we can integrate this material much more easily into our existing imaginative wholes, making valuable and compelling intuitive judgments in the process. Of course, Burke is relying on the fact that his listeners' imaginations can readily recognize good and bad character traits, and that their assessments will be similar to Burke's. That is, they must possess relatively well-developed, and similarly developed, moral imaginations in order to respond as Burke hopes they will.

Burke's use of character portraits should not be taken purely as a rhetorical device. He actually does see politics and public policy as an outgrowth of the character of political elites and of the broader populace. It is therefore natural for him to associate various policies of the British government with the personal qualities of the backers of those policies. In the context of a variety of different political issues, Browne finds that a focus on key political personalities "allows Burke to account for political crises in the human terms of individual character."[51] In the particular case of India, Browne finds that Burke paints Hastings (perhaps unfairly) as possessing an "essentially criminal will."[52] In his writings on the French Revolution Burke spends as much time describing the personal character of the Revolution's heroes and supporters in France and Britain as he does discussing specific events in France. The "ad hominem" quality of many of Burke's speeches and writings is not a trick to divert his audience from the "real facts" of the case. Burke possessed impressive knowledge of the events of his day, and often conducted extensive, detailed research. He shared this information with his readers and listeners. Many of his speeches in Parliament are full of facts and figures, and some are even supplemented by tables of quantitative data. Burke knows, however, that this is not enough. Technical information will not by itself convince skeptical listeners, because it does little to stimulate the imagination. This is quite distinct, it should be understood, from the conventional view, which Lock attributes to Burke, that "emotional and ethical appeals are subordinate means to enforce a rational judgement."[53] It is not a matter of approaching a question "rationally" or "emotionally." Rather, it is the case (in this example, as in many others) that technical information is inadequate to provide a real understanding of a complex situation. The character of individuals really matters; it shapes public policy, and it is shaped by public policy as well. Although Burke certainly could have qualified as what is today sometimes called a "policy wonk," he detests the stereotypical "policy wonk" or "technocrat" mentality. He criticizes those who are "too much confined to professional and faculty habits" because "they are rather disabled than qualified for whatever depends on the knowledge of mankind, on experience in mixed affairs, on a comprehensive, connected view of the various, complicated, external and internal interests which go to the formation of the multifarious thing called a state."[54]

Burke's use of character portraits as "interpretive keys" for his listeners, as well as his great concern for the role of customs, symbols, and the like, reflects his understanding of how the moral imagination works, and of the cognitive and ethical role it plays. This understanding includes a recognition of the importance of metaphor. One contemporary work that discusses metaphor and its relationship to the moral imagination is *Moral Imagination: Implications of Cognitive Science for Ethics* by Mark Johnson.[55] Of the many books of the past two decades with "moral imagination" in their titles, this is one of the few that makes some attempt at a serious treatment of the subject. Like many of the contemporary writers who in some way write on the moral imagination, Johnson makes no reference to Burke, and offers no provenance at all for the term. However, Johnson touches explicitly on some points that are compactly present in Burke. Johnson's central claim, which he seems to regard as novel, is that "human moral understanding is fundamentally imaginative."[56] For him, part and parcel of moral understanding being fundamentally imaginative is its being fundamentally metaphorical. According to Johnson, "the metaphoric character of our moral understanding is precisely what makes it possible for us to make appropriate moral judgments." Metaphor "gives rise to different ways of conceptualizing situations" and "gives us constrained ways" to move "beyond the 'clear' or prototypical cases to new cases."[57] That is, it serves as a means to bring experience to bear on new situations. For Johnson, "We understand morally problematic situations via conventional metaphorical mappings."[58] Johnson lays out his moral-imaginative understanding of morality in the following way:

> 1) We are basically beings in process, synthesizing creatures, whose bodies locate us within a world that is at once physical, social, moral, and political all intertwined. (2) We are situated within a tradition and culture that supplies a stock of roles, scripts, frames, models, and metaphors that are our way of having a world, understanding it, and reasoning about it. (3) Moral judgments occur within this biological-cultural background and make use of these imaginative tools. . . . (4) As the most comprehensive synthesizing process, narrative plays a role in organizing our long-term identity and in testing our scenarios in making moral choices.[59]

Burke, like Mark Johnson, understands that moral understanding operates much more on a metaphorical level than on an abstract conceptual level; the limits of abstract conceptual thought, of course, he mentions repeatedly. Johnson emphasizes, along with metaphor, the importance of prototypes,[60] a fact of which Burke was also clearly aware. For Burke, we may not always be able to provide good conceptual definitions of various virtues and vices, but we can usually tell the good guys from the bad guys. He tells us that the imagination possesses great creative power and great power for finding similarities; through these powers we can metaphorically apply particular examples and prototypes to very different circumstances. This is one reason why he offers character profiles of political leaders; the profiles link metaphorically to public policies. Likewise, the symbols and traditions he wishes to strengthen and preserve serve metaphorically as anchors for our moral understanding. They give us "constrained ways" to address new situations (to use Johnson's language), providing a bulwark against caprice. Johnson also maintains that "fiction provides experimental settings in which to make our own moral explorations,"[61] just as Burke found that "the theatre is a better school of moral sentiments than the churches."

Although Mark Johnson makes useful observations, it should be noted that his approach to the moral imagination lacks the richness of Burke's. Johnson devotes his energies to fighting against what he calls "moral law" approaches to ethics, but his own approach is one that Burke would probably consider to be strangely rationalistic. According to Johnson, a moral-imaginative approach to morality suggests we have "a task of refining our perception of character and situations and of developing empathetic imagination to take up the part of others."[62] The implication seems to be that we should just set about doing this. There is comparatively little information given about how the moral imagination is developed. In particular, while there is some mention of the role played by cultural elements, there is little exploration of precisely how these elements contribute to a sound moral imagination, and little recognition that traditions are important. Akin to the downplaying of the need for traditions, there is no discussion of how one's moral perception may deteriorate as in the case of Burke's monster metaphysicians who ignore traditional touchstones. Very significantly, there is no emphasis on the need for a sense of a moral order that is greater than the will of any individual or group, or of the role of the sacred and sublime. Johnson's approach is much more reflective of late modernity than is Burke's, in that Johnson places more emphasis on individual autonomy and much less emphasis on humility.

In addition, Johnson seems to contradict himself. Or the precise meaning of "moral imagination" seems to shift throughout his work. Although his stated thesis is that "human moral understanding is fundamentally imaginative," when explicitly discussing the moral imagination he tends to focus on the need to develop particularly "imaginative" approaches to moral and social problems. If moral understanding is *fundamentally* imaginative, one would not think that it would be necessary to make a particular effort to think imaginatively in order for the moral imagination to be in play. In direct contradiction of his thesis, Johnson sometimes gives the impression that if one employs one's moral imagination in addressing an ethical question, one is approaching that question in a special way that is categorically different from the manner in which people normally approach ethical questions. Similarly, Johnson sets up a very sharp contrast between a moral-imaginative approach to ethics and a "moral law" approach to ethics, implying that these approaches are mutually exclusive. Such a sharp contrast would not be drawn by Burke. On the one hand, Burke seems to understand that there is really no such thing as addressing an ethical question purely though the "rational" application of moral laws, and seems to understand that the moral imagination is always in play. Some sort of imaginative framework for understanding reality is always present and functioning. On the other hand, Burke would never advocate an attempt to approach morality in a manner that ignored moral laws; these contribute in important ways to our imaginative conceptions of reality.

Johnson's emphasis on metaphor and prototypes is nonetheless helpful in understanding Burke. It is in part because of the role of metaphor and prototypes in morality that Burke emphasizes the importance not just of old customs but of theater, fiction, poetry, art, and the like. As was mentioned in chapter 2, from his very first public writing in the *Reformer* Burke demonstrates awareness of an intimate connection between the "Morals of a Nation" and the "Taste and Writings" of its people. Attention to the theater and to literature is for him no less than "the first and surest Method" of attending to public morality and, by implication, to politics. Cultural elements such as these form part of the "wardrobe of a moral imagination" to which Burke would refer decades later. In chapter 1 it was noted that Burke believes that we learn primarily by imitation, rather than by "precept." This is one aspect of the mind's tendency to operate through prototype and metaphor, rather than through the application of abstract conceptual criteria. Abstract concepts typically play a part in framing our imaginative wholes; they may in some cases play an extremely important part, but those wholes are mostly formed from concrete experiential data. Consequently, the plays we see, the stories we read, and all of our experiences can shape us in powerful ways, by equipping our imagination for good or for ill.

It should be noted that even abstract concepts often tend to be utilized more in metaphorical and intuitive ways than in a strictly "rational" manner; it is in fact not uncommon for a particular conceptual framework or maxim to influence thought in ways that do not actually follow logically. For example, Plato noted in the *Republic* a relationship between democracy, with its emphasis on equality, and a belief that all actions or ways of life are of equal value; Tocqueville noted in *Democracy in America* that democracy, with its majoritarian basis, tends to lead to a belief that the majority view is necessarily the "correct" one, morally or otherwise. Neither belief follows automatically from support for democracy as a political system, yet the connection is there. The metaphorical power of abstract concepts, and of political practices of all sorts, suggests a need for great caution when adopting new doctrines or policies.

The importance of "narrative," discussed by Johnson, is of course not lost on Burke. Burke's interest in this area is demonstrated by his emphasis on the theater and on literature, and his discussion of the role played by narrative in societies without philosophical discourse. Moreover, Burke's interest in tradition, and in the building up of historically based models for imitation, ties closely to an interest in narrative. The linkage between narrative and tradition is shown by Alasdair MacIntyre. For him, "there is no way to give us an understanding of any society, including our own, except through the stock of stories which constitute its initial dramatic resources. Mythology, in its original sense, is at the heart of things."[63] He speaks of the "narrative view of the self," and states that "what I am, therefore, is in key part what I inherit, a specific past that is present to some degree in my present."[64] Despite making such highly Burkean observations, MacIntyre goes on to disparage Burke, maintaining that "when a tradition becomes Burkean, it is always dying or dead."[65] This seems an odd claim. MacIntyre never explains how a tradition can "become Burkean"; while forms of political, social, or philosophical thought can be "Burkean" if they resemble Burke's, it is not clear what a "Burkean tradition" may be. MacIntyre states that "traditions, when vital, embody conflict"; presumably he believes that for Burke they cannot. He offers no evidence of any sort to support this implied claim. The British political tradition was for Burke certainly one that "embodied conflict": it was neither static nor reflective of a single approach to government. Burke states, in fact, that the obliteration of that tradition in favor of new rationalistic schemes would "render us unfit for rational liberty."[66] One of the benefits of attending to tradition is that tradition does in fact embody conflict, while rationalistic approaches generally attempt to ignore or suppress conflict. Writing on Russell Kirk, who was much influenced by Burke, Gerald Russello draws on Jean-François Lyotard to note that for Kirk "the patterns of narrative knowledge allow a culture always to be reintegrating its past into its present."[67] Like Kirk, Burke gives no indication of perceiving tradition as something static and "dead."

In another work MacIntyre veers into another odd, offhand-appearing attack on Burke, stating that

> in part the invisibility of the rationality of tradition was due to the lack of expositions, let alone defenses, of that rationality.
>
> Burke was on this matter, as on so many others, an agent of positive harm. For Burke ascribed to traditions in good order, the order as he supposed of following nature, "wisdom without reflection." So that no place is left for reflection, rational theorizing as a work of and within tradition.[68]

Again MacIntyre offers no documentation to support his view, other than the single quotation of the brief phrase "wisdom without reflection" from the *Reflections*. Burke's use of this phrase, however, simply denotes the fact that traditions potentially offer individuals sources of wisdom that are available without those individuals engaging in special reflection or theorizing. It certainly does not imply a belief that tradition leaves no room for reflection or for rational theorizing, or that reflection and theorizing are not a part of tradition. Burke, in fact, goes out of his way to make clear that he does not reject theorizing:

> I do not vilify theory and speculation: no, because that would be to vilify reason itself. . . . [W]henever I speak against theory, I mean always a weak, erroneous, fallacious, unfounded, or imperfect theory; and one of the ways of discovering that it is a false theory is by comparing it with practice. This is the true touchstone of all theories which regard man and the affairs of men,—Does it suit his nature in general?—does it suit his nature as modified by his habits?[69]

Likewise, there is the famous statement, quoted in chapter 1, that "many of our men of speculation, instead of exploding general prejudices, employ their sagacity to discover the latent wisdom which prevails in them. If they find what they seek, and they seldom fail, they think it more wise to continue the prejudice, with the reason involved."[70] Burke does not oppose philosophical thought or social criticism. And for him, tradition embodies wisdom in a dynamic, not a static, way. "Tradition" includes traditions of inquiry, and tradition supports sound inquiry by equipping the moral imagination. MacIntyre's mischaracterization of Burke flows from a misunderstanding of "Burkean conservatism," which in turn flows from a failure to appreciate Burke's moral-imaginative approach to epistemology and ethics.

The very future of society can be seen for Burke to rest upon the moral imaginations of the people and their leaders. The project he began in his youth of attending to character through the cultural elements that furnish the moral imagination, he continued throughout his life. This chapter has explicated and developed aspects of Burke's epistemological and ethical thought, has indicated the role that the moral imagination plays in that thought, and has touched on the relationship of that thought to Burke's politics. Relatively little attention, however, has been devoted to the question of precisely what constitutes a sound moral imagination for Burke, or to the question of what factors he believes help to support or undermine that imagination. These will be addressed in chapter 4.

4
Characteristics of
a Moral Imagination

IN CHAPTER 3 KEY MORAL and epistemological ideas, including the concept of the moral imagination and its role, were developed from Burke's thought. A healthy, stable, liberal society requires a people with a particular kind of character, and this requires that they possess moral imaginations of a particular type. That is, their imaginations must be the sort that contribute to the kinds of judgments and behaviors that make for good living within such a society, and that reinforce that society's desirable norms. It has been shown that because our reason, our intuition, our feelings, and such all must operate within imaginative wholes that we create, the forms these wholes take have a profound effect on how we reason, how we intuit, and what we feel. Because we tend to think metaphorically, our understanding of reality is shaped strongly by symbols, and by associations we make among diverse elements. What is often called "moral education" or "political education" in academic discourse today can be seen, in large part, as the equipping of the moral imagination. The terms "moral education" and "political education" have varying uses, however. Burke would agree with the broad, descriptive usage of these terms, which tends to emphasize the experiential nature of such learning. He would likely have concerns about those who believe that morality or proper political behavior can simply be taught in the same manner in which one teaches, for example, the alphabet.

For Burke, people learn largely through imitation, through experience, and through the absorption of prejudices; while there is a potentially important role for deliberate tutelage, one cannot simply create sound character in this manner. Care, then, must be taken to identify the kinds of elements that for Burke would contribute to a well-equipped moral imagination. To identify these elements, it is necessary also to determine how he characterizes a desirable imaginative framework.

Theater and Art as Moral Shapers

In previous chapters Burke's early concern about the effect of theater on morality and politics was mentioned. The morals of a nation, the first issue of the *Reformer* states, have a great dependence upon the "taste and writings" of its people. People are naturally imitative and learn primarily in this manner; as a result, the theater may have a great impact on how people behave. Interestingly, one of the works Burke reviewed for the *Annual Register* was *A Letter from M. Rousseau of Geneva, to M. d'Alembert, of Paris, concerning the Effects of Theatrical Entertainments on the Manners of Mankind.* Burke takes the opportunity to denigrate Rousseau, attributing to him "a splenetic disposition carried to misanthropy," and stating that his treatments of "civilized society" and "learning" are likely to "lead by degrees to universal scepticism [*sic*]."[1] Nonetheless, he gives this particular work a favorable review, and remarks on the importance of the topic. Burke's interest in the impact of the theater did not fade over time. As has been seen, in the *Reflections* he remarks at one point about the theater's role in moral education. Despite recognizing the potential for the theater to play a positive role, he is more often concerned about its negative effects.

The second issue of the *Reformer* expresses concern about the characters whom a playwright "plainly proposes for Imitation."[2] In the third issue Burke remarks particularly on players who contribute to "Propagation of Vice, or what is near as bad, Folly, by their Manner of acting."[3] This remark repeats a concern expressed in the first issue regarding "Vice and Folly" going "round the Nation hand in hand."[4] Burke's concern regarding portrayals of vice in the theater is readily understandable; his complaints regarding lewdness and "smutty Entendre" are echoed by critics of the media today. But why should "folly" be such a concern, and why does it travel "hand in hand" with vice? The *Reformer* makes clear that the objection is not to humor per se, but specifically to "folly" or "buffoonery."[5] Interestingly, it quickly becomes evident that what Burke is really most concerned about is the insertion of folly, buffoonery, entendre, and the like into venerable plays by great playwrights:

> It was one of the greatest Charges on *Zoilus* the Detracter [*sic*] of *Homer*, that he dare abuse a man by whom so many lived; how much more might it be objected to those Players, who daily more than burlesque by their vile Alterations, the Authors from whom they have their daily Bread; and, not content with the many Pieces they have already of that Nature, they turn all that we have, great or noble, to Farce: To give but one Instance from a thousand, the Scene of the Witches in *Macbeth*, perhaps the most solemn that can be represented, is burlesqued in such a Manner, that it is surprizing [*sic*] how the People bear, much less applaud it.[6]

Something very important is lost when we "turn all that we have, great or noble, to Farce." Once they are parodied or made into opportunities for jokes and silliness, the great and noble things, by which "so many lived," no longer have the same significance they once had. The scene of the witches is a solemn one because it deals with fate, with mystery, and with great matters affecting people and nations. To turn this scene into an occasion for "ridiculous Jiggs" and "smutty Entendre"[7] is to deny the seriousness of the matters that are addressed. If such grave matters as those the scene addresses cannot be taken seriously, what can be? Can duty, honor, and country be taken seriously? The sense emerges that nothing is sacred, and, ultimately, that nothing has meaning. One can see how "folly" and "vice" will therefore travel "hand in hand." As in Plato's model of the degeneration of society in the *Republic,* vice grows as a sense of order and meaning declines, and everything becomes equal. The friends of the young "democratic man" promote vice by making fun of virtues and of those who possess them. By ridiculing that which is most important in life, a hierarchy of values is lost, and we all become "democratic men."

Plays, literature, and other creative works, especially venerable ones, constitute an important part of one's moral imagination. The vicarious experiences we have in the theater, and the characters we observe, provide touchstones that guide our judgment in matters of all kinds, especially the ethical. If we undermine those experiences by failing to take them seriously, we impair the moral imagination that is partly based upon them. A relationship is evident between Burke's early concern regarding "folly" in the theater, particularly when inserted into venerable works, and his praise of Pope Gregory for taking care to ensure "that the prejudices of the people might not be too rudely shocked by a declared profanation of what they had so long held sacred" when England was converted to Christianity. Likewise, because Homer was "a man by whom so many lived," his detractor caused harm by causing people to lose their bearings. Those who spread "folly" in the theater are committing a similar crime. The harm they are inflicting can be characterized as deforming the moral imaginations of their audience. The doors are opened to cynicism and nihilism, and to irresponsible, capricious behavior. What the modern writers and adapters of these plays are doing is destroying the sense of standards, and making any standards that do exist in the community appear arbitrary, with no linkage to a greater, mysterious order beyond human whim.

Several years after his *Reformer* project, in his *Hints for an Essay on the Drama*, Burke argues for what we would call "decorum" in the arts. He rejects the arguments of those who claim that anything that is "natural" may be introduced into a story, with "natural" meaning, in this case, anything that might possibly be found if the events portrayed were happening in the real world. Burke insists that one of the criteria of a good play is not "naturalness," but the sense that all of the elements have something to do with the end for which the work is written. For one negative example Burke turns from the theater to the visual arts, criticizing a famous painting of the Last Supper by Rubens in which a dog gnawing bones is shown under the table.[8] He does not explain precisely what is wrong with this painting, but from the context one may presume that Burke believes that the mundaneness and ugliness of the realistic or "natural" image of a dog gnawing bones sets up a jarring contradiction to the feelings associated with the Last Supper itself. It serves to drag the event down to the level of ordinary human experience, transforming it into a dinner party. In the process, it diminishes one's sense of reverence towards this profoundly sublime "larger than life" event.

Whether or not one agrees with Burke's assessment of the Rubens painting, it is easy to see what he is getting at. The strong linkage between aesthetics and ethics is once again evident. This linkage occurs because of the role of the imagination. While to a degree the imagination operates "aesthetically," it is also a key to morality. It helps establish standards and it gives them weight. A very strong relationship is of course also evident to Burke's interest in the sublime. The scene of the witches and the Last Supper are both, in different ways, sublime. They involve powers and mysteries beyond human understanding or control, thereby providing a point of contact with the infinite and provoking a sense of humility in the face of a greater order. Burke is concerned about the insertion of the ridiculous, or of the mundane, into the sublime, since this has the effect of undermining the sublime. The above examples demonstrate additional aspects of the synthesis that Burke effectively establishes between "romanticism" and "classicism." Burke's interest in mystery and his belief in the ability of the imagination to penetrate, to a limited extent, that mystery, has a romantic quality, but it is paired with a classical support for decorum in the arts. Decorum actually helps maintain the "romantic" sublime, by disallowing those artistic elements that would undermine it. Conversely, Burke's "romantic" interest in the sublime can be seen as part of a "classical" interest in upholding standards, since the feelings we get from the sublime encourage us to maintain and work toward standards by giving them meaning and importance that go beyond simple human convention. One's aesthetic approach to important things helps to determine whether or not those things really *matter.*

Religion, Humility, and Standards

An emphasis on standards is one of the central elements of Burke's moral and political outlook. An awareness of something greater than oneself, expressed through reverence or awe, is also central to his thought. These two key elements are linked through Burke's emphasis on humility. In Burke's words, "true humility, the basis of the Christian system, is the low, but deep and firm foundation of all real virtue."[9] The humility that Burke calls for is an uplifting, rather than demeaning, sort of humility. It is humility in the face of a greater order, but this humility includes a recognition that one plays a part in that order. Rather than rendering one's actions futile, it gives them new importance.

At a mundane level, a practical demonstration of Burke's emphasis on humility is provided in his observation that "turbulent, discontented men of quality, in proportion as they are puffed up with personal pride and arrogance, generally despise their own order. One of the first symptoms they discover of a selfish and mischievous ambition, is a profligate disregard of a dignity which they partake with others."[10] Proud and arrogant members of the upper classes who disregard the "dignity which they partake with others" behave in "selfish and mischievous" ways; virtuous behavior flows from those who have the humility to recognize the role they play in their class and their society, and who realize that they owe much to their class and to their society. These things have helped make them who they are. Burke would certainly agree with the maxim that there is no such thing as a "self-made man." Elites who reject or denounce their class in favor of a professed egalitarianism are not being humble but are displaying a kind of arrogance and vanity. They are demonstrating (at least, in their own minds) their independence from, and their moral superiority to, the other members of their class. While this example demonstrates one linkage between humility and virtue in Burke, the particular kind of humility he is most concerned about is that which is "the basis of the Christian system," which is humility before an order that is greater than any merely human order or system. Humility with regard to the social order and humility before a greater mysterious order are, however, closely linked in Burke's thought, and operate in similar ways.

As was mentioned in chapter 1, Burke famously gives credit for "our manners, our civilization, and all the good things that are connected" with them to "the spirit of a gentleman, and the spirit of religion."[11] In the particular context of this quote Burke explicitly credits the nobility and clergy with preserving and promoting learning. However, the "spirits" of which Burke speaks are much more than spirits of learning. He states that he favors the British tradition of education by ecclesiastics, which promotes "learning, not debauched by ambition."[12] The spirit of a gentleman and spirit of religion are both, more than anything, a spirit of standards, grounded in a spirit of humility and reverence. To be a gentleman is to have certain standards. These standards are at once internal and external. They have been internalized, and have been willingly adopted and taken to heart. They are one's own standards. But, they are not simply one's own standards. They are external in that they are understood not to spring entirely from one's own will, but from a greater social and, indeed, universal order. Linked to these standards is a sense of a kind of sacred trust that one has from one's class and one's society, as well, perhaps, as from humanity as a whole. In the case of religion, the sense of the sacred is of course much more explicit.

The importance of religion comes up frequently in Burke's writings. He states that "we know, and what is better, we feel inwardly, that religion is the basis of civil society, and the source of all good and of all comfort."[13] Like many commentators of his time period, Burke occasionally makes reference to the straightforward connection between Christianity and a good society that arises from Christianity's promotion of morality through promises of rewards or punishments in the afterlife. One early reference appears in the *Reformer,* where it is stated that "there are a Set of Men not infrequent in this City, who tho' they allow of Morality, cry down reveal'd Religion, yet in their Practice, they make them equal, neglecting both; how weak an Obligation, Morality consider'd in itself would be, may be seen, by supposing Laws imposed on a Nation, without Rewards for those who kept, or Punishments for those who broke them."[14] However, Burke's appreciation of the role of religion goes much beyond the simple incentive of rewards and punishments. Religion inspires in us a sense of a greater order of which we are a part. This in turn inspires humility and restraint, while also inspiring us to be our best.

Burke gives religion the greatest importance among the many factors that contribute to a sound moral imagination. He also gives it an important political role. The church establishment, Burke says, is "the first of our prejudices."[15] He emphasizes the need for some sort of a tying of church and state, "like a provident proprietor, to preserve the structure from profanation and ruin, as a sacred temple purged from all the impurities of fraud and violence and injustice and tyranny, hath solemnly and forever consecrated the commonwealth, and all the officiate in it."[16] Burke's view of the commonwealth as something "consecrated" is striking. Casual and unsympathetic readers of Burke sometimes interpret his idea of the church "consecrating" the state as a cynical plan to dupe the masses into providing unconditional support for their government.[17] Burke is anything but cynical, however. And although his concern extends to the behavior of the general population, he is at least as concerned about the behavior of elites, especially those holding high office. The linking of church and state does not keep a population submissive to oppressive rulers, but helps discourage "fraud and violence and injustice and tyranny" in government. Burke explains:

> This consecration is made, that all who administer the government of men, in which they stand in the person of God himself, should have high and worthy notions of their function and destination; that their hope should be full of immortality; that they should not look to the paltry pelf of the moment, nor to the temporary and transient praise of the vulgar, but to a solid, permanent existence, in the permanent part of their nature, and to a permanent fame and glory, in the example they leave as a rich inheritance to the world.[18]

A key to good government is the attitude that those in office display toward their citizens, toward their commonwealth, and toward their own roles in society. The commonwealth is, in some ways, a sacred thing, and a position of government office is a sacred trust. A sense that those in government "stand in the person of God himself" does not, of course, imply unthinking obedience to an absolute monarch; Burke's own parliamentary record of opposition to the king should dispel any such interpretation. Nor, of course, does this sense imply a freedom for those in government to exercise arbitrary power. What Burke strives for is the exact opposite of arbitrary power. He is calling for the constrained, measured use of power. No simple formula exists for such a well-run government, but it is for Burke the kind of government that flows from leaders with reverence for God and for the commonwealth. Such persons, Burke believes, are likely to have high standards, and to think not of momentary personal advantage but of the permanent things. What they possess is the proper sort of humility, thinking of the awesome role they play and of the sacredness of their trust. This humility imposes a sense of constraint on the will, since one recognizes that one is not free to exercise arbitrary power. Similarly, this humility inspires dutiful action.

Once again Burke's early interest in the sublime is manifest in his politics; in speaking of the importance of the "consecration" of the state he adds that "such sublime principles ought to be infused into persons of exalted situations, and religious establishments provided, that may continually revive and enforce them."[19] Although Burke certainly views the prospect of divine punishment or reward as a motivator, he is at least as concerned with the powerful way in which a sense of the sacred helps convey meaning, order, and standards to political life. In the introduction to his early *Vindication of Natural Society* he explains that in writing this work "the Design was, to shew that, . . . the same Engines which were employed for the Destruction of Religion, might be employed with equal Success for the Subversion of Government."[20] Burke gives an indication of what he considers those "engines" to be when he states that "the Editor is satisfied that a Mind which has no Restraint from a Sense of its own Weakness, of its subordinate Rank in the Creation, and of the extreme Danger of letting the Imagination loose upon some Subjects, may very plausibly attack every thing most excellent and venerable; that it would not be difficult to criticize the Creation itself."[21] If we lose the "constrained ways" (as Mark Johnson puts it) that a moral imagination provides for evaluating situations, we find ourselves hurtling toward an abyss in which anything and everything is questioned, and in which much that is "excellent and venerable" is destroyed, along with any sense of meaning. This occurs if we lose the "sublime principles" by which we remove ourselves from the center stage and treat the world with a measure of awe and respect, instead of treating it as no more than raw material to be made subject to our capricious will.

Burke holds that, in addition to shaping the attitudes of those holding high offices, "the consecration of the state by a state religious establishment is necessary, also, to operate with a wholesome awe upon free citizens, because, in order to secure their freedom, they must enjoy some determinate portion of power. . . . All persons possessing any portion of power ought to be strongly and awfully impressed with an idea that they act in trust."[22] The "consecration" of the state helps to maintain not a subjugated citizenry, but a free citizenry. Since ordinary citizens hold some of the political power, they, no less than high office holders, must possess the right kind of moral imagination, which helps them to exercise restraint and prompts them to think of what Russell Kirk calls "the permanent things." Burke maintains that "it is therefore of infinite importance that they should not be suffered to imagine that their will, any more than that of kings, is the standard of right and wrong."[23] A sense among the general public that standards exist, and that the will must be checked with reference to those standards, is for Burke central to political order; he finds this to be true for any form of government.[24] He explains:

> When the people have emptied themselves of all the lust of selfish will, . . . they will not appoint to the exercise of authority, as to a pitiful job, but as to a holy function; not according to their sordid selfish interest, nor to their wanton caprice, nor to their arbitrary will; but they will confer that power . . . on those only, in whom they may discern that predominant proportion of active virtue and wisdom, taken together and fitted to the charge, such as in the great and inevitable mixed mass of human imperfections and infirmities is to be found.[25]

Political order rests upon the character of both the rulers and the ruled. In a society that is in any way democratic it is especially important that the citizenry possess the kind of character that allows them to move beyond immediate self-interest and to think of the "big picture." This requires a well-developed moral imagination. Only a population that sees government as a "holy function" and is equipped to check its own "arbitrary will" will place the right sort of persons in power. If the citizenry is not so formed, it will, Burke explains, become "prey to the servile ambition of popular sycophants."[26] Burke is well aware of the prevalence of "human imperfections and infirmities"; consequently he knows how precarious a sound political order is. It is therefore not surprising that he focuses on seeing to it that the citizenry is morally well equipped. If "folly" in the theater may indirectly contribute to a loss of the sense of government and society as sacred trusts, and to the loss of an appreciation of the need for meaningful personal and political standards, it is no wonder that the theater and other avenues of the imagination would occupy his interest.

It is perhaps worthwhile to emphasize that Burke's goal here is not an authoritarian state, but its opposite. It is the right sort of character and culture that makes a reasonably liberal order possible. Speaking of the new French republic of the revolutionaries, Burke notes that "every thing depends upon the army in such a government as yours; for you have industriously destroyed all the opinions, and prejudices, and, as far as in you lay, all the instincts which support government. Therefore the moment any difference arises between your national assembly and any part of the nation, you must have recourse to force."[27] In Burke's view a thoroughly "modern" state, in the sense of a state in which the usual moral-imaginative touchstones have been stripped away, is bound to be a tyranny. Famously, Burke remarks:

> Men are qualified for civil liberty, in exact proportion to their disposition to put moral chains upon their own appetites; in proportion as their love to justice is above their rapacity; in proportion as their soundness and sobriety of understanding is above their vanity and presumption; in proportion as they are more disposed to listen to the counsels of the wise and good, in preference to the flattery of knaves. Society cannot exist unless a controlling power upon will and appetite be placed somewhere, and the less of it there is within, the more there must be without. It is ordained in the eternal constitution of things, that men of intemperate minds cannot be free. Their passions forge their fetters.[28]

If people cannot control themselves, an authoritarian state will be required to maintain order. To a large extent Burke's general project can be seen as one of fostering the kinds of societies that make civil liberty possible. Burke's politics can therefore be seen as a kind of politics of virtue. The contemporary scholar Bruce Frohnen maintains that "the conservative seeks to preserve existing institutions *because* they allow for and foster the practice of virtue."[29] As previously noted, identifying Burke's views with conservatism may be problematic in some ways, and Burke does not always seek to preserve existing institutions. But, this linkage between virtue and the preservation of institutions is an important one. Frohnen also notes that "Prudence is the necessary tool for the attainment of virtue; it is the practical wisdom necessary if one is to judge rightly how to respond to particular circumstances."[30] Burke's emphasis on "prudence," noted by Strauss in a quote early in this book, is reflective of his belief that the state rests upon virtue and practical wisdom, and that these in turn rest upon the various sorts of social frameworks that are in place. Alasdair MacIntyre has stated that "practical reasoning is by its nature, on the generally Aristotelian view that I have been taking, reasoning together with others, generally within some determinate set of social relationships. Those relationships are initially formed and then developed as the relationships through which each of us first achieves and is then supported in the status of an independent practical reasoner."[31]

In this context it is not surprising that the importance of religion to Burke is not limited to its role in the "consecration" of the state. Chiding the French revolutionaries, he argues:

> All other nations have begun the fabric of a new government, or the reformation of an old, by establishing originally or by enforcing with greater exactness some rites or other of religion. All other people have laid the foundations of a civil freedom in severer manners, and a system of a more austere and masculine morality. France, when she let loose the reins of regal authority, doubled the licence, of a ferocious dissoluteness in manners, and of an insolent irreligion in opinions and practices.[32]

His coupling of religion with manners here is significant. As previously discussed, manners are very important to Burke; he states that they help constitute the "wardrobe of a moral imagination," shaping character, supporting morality, and making a civil society possible. Burke's interest in manners is not unique; there was in fact a great deal of interest in the role of manners and politeness among intellectuals in his day, especially among the Scottish historians and moral philosophers with whom Burke was in contact.[33] J. G. A. Pocock explains that manners and politeness were seen as important civilizing agents: "By observation, conversation, and cultivation, men and women are brought to an awareness of the needs and responses of others and of how they appear in the eyes of others," so that manners and politeness are closely linked to morality. Moreover, Pocock finds that the French "deist philosophes were seeking to substitute manners for religion as the key to the history of mankind."[34] Burke, however, does not seek to substitute manners for religion; he presents manners partly as functioning side-by-side with religion, and partly as rooted in religion.

Burke's grouping of religion with manners, and his general focus on the practical, and especially the political, value of religion, have led to some speculation that Burke's religious beliefs were not sincere. A wide variety of Burke scholars, however, have taken his religiosity seriously. Michael Freeman, for example, writes that "although Burke's commitment to religion was strong, he did emphasize its social utility much more than its truth. . . .

Yet the social advantages of religion touched such fundamental aspects of human existence that they constituted, for him, proof of its truth."[35] Rather than saying that Burke did not emphasize the "truth" of Christianity, it may be better to say that he did not emphasize explicit doctrine or dogma, or that he did not devote attention to efforts to make or prove particular religious points. This may be traced in part to Burke's humility, to his sense of mystery, and to his recognition of the limits of human knowledge, especially regarding ultimate things. The ambiguities and contradictions of Burke's own religious upbringing would have certainly discouraged in him belief in a single "true" religion that alone had value. Although Burke professed to be an Anglican and was a staunch defender of the church establishment, his mother, sister, and wife were Roman Catholic. Moreover, although Burke's father was officially a member of the Church of Ireland (the Anglican Church's Irish equivalent), he may have been a recent "convert," and would have been like the many other Irish Catholic attorneys who found it necessary at that time to "convert" nominally to Anglicanism due to the barring of Catholics from most practice of law.[36] Because of the severe restrictions that existed on Catholics, it was common to baptize sons secretly as Roman Catholic and then to baptize them publicly as Anglican. Daughters in such families were generally simply baptized Catholic, since the professional and economic constraints on Catholics usually had little bearing on women. While it is impossible to know precisely what was going on privately in Burke's family, the pattern of Irish families with Catholic mothers and daughters and "Protestant" fathers and sons was a common one. Burke spent portions of his childhood living with his Catholic cousins, and then was sent to a Quaker school. His best friend, Richard Shackleton, was the son of the schoolmaster. While, as an Anglican, Burke attended Trinity College, his friend was not permitted to attend due to his dissenter status.[37] Burke's intense personal experience of so much religious diversity, and his direct personal observation of the exploitation of such diversity for purposes of oppression, probably contributed to his deemphasizing of doctrinal details and his emphasis instead on mystery, and on "religion" in general.

For Burke, the importance of religion extends far beyond particular doctrines. Religion consists not just of doctrine, but of rites, narratives, and other trappings that help to form the moral imagination and to shape character on an inarticulate, intuitive level. Burke demonstrated an awareness of the importance of such elements in his early discussion of the gradualism of Christianity's introduction into England. Much later, in the *Reflections*, he writes approvingly that "there is no rust of superstition, with which the accumulated absurdity of the human mind might have crusted it [religion] over in the course of ages, that ninety-nine in a hundred of the people of England would not prefer to impiety."[38] Early in his career, Burke had with the *Vindication* taken on those who would replace traditional Christianity with new and improved, "natural" or "reasonable" forms of religion. Burke's concern is not with attaining or preserving some sort of purity of doctrine, but with piety. The "rust of superstition" is fine with him, just as much earlier he approved of the preservation of those elements of pagan rites that were not incompatible with Christianity. Much of religion's value for Burke lies in its experiential nature, since for him we learn more experientially than "by precept." It is the sense of the sacred, the awareness of a mysterious greater order into which we fit, that Burke considers most important. He knows that this sense of a universal order is transmitted in part through the venerable nature of religion. Simply to make up a religion for oneself is the height of hubris. Such a religion cannot be very successful in inspiring piety, since that which we fully understand, or that which is wholly the product of one's own will, cannot in Burke's view be sublime.

The Venerable as a Bridge to the Universal

The tying of the venerable to the sublime and, hence, to the moral, is a dominant theme in Burke. The state is not "consecrated" merely by religion but by its own timeless nature. The constraints needed on behavior in order to maintain a well-functioning liberal society are not imposed only by religion but by respect for one's political forefathers. Most important is a strong historical sense of one's place in an ongoing society. Burke maintains that

> one of the first and most leading principles on which the commonwealth and the laws are consecrated is, lest the temporary possessors and life-renters in it, unmindful of what they have received from their ancestors or of what is due to their posterity, should act as if they were the entire masters; that they should not think it among their rights to cut off the entail or commit waste on the inheritance by destroying at their pleasure the whole original fabric of their society; hazarding to leave to those who come after them a ruin instead of an habituation—and teaching these successors as little to respect their contrivances as they had themselves respected the institutions of their forefathers.[39]

This passage can of course be seen as a manifestation of "Burkean conservatism." As was explained in chapter 1, Burke's true perspective is not a conviction that the old ways are always, or nearly always, better. His view does include the belief that what is old has, to a degree, been proven and tested, and that we make drastic changes at our peril, since life and human nature are complex and somewhat mysterious and our knowledge is always limited. This is a point that Burke is making here, but it is not his main point. He goes on to talk about "the evils of inconstancy," explaining that a society with ever-changing laws, customs, and such would be one of "barbarism." The legal system would break down; education would break down since one could not know what sort of society and role for which to prepare young people; "unskilfulness" [*sic*] would reign, and "the commonwealth itself would, in a few generations, crumble away, be disconnected into the dust and powder of individuality."[40] In other words, a world would be created in which no one would really know what to do or how to do it properly, and the close ties among people would be replaced by atomization.

Change made without proper respect for what has been handed down is likely to create a culture of "inconstancy," since if dramatic changes can be made once, they can be made again. Why should the first set of changes be respected? Nothing is sacred; no inherent value or weight is attached to that which is long-established. In such an atmosphere, everything is up for grabs. Why should any convention be respected? Politics becomes more and more the exercise of brute power, since traditional boundaries and constraints on the use of power vanish. Just as, for Burke, a made-up religion cannot be very successful in inspiring piety, so a radically new, made-up social order or political structure is also an act of hubris that is likely to fail. In chapter 2 mention was made of Heidegger's observation that a world in full conformity to one's will is one of insignificance. Similarly, a highly malleable social and political order is for Burke one that carries no meaning. That which is ancient is, in a way, sublime; it has an existence beyond the individuals of the present generation, inspiring a degree of awe and respect. It serves as a fixed point anchoring the moral imagination. Just as, Burke noted in his aesthetics, an inability to see clearly the edges of an object suggests infinite size; so too does an old political order suggest infinite time. If our imaginative wholes center on what seem to be permanent things, they may offer a source of standards that acts powerfully to help check the will. That which is seen merely as the product of our arbitrary will is unlikely to inspire humility, and is therefore unlikely to be very helpful in checking additional arbitrary willfulness. Such concerns about the need for a sense of permanence helped fuel Burke's opposition to relatively modest parliamentary reform, as will be discussed later.

What destroys the fabric of society is not necessarily a bad change, but any change, good or bad in itself, that is accomplished without due reverence for what has come before. This is the nature of Burke's "conservatism." This is one reason why Burke sharply distinguishes between "innovation" and "reform" in his writings, with the difference being found less in the *scope* of a change than in the *spirit* in which the change is made. "Innovation" is, of course, regarded by Burke as a bad thing, while proper reform is good. Burke was not unique in emphasizing this distinction, or in regarding innovation as undesirable. Suspicion of radical change was so ingrained in British society and politics at the time that it was common for politicians to pin the label "innovation" on proposals they wished to disparage. Francis Canavan maintains that "no politician would admit that he favored 'innovation.'" He points out that even the relatively radical Whig Charles Fox was, out of political necessity, very careful to distinguish between "innovation" and "improvement" when describing his own proposals.[41]

Writing on Burke, Bruce James Smith maintains that "the 'miracle' of custom was not that it remained unchanged (which it didn't), but that it somehow succeeded in hiding change (even the cataclysmic variety), purging the mind of the memory of dangerous examples of innovation."[42] He adds that for Burke "if we are to save the future, we must hide the fact that the present is not like the past," and that therefore "the first task of conservatism must be the obliteration of such remembrance."[43] While Burke does not clearly articulate such a view, it certainly aligns with the emphasis he appears to place on maintaining a sense of continuity with the past.

Burke insists that "people will not look forward to posterity, who never look backward to their ancestors."[44] In looking backward, in honoring those who came before and acknowledging our ties to them, we learn to think in terms of the permanent things; we look beyond our immediate self-interest and view our concerns in light of the "big picture." The effect is similar to that of the consecration of the commonwealth by religion. In reflecting on what our ancestors—whether biological or merely cultural/political—have done for us, we are inspired to do well by our descendents. Traditionalism and reverence for the past are portrayed, in fact, as necessary components of a successful liberal society: "Always acting as if in the presence of canonized forefathers, the spirit of freedom, leading itself to misrule and excess, is tempered with an awful gravity."[45] Idealized images of past statesmen provide examples to live up to, standards to follow, and a proper measure of constraint when conceiving future actions. A moral imagination is built up, which equips citizens both to make sound political decisions and to check excesses in their own day-to-day behavior. As Hayek noted, internalized moral checking is far more effective than attempts by an elite to control behavior, and it permits a freer society.[46] In addressing the Jacobins and their supporting "metaphysicians," Burke argues that "all your sophisters cannot produce any thing better adapted to preserve a rational and manly freedom than the course that we have pursued, who have chosen our nature rather than our speculations, our breasts rather than our inventions, for the great conservatories and magazines of our rights and privileges."[47]

Education and the Moral Imagination

Given Burke's strong interest in character and in moral education it is not surprising that he should have something to say about the role that the formal education of young people plays in society. What he says about education is fully in keeping with his views about the other elements that contribute to what we can identify as a sound moral imagination. Burke finds that "nothing ought to be more weighed than the nature of books recommended by public authority. So recommended, they soon form the character of the age." Assessing the state of education in revolutionary France, Burke finds that "instead of forming their young minds to that docility, to that modesty, which are the grace and charm of youth, to an admiration of famous examples, and to an averseness to anything which approaches to pride, petulance, and self-conceit . . . they artificially foment these evil dispositions, and even form them into springs of action." A good education is one that promotes humility and self-restraint, and that encourages these and other virtues through emulation of honored historical figures. Such humility as Burke recommends is not considered virtuous by the new leaders of France and, perhaps more important from their perspective, it is not regarded as politically advantageous. Consequently, "their great problem is, to find a substitute for all the principles which hitherto have been employed to regulate the human will and action."[48]

Faced with the problem of developing and promoting a new set of social standards, "the [French National] Assembly recommends to its youth a study of the bold experimenters in morality," particularly Rousseau. Rousseau is for Burke the foremost *"philosopher of vanity,"* glorying even in the publication of his own vices.[49] Rousseau flatters humanity and discounts the role of culture, social ties, and civilization by portraying humans as inherently good but corrupted by society. The new Rousseauesque public ethics of France are,

Burke maintains, "*the ethics of vanity.*"[50] Instead of learning restraint, a sense of duty, and respect for others living and dead, youth are taught to assert themselves however they will, and to exhibit disrespect for those around them. This contrasts with the "more austere and masculine morality" found in other nations.[51] Criticizing Rousseau's *La Nouvelle Héloïse*, Burke finds that the French youth are now being taught "a love without gallantry; . . . Instead of this passion, naturally allied to grace and manners, they infuse into their youth an unfashioned, indelicate, sour, gloomy, ferocious medley of pedantry and lewdness; of metaphysical speculations, blended with the coarsest sensuality."[52] In contrast, "the last age had exhausted all its powers in giving a grace and nobleness to our natural appetites."[53] These remarks are strongly evocative of Burke's passage regarding the "moral imagination" and the need to fight a reductionism that would strip away all elegance, all meaning, and ultimately, humanity itself.

Significantly, Burke finds that "benevolence to the whole species, and want of feeling for every individual with whom the professors come in contact, form the character of the new philosophy."[54] This sort of detached benevolence is exemplified by Rousseau, who "melts with tenderness for those only who touch him by the remotest relation," while sending his own illegitimate children to orphanages.[55] Burke finds the new "universal benevolence" repugnant because it places no demands upon the will, but instead gives it free rein. This is another manifestation of the problem of abstraction. Love for a real person, such as for one's own child, imposes many duties and constraints, at least in one who has had proper moral development. Love for humankind in the lump, however, imposes no duties or constraints. Or, any duties and constraints it imposes are very much open to interpretation, and are hence essentially voluntary. Almost any project or activity one wishes to undertake can be justified by such "love" for an abstraction; one is not subject to the inconveniences of dealing with the needs and desires of a particular real-life person. Because the "duties" associated with love of mankind tend to be subject to one's self-indulgent will, they do not serve to impose meaningful limitations on it. As Burke found in the case of the monster metaphysicians, great crimes, against particular people and against humanity itself, can be justified under the rubric of "universal benevolence."

Personal Relationships and the Liberal State

The shaping of a moral imagination through different kinds of "benevolence" is an important theme in Burke. One of the most oft-quoted passages from the *Reflections* is Burke's insistence that "to be attached to the subdivision, to love the little platoon we belong to in society, is the first principle (the germ as it were) of public affections. It is the first link in the series by which we proceed towards a love to our country and to mankind."[56] Today this passage is quoted frequently by those extolling the virtues of families, but in the specific context in which this quote appears Burke seems primarily to have not families in mind but social classes, particularly the aristocracy.[57] Nevertheless, one may reasonably maintain that Burke has more than social classes in mind; there are all sorts of "little platoons" within society, and we owe much to all of them. Elsewhere, Burke makes explicit reference to the role of families and other subunits of society. As he explains, "We begin our public affections in our families. . . . We pass on to our neighborhoods and our habitual provincial connections. These are inns and resting-places. Such divisions of our country as have been formed by habit, and not by a sudden jerk of authority, were so many little images of the great country in which the heart found something which it could fill." Our affection and care for that which is close to us "is a sort of elemental training" for affection and care for our nation as a whole.[58]

Here Burke brings to mind the argument made by Robert Nisbet in *The Quest for Community* that "from innumerable observations and controlled studies we have learned that the discipline of values *within* a person has a close and continuing relationship with the discipline of values supported by human inter-relationships."[59] The development of character, of the right sort of discipline, requires interaction with real people on a continuing basis. The kind of "benevolence" or affection for one's country that yields truly moral results cannot be acquired without playing a part in "little platoons" of various sorts, since this is how we learn to develop the right kind of unselfish affection for those around us. This furnishes us with the touchstones and frames of reference needed to extend our affections to the larger society in a meaningful way; we become imaginatively grounded not in the abstract, but in the concrete, and this provides us with much more useful, internalized guidance on how to behave. Nisbet closely links the success of liberalism with the moral education provided and sustained by established social relationships and by traditions:

> [I]t is important to stress the close dependence of the whole conscious liberal heritage, with all its basic propositions, upon the subtle, infinitely complex lines of habit, tradition, and social relationship that have made this conscious heritage more than a mere set of formal propositions, that have made it

instead a potent body of evocative symbols, striking deep chords in human appreciation and remembrance. The formal, overt judgments of liberalism have rested, historically, not merely upon processes of conscious reason and verification, but upon certain prejudgments that have seldom been drawn up for critical analysis until the most recent times. And these prejudgments have, in turn, been closely linked with a set of social relationships within which their symbolic fires have been constantly kept lighted through all the normal processes of work, function, and belief.[60]

Nisbet's reference to "a potent body of evocative symbols" is strongly suggestive of Burke's "wardrobe of a moral imagination," and his reference to "prejudgments" can of course be compared to Burke's "prejudice." Burke's opposition to "abstraction" and "metaphysics" is in part a rejection of those who would rely upon, as Nisbet says, "a mere set of formal propositions" while destroying the "potent body of evocative symbols" necessary to make those propositions meaningful and compelling on a personal level. These symbols become available to us and become meaningful for us in myriad ways, including "infinitely complex lines of habit, tradition, and social relationship." They constitute a kind of "cultural capital" upon which liberalism and political modernity depend in order to function, but which they are often loathe to acknowledge, except perhaps as negatives. This cultural capital gives reasonably precise and concrete meaning—as well as "affection" and a kind of moral force—to the doctrines and precepts that characterize liberalism and political modernity. Without such support, liberalism's ideals and maxims possess little meaning, are highly mutable, and carry little weight when it comes to directing real-world behavior.

For Burke, an important dimension of many personal relationships is the fact that they are not entirely voluntary. One of the errors of the Jacobins is that they neglect that many of our associations and, consequently, our obligations, do not arise through our own volition, and that the political order likewise cannot be seen as simply the product of individuals' election. Burke uses the example of the relationship between parents and children to criticize the voluntaristic mindset of the Jacobins, stating that "Your masters reject the duties of this vulgar relation, as contrary to liberty; as not founded in the social compact; and not binding according to the rights of men; because the relation is not, of course, the result of *free election*; never so on the side of the children, not always on the part of the parents."[61] While the Jacobins' ethic is purely one of right, Burke's is primarily one of obligation. The Jacobin ethic, Burke endeavors to show, is based on a fiction. Just as the physical limitations of our bodies constrain us and impose various requirements, our relationships with others constrain us and impose obligations and limitations. This is the human condition. Burke maintains, moreover, that just as our relationships with our children are not completely voluntary, neither is our membership in the state. As Aristotle observed, only the superhuman or subhuman exists outside of society. This is why Burke rejects the Lockean, or (so as not to mischaracterize Locke) the Locke-derived concept of a purely voluntary social contract. This does not mean that for Burke one cannot make changes in the state, or, in the most extreme circumstances, even reject the state. His response to the American Revolution demonstrates this. Burke, though unhappy to see Britain lose her colonies, does not begrudge the Americans their break.

It is perhaps appropriate to make clear that for Burke arguments based upon obligation rather than right do not necessarily come down on the side of the state or of elites, as opposed to the side of ordinary people. As will be seen, he especially emphasizes the obligation of those in power to do right by their citizens or subjects. One could say, in fact, that it is generally not elites, but those most lacking in power (such as the lower classes in a state, or children in a family) who tend to have the most to lose from a rejection of obligation in favor of voluntary relationships. For Burke a denial of obligation and an overemphasis on free volition can be politically and socially devastating. The manner in which we respond to those relationships that are not entirely voluntary may in fact be one of the most important measures of, and contributors to, the development of the sort of moral-imaginative framework that equips us for life in the real world. In response to the advocates of social contract theory of a highly voluntaristic sort, Burke opines:

> Society is indeed a contract. Subordinate contracts for objects of mere occasional interest may be dissolved at pleasure—but the state ought not to be considered as nothing better than a partnership agreement in a trade of pepper and coffee, callico [*sic*] or tobacco, or some other such low concern, to be taken up for a little temporary interest, and to be dissolved by the fancy of the parties. It is to be looked on with other reverence; because it is not a partnership in things subservient only to the gross animal existence of a temporary and perishable nature. It is a partnership in all science; a partnership in all art; a partnership in every virtue, and in all perfection. As the ends of such a partnership cannot be obtained in many generations, it becomes a partnership not only between those who are living, but between

those who are living, those who are dead, and those who are to be born. Each contract of each particular state is but a clause in the great primeval contract of eternal society, linking the lower with the higher natures, connecting the visible and invisible world, according to a fixed compact sanctioned by the inviolable oath which holds all physical and all moral natures, each in their appointed place.[62]

Everything is bound up together; the state, though changeable and somewhat arbitrary in its particular form, both reflects and contributes to a greater order. To function as it ought, it must be treated with the reverence due to all matters pertaining to the highest aspects of human existence.

Personal relationships, religion, respect for ancestors, appropriate literary and theatrical material—all for Burke contribute to the development of the right sort of worldview and the right sort of will. As has been suggested, this is a will that is properly bounded. One of the great failings of the "metaphysicians" is their failure to place proper limits on the will. The "spirit of a gentleman," examples of great ancestors, religion, and the like help to encourage such willing. Willing in the right way is of course willing to do the right thing. This, however, requires a proper understanding of the "right thing," which recognizes limits, and which is informed less by lofty goals than by an intuitive sense of what actually is the right thing to do in various particular circumstances in the here and now, the practical wisdom associated with virtue. This intuitive wisdom arises through the many small judgments made as our imagination forms wholes and creates a picture of the world.

Of course, almost everyone wants to feel that he or she is doing the right thing. One product of a healthy moral imagination is a desire to feel this way. But the desire for such a feeling can have a narcissistic or selfish quality, and even the most well-meaning actor can end up taking actions that cause more harm than good, no matter good they make him feel. Burke's metaphysicians suffer from this malady, among others. A truly well-equipped moral imagination provides the kinds of anchors in reality that ensure that one's actions are truly sound on both a moral and a practical level, so that what *feels* good actually *is* good, and yields good results.

Political scientist James Q. Wilson has famously written on "the moral sense."[63] Wilson emphasizes the innate aspect of this sense, although he recognizes a learned aspect also. Burke, in contrast, emphasizes what is learned. This is not to say that Burke believes that morality is entirely learned. Since there is no reason to believe that Burke was not a pious and orthodox Christian, he very likely believed in conscience as it is traditionally understood; his mention of the "compunctious visitings of Nature" may suggest this. He does not much engage in explicit speculation regarding human nature, so it is difficult to know precisely how much he considered innate and how much learned. He would perhaps have regarded such "metaphysical" speculation as an unproductive exercise, since what is innate is beyond our control. Burke's interest is in what is, at least to some degree, within our control, which is the learned aspect of moral sense. Clearly, he regards learning as extremely important in the development of a well-functioning moral sense or intuition. Such a sense cannot be learned very well through "precept," but is acquired largely through imitation and experience, building the moral imagination. Compactly present in this form of knowledge is information that is useful beyond that contained in a maxim, even if that information is not readily expressible through abstract conceptual language. It is generally impossible for any moral code to spell out precisely how it should be applied in various different real-world circumstances; we rely on our judgment to make such determinations, and our reason must rely upon the imaginative whole that we have created.

According to Irving Babbitt,

> The forms and traditions, religious and political, that Burke . . . defends, on the ground that they are not arbitrary but are convenient summings up of a vast body of past experience, give support to the imagination of the individual; the imagination, thus drawn back as it were to an ethical center, supplies in turn a standard with reference to which the individual may set bounds to the lawless expansion of his natural self (which includes his intellect as well as his emotions).[64]

Tradition and other cultural elements embody wisdom, but they do more than simply convey information. They supply standards, and, in so doing, help one to develop an ethical will. In equipping the moral imagination, they help one to actually become a better person. One comes to exercise better judgment because one operates within a more sound moral universe.

Most of the elements supporting the moral imagination that have been discussed here are largely nonpolitical, if one uses this term in its most narrow sense. Broadly speaking, however, they are all very political, and they do much to shape the politics of a country and the character of society as a whole. The importance of these elements to Burke demonstrates his sensitivity to the fact that explicitly political action is largely the product of predispositions that have already developed among the public and among elites. This connection between the moral imagination and politics is not one-way. While the moral imagination profoundly shapes politics, politics itself also helps shape the moral imagination. Through an exploration of some of Burke's specific public policy positions, a better understanding of some of the interplay between imaginative frameworks and political action can be developed.

5 Moral Imagination and Public Policy

EDMUND BURKE WAS ONE OF THOSE rare figures who combined profound political-philosophical observation with a highly active political career. After he entered Parliament, almost all of his writings and speeches addressed some sort of pressing public policy concern. Although Burke's policy focus provides a great deal of material for political historians and biographers, it poses challenges for political theorists, who must tease political philosophy out of works that were not explicitly written as such. But Burke's policy focus also offers important advantages. First, one can argue that Burke's public career helps keep his thought attuned to "real-world" issues in all their messiness and complexity, and forces him to consider information that more speculative thinkers might disregard. Second, Burke's writings and speeches clearly demonstrate the application of particular political-philosophical perspectives to public policy questions. An exploration of the role of Burke's moral-epistemological outlook in his political activities thus serves to better explicate that outlook and to illustrate how it can shape public policy.

Because Burke was, first and foremost, a practicing politician, any claim that a particular ethical and epistemological outlook is central to an understanding of him should be supported by evidence from his "real-world" political engagements. The fact is that the policy positions, speeches, and writings of Burke, throughout his long parliamentary career, may be used to illustrate the application to practical politics of ideas centered around the concept of the moral imagination. For Burke, those in office need to consider the worldviews of those whom they govern, worldviews we can best understand as moral-imaginative frameworks. Those frameworks shape how governmental actions are perceived, and received, by the public. And, directly or indirectly, public policy helps to shape the moral imagination of a country, for better or for worse. The activities of political actors impact political culture, and public policies can end up shaping societies in profound ways. By influencing the moral imagination and hence society, current public policies have the effect of influencing the sort of public policies that will be adopted in the future.

The policy areas to which we will devote the most explicit attention are American policy, Indian policy, Irish policy, and constitutional reform. These are in fact among the policy areas that receive the most attention in most studies of Burke, and they are widely recognized as most important for developing an understanding of him. Three of these areas—American, Indian, and Irish policy—could of course also be grouped together as "imperial policy." The importance of Indian policy and Irish policy is certainly unquestionable; these were major areas of concern for Burke for the bulk of his career, as is evidenced by his copious writings on these subjects. Matters of American policy and of constitutional reform make up much smaller portions of his works and activities, but were also demonstrably important to Burke. His writings and speeches in these areas are frequently cited by scholars, whether they are approaching Burke from the perspective of political theory, of rhetoric, or of political history. It was the American crisis that first established Burke's reputation in Parliament. And his writings on constitutional reform, particularly those on reform of representation in Parliament, offer a picture of a "conservative" Burke that seems to contrast with the liberal or reformist Burke evidenced in the other policy areas. One notable area of Burke's public policy that is not treated in this chapter is of course his effort, ultimately successful, to bring about a strong British response to the French Revolution. One reason why this subject is not treated here is that, throughout this book, Burke's remarks on the French Revolution and related subjects are drawn upon more than on those in any other single policy area when explicating a general interpretation of his thought. Consequently, a focus here on Burke's views on the French Revolution would be duplicative of material found in other chapters. It is in the other policy areas that the role of the moral imagination in Burke's thought is less likely to be immediately evident. Also, it is the other policy areas that require the sort of framing and explication that demand independent narrative treatments.

America and Legalism

When Burke first took his seat in Parliament in January 1766, tensions with the American colonies were already high. Burke's maiden speech in Parliament was a brief unrecorded address supporting repeal of the Stamp Act, a position around which the Rockingham Whigs were coalescing.[1] In 1770 Burke was named New York's agent in Parliament, and in 1774 and 1775 he would make his major speeches on American policy, urging British conciliation on taxation and other issues that were contributing to the Americans' unrest. Although Burke's stated positions were in line with his party, there seems to be general agreement among scholars that Burke's interest in the American situation went beyond simple party loyalty. There is disagreement, however, as to whether Burke was motivated more by sympathy for the Americans or by desire to preserve Britain's holdings. Burke is sometimes viewed as a supporter of the American Revolution. Conor Cruise O'Brien does not quite go so far as to make this claim, but he does paint Burke as a zealous defender of the Americans, spurred on by his exposure to oppression in Ireland. James Conniff emphasizes that Burke "was among the first of the Rockingham Party to recognize the inevitability of American independence, and to advocate separation on terms of mutual benefit."[2] Frank O'Gorman portrays Burke as an "imperial statesman" who eventually came to be a strong supporter of American independence because "for Burke, the imperial conflict had become a struggle for liberty."[3] While there is some truth in such statements, it is important to recognize that prior to 1777 Burke's efforts were clearly devoted not to securing American independence, but to the opposing project of keeping the Empire together.[4]

However one wishes to characterize Burke's views and motivations in the American case, certainly his speeches and correspondence provide ample evidence of sympathy for the Americans' complaints. After hearing of the Declaration of Independence, he was in fact at a loss as to where his sympathies should lie, writing in a private letter, "I do not know how to wish success to those whose Victory is to separate from us a large and noble part of our Empire. Still less do I wish success to injustice, oppression, and absurdity."[5] Once the Revolution is over, however, Burke seems to lose interest in America. He never offers any extended commentary on the

American regime; of course, once America was no longer tied to Britain there would have been no practical political reason for him to have done so. Interestingly, in 1785 an acquaintance of Burke's noted with surprise the "contemptuous terms" in which he spoke of the Americans, and recorded that Burke feared that the weak union would collapse and that "the democratic party" in America would overpower the Federalists.[6] If Burke's remarks were correctly understood, this would seem to contradict, at least a bit, the view, typically associated with him then and now, that he was broadly supportive of the Americans. Unfortunately, we do not know if the 1787 Constitution made his view of the American experiment more positive, or if he thought much about it at all. By the time the formal adoption of the U.S. Constitution was announced in 1789, the European world was of course consumed with the events in France.

Whatever Burke's precise views were regarding the Americans and their revolution, his remarks on American policy are strongly informed by his sensitivity to how people think and judge. It has already been observed that Burke's speeches and writings, including some on American policy, evidence a moral-imaginative approach in the manner in which Burke tries to persuade his readers. One such approach was Burke's tendency to identify specific past policies with specific historical or contemporary individuals, drawing connections between failures and successes and the widely recognized character flaws or positive traits of the individuals who had pursued those policies. It is, however, not just Burke's rhetoric on America that reflects his epistemological and moral perspective, but his actual policy recommendations and the ways in which he comes to them.

Burke was a leader in urging conciliation with America, but he was also very much within the mainstream of his party. The Rockingham Whigs had advocated and pursued a conciliatory policy; they had, for example, repealed the Stamp Act during their brief period in power. The Rockingham administration had fallen, however, in 1766, and would not return to power until after American independence was assured. (The Whigs' later brief increase in popularity was, in fact, partly due to the Tories' embarrassing loss of the American colonies.) In the early to mid-1770s Britain's American policy was following the confrontational line of the Tories and George III, and in arguing for conciliation Burke found himself fighting a losing battle, as he would so often in his career. The American problem centered primarily on taxation by Parliament and the colonists' resistance to that taxation. Parliament believed it had a right to tax the colonies in any manner it chose, since the colonial charters made those colonies subject to the Crown.

The Americans, as a general rule, recognized Parliament's legitimacy in governing them, but believed that the imposition of taxes without their consent or participation violated basic rights of Englishmen.

As a problem of conflicting rights claims, the American crisis may have helped convince Burke of the limitations of rights-based frameworks and of the drawbacks of abstract conceptual arguments that disregard real-world circumstances. In his 1775 *Speech on Conciliation* he suggests that it is not entirely clear whose claim of right—that of Parliament or of the Americans—should predominate. The general issue as to whether "a right of taxation is necessarily involved in the general principle of legislation, and inseparable from the ordinary supreme power" or whether, as a taking of property, it falls into a special category and requires special consent, involves "deep questions" that are difficult to resolve, a "Serbonian bog" in which Burke does "not intend to be overwhelmed." He points out that, if one debates the question with reference to historical writers and statesmen, one finds that "high and reverend authorities lift up their heads on both sides, and there is no sure footing in the middle." The theoretical arguments come down on one side or the other, and leave no room for compromise; they feed the conflict instead of moving it toward a resolution. The solution Burke offers is to abandon the rights debate and to focus simply on creating good public policy: "The question with me is, not whether you have a right to render your people miserable; but whether it is not your interest to make them happy? It is not, what a lawyer tells me I *may* do; but what humanity, reason, and justice tell me I ought to do." His controlling ethic is one of obligation, not of right. Indeed, Burke argues that even if he were certain that "the colonists had, at their leaving this country, sealed a regular compact of servitude, that they had solemnly abjured all the rights of citizens," he would still argue for conciliation, since the real issue is not one of legal technicalities or past agreements, but of governing a particular population with particular viewpoints in the here and now.[7]

In both the *Speech on Conciliation* and the *Speech on Taxation* a year earlier Burke endeavored to convince the Tories of the need for any American policy to take into account what we would call the political culture, or worldview, or imaginative framework of the colonists. Britain and America had, to a degree, grown apart, and the Americans' perception of the circumstances at hand was very different from that of the king and of most members of Parliament. Effective governance required a sensitivity to those differences. Burke explains that there is a consideration that should guide policy regarding America "even more than its Population and its Commerce, I mean its *Temper and Character*."[8] According to Gerald Chapman, Burke "painted his famous 'view' of the American character and its driving force, . . . to waken a sense of American practice as conditioned by in-grown values and principles, fixed, and lively, though more or less unconscious, and suspended in the dearest web of moral feelings."[9] The dominant element of this character is a "love of freedom" and "fierce spirit of liberty," a quality that derives in large part from the colonists' British roots: "England, Sir, is a nation, which still I hope respects, and formerly adored, her freedom. The colonists emigrated from you, when this part of your character was most predominant."[10] Presumably Burke is referring to the latter part of the seventeenth century and the beginning of the eighteenth century, when the Civil War, Restoration, Revolution of 1688, and Act of Settlement had helped reinforce a political culture characterized by belief in strict limitations on the monarchy and in the importance of the rule of law. In particular, the 1689 Bill of Rights emphasized the need for the monarch to obtain the people's consent, through Parliament, for any taxation. Since the time of the Magna Charta, in fact, the taking of property without consent had been regarded as unacceptable behavior in a monarch and a mark of tyranny. The colonists' fixation on the taxation issue, which Parliament regarded as unreasonable, was in fact very British—although perhaps late seventeenth-century British—since taxation only by consent amounted to a key traditional British test of liberty. Significantly, Burke explains: "Abstract liberty, like other mere abstractions, is not to be found. Liberty inheres in some sensible object; and every nation has formed to itself some favorite point, which by way of eminence becomes the criterion of their happiness. It happened, you know, Sir, that the great contests for freedom in this country were from the earliest times chiefly upon the question of Taxing."[11]

There is no such thing as liberty in the abstract; it exists in concrete circumstances. We understand the idea of liberty because it is imaginatively linked to various particular things. The Tories fail to understand how closely the older British cultural framework, still strong in the colonies, associates liberty with consent for taxation. They see the American response as simple defiance, a challenge to the legitimacy of their rule. Consequently they believe they must insist on their taxes in order to maintain their authority; if they give in on this matter, more defiance will follow. Burke's point is that taxation is, in the colonists' minds, a special case, and a rejection of taxes is not a part of a blanket rejection of the Crown. Not that the colonists do not have a particularly strong "love of freedom"; they do, and Parliament must take this into account. Burke traces this love culturally. Many of the emigrants to America, he explains, were Protestant dissenters, and they rested their dissent "on a strong claim to natural liberty."[12] This has shaped the American psyche. O'Brien makes reference to the extremely "Protestant" nature of American Christianity, including its Anglicanism. He points out that attempts to send Anglican bishops to the colonies were rebuffed, and that Burke was well aware of this phenomenon.[13] Moreover, although the south does not share the north's shaping by dissenters, and most southerners are members of the Church of England, the practice of slavery, Burke argues, actually enhances the southerners' love of liberty.[14] Burke also points out that an astonishingly large number of Americans have studied law, and that the colonial legislatures are made up almost entirely of lawyers. This legal study heightens the Americans' sensitivity to infractions on liberty, even if those infractions have little practical impact: "In other countries, the people, more simple, and of a less mercurial cast, judge of an ill principle in government only by an actual grievance; here they anticipate the evil, and judge of the pressure of the grievance by the badness of the principle."[15] Legalistic approaches to social and political questions, like "metaphysical" approaches and the reliance on "high and reverend authorities," tend to yield polarizing results and to make compromise difficult. Once one finds a policy or practice to be a violation of a particular articulated principle, nothing less than the complete reversal of that policy or practice is acceptable.

Along with all of the above factors, the worldview of the Americans has been shaped by precedent and prescription of a particular sort; it has been shaped by the history of their relationship with Britain. The imposition of taxes in 1764, Burke argues, appeared to the Americans as "a great innovation."[16] As has been observed, "innovation" was, not just in Burke's view, but in general usage, a loaded term in eighteenth-century British political debate; to tag a policy with that label was to suggest that it was highly questionable, and perhaps of dubious legitimacy. To Burke it is Parliament that bears most of the blame for the present situation by changing its American policy at midstream. There are, he explains, two basic ways to derive economic benefit from colonies: through the establishment of commercial monopolies, or through taxation. The method that Britain has historically chosen is the mercantilist model of a commercial empire. The imposition of trading monopolies clearly demonstrates Parliament's authority, in a manner to which everyone is accustomed: "Be content to bind America by laws of trade: you have always done it. Let this be your reason for binding their trade."[17] To the extent that revenues are required to provide services to the colonies, the Crown should follow the same model with the colonies that the king has traditionally followed with Parliament: the colonial legislatures should be asked to raise funds and to grant them to the Crown.[18] By sticking to tradition, Parliament will defuse the question of the scope of its authority. Burke's recognition of the authority of the venerable, and of the dangers inherent in abrupt change, is clearly evident here, long before he would comment on the French Revolution. In Burke's words, Parliament should "leave America, if she has taxable matter in her, to tax herself. I am not here going into the distinctions of rights, nor attempting to mark their boundaries. I do not enter into these metaphysical distinctions; I hate the very sound of them. Leave the Americans as they anciently stood, and these distinctions, born of our unhappy contest, will die along with it."[19]

Perhaps the biggest mistake made by members of Parliament is their insistence on labeling the colonists' actions as "treason" and "rebellion." Most colonists, Burke argues, do not view themselves as in a general state of rebellion; they are British subjects who are opposed only to one line of governmental action, and who are frustrated by Parliament's refusal to enter into a dialogue with them. They are claiming what they consider to be well-established, traditional rights of Englishmen. The Americans have not denied all of Parliament's authority; it is Parliament that maintains that its authority is being denied. In telling the Americans that this one disagreement constitutes "rebellion," Parliament is indicating to them that it does not recognize basic liberties. It is, effectively, teaching the Americans to rebel.[20] It is prompting a paradigm shift, reshaping the Americans' self-perception. Their imaginative frameworks, we can say, are being re-formed in a manner in which their limited actions are being identified with a general state of rebellion. If Parliament continues to tell the Americans that they are committing treason, the Americans will eventually agree.

Burke was not just concerned about the impact of Parliament's policies on the American colonies and on Britain's relationship with them. According to O'Gorman, for Burke "liberty throughout the empire was indivisible. If it died in America, it would not be long before it would be extinguished in Britain: 'you cannot have different rights and a different security in different parts of your dominions.'"[21] Ultimately, in claiming new powers over the colonists, and bringing military power to bear to assert that authority, Parliament could end up altering British political culture and bringing about despotic domestic government.

What makes Burke's handling of American policy striking is his emphasis on what we are referring to as the moral imagination. Burke understands that the colonists and the Tories in Parliament are getting at reality in slightly different ways; time, distance, and circumstances have made their imaginative conceptions of the world somewhat different. These include their conceptions of liberty and of the nature of good government, which are tied intuitively, or imaginatively, to particular elements of concrete historical experience. What has made Britain's American policy a failure has been the failure to take these differences into account, as well as a failure to take into account how current policies may continue to shape the Americans' imaginations in adverse ways. Good governance, Burke explains, does not arise through adherence to questionable legalisms but through sensitivity to one's subjects and their worldview. In language that foreshadows that which he will employ years later in the context of the French Revolution, Burke tells Parliament, "the question . . . is;—whether you will chuse to abide by a profitable experience, or a mischievous theory . . . ?"[22] Parliament's error is similar to the error Burke would later see in the Jacobins and "metaphysicians" who focus on abstract rights and on legalistic political theories without bothering to consider human nature or the specific circumstances at hand.

It is worth noting that although Burke's positions on America are generally considered to represent his "liberal" or "reformist" side they are quite compatible with his "conservatism." For one thing, he is trying to protect traditional "rights of Englishmen," both in America and in Britain. Also, he faults Parliament for its abrupt policy changes and argues largely for a return to the policies that had traditionally been applied to America. This is not so much because the old policies are "better," on either a moral or a practical level. It is because those are the policies to which everyone is accustomed; their venerability confers legitimacy. They have that sublime quality that age, with its suggestion of the infinite, can convey. They have an implied connection to something that goes beyond simple human agency. They are not seen as arbitrary or capricious, but as part of an established order. While the old policies may not be "better" if they are considered abstractly or in isolation, they are very much better—on both a practical and a moral level—than the policies that Parliament is now pursuing, when considered in light of the concrete circumstances at hand. They are more moral because they would work; they would resolve the situation in as desirable a manner as can be expected. The dropping of the technical "right" of Parliament's taxing power over the colonies would yield a result that would surely be considered to accord with what is understood as good under the broader British tradition. Burke's criticisms of the "metaphysicians" make it clear that he is not a pure consequentialist who believes that "the end justifies the means," in the sense that otherwise immoral or unscrupulous methods can be justified by admirable goals. But for him, the rightness of a policy or action cannot be divorced from the results that are likely to flow from it. It is impossible for a public policy to be good or moral or right if its results are largely bad.

The approach to politics here demonstrated by Burke is not one that starts from clearly articulated, general political principles or moral principles, and then seeks to bring those principles to bear on particular situations. This does not mean that Burke does not use "principles" of his own, and it certainly does not mean that his approach is not "moral." He recognizes that good public policy is not grounded primarily in abstract principles. As previously noted, Joseph Pappin states that Burke finds that "rational man acts without regard to abstractions and universals."[23] Good public policy reflects both attention to actual circumstances and the right knowledge, attitudes, and character on the part of the actors. In the case of American policy, Burke both devotes considerable time to technical and factual matters and, more notably, calls for the display of the right kinds of virtues, such as humility, empathy, and magnanimity. Humility is required because Parliament needs to recognize that its perception of reality—specifically, its understanding of its political rights and of the need to assert those rights in order to keep the Americans in the fold—is not unimpeachable. Parliament does not possess absolute knowledge, and cases may be made by others for alternative understandings. Empathy is required to foster an understanding of the Americans' differing perception of the situation. And Burke calls on Parliament to be magnanimous and to drop its legalistic arguments in favor of the pursuit of an amicable solution. This, we can say, is a solution informed by proper attention to the moral imagination.

India and Imperialism

In sheer volume, Burke's writings and speeches on Indian policy make up a much greater part of his works than those on any other subject. Burke himself seems to view his actions regarding India as the most important of his career. In his *Letter to a Noble Lord* he maintains that his (ultimately unsuccessful) pursuit of the impeachment and removal of Warren Hastings of the East India Company would alone justify his pension from the Crown. Significantly, Burke makes this observation shortly after he notes, in an important passage, that government is "made for the very purpose of opposing that [sovereign] reason to will and to caprice, in . . . the governors or in the governed."[24] Many commentators on Burke have seen in his Indian speeches a particularly strong demonstration of his opposition to arbitrary power.[25] Close linkages are also widely seen among Burke's positions regarding India, America, and Ireland.

In the sphere of Indian policy Burke is best known for his pursuit of the Hastings impeachment, but his concern with Indian matters began long before that. In his first years in Parliament Burke helped to promote the established Whig party line on India. At that time the Whigs opposed any reform of Indian policy, including closer government oversight of the East India Company, fearing that the actions to be taken to curtail the Company's independence would amount to a power grab for the Crown and for members of the administration. While in the 1760s Burke appears to be solidly behind the Whig position, in the 1770s strong tensions become evident within his speeches on India. While ostensibly supporting the Whig party line, he nevertheless launches, on occasion, attacks on the East India Company. O'Brien maintains that what Burke advocated during much of 1772–1773 amounted to comprehensive regulation of the Company, a position that "was directly opposed to party policy."[26] Russell Kirk likewise finds that by 1773 "reports of corruption and arbitrary abuse of power by the Company's servants could not be dismissed" by Burke.[27] Gradually, Burke found himself becoming an opponent of the status quo with regard to India.

By the late 1770s the Whigs' consensus view on India was looking more and more like Burke's. In 1783, Charles James Fox, with Burke's assistance and support, introduced bills designed to reform British activities in India. Unlike the American colonies prior to the Revolution, India at that time did not have official colonial status; it had no clear status at all, and was an almost accidental empire. The French had established a toehold in India, and fears that they might build their own empire there caused Britain to rush in in a rather haphazard manner. The East India Company, theoretically created to engage in commercial activities, had stepped into a power vacuum in India and, with British might behind it, had assumed control over much of the subcontinent. The Company's strong-arm tactics were perceived by many as necessary, at least in the beginning, since India at that time consisted of a confused patchwork of weak principalities, often corrupt and hostile to one another, and sometimes with overlapping jurisdictional claims; this made commerce difficult. However, by the 1770s the manner in which most fortunes were being made in India was not, strictly speaking, commerce. Instead, by exerting their influence over local rulers, officials of the Company were essentially extorting vast sums from the local population.

Such activities were not highly coordinated; officials of the Company frequently acted on their own, sometimes against one another. When the Company's London directors, in an attempt to address the situation, sent a new governor to Madras, a local Company official had him imprisoned, where he died.[28] If the Company was the closest thing India had to a de facto government, it was not really a government at all, or else was an especially haphazard and lawless one. Kirk writes that "the East India Company, as its territories and power grew, had become incapable of governing well an empire acquired almost in a fit of absence of mind: many of its servants, intent upon making immense fortunes in a few years, ignored the laws of the Indian principalities and peoples, the laws of England, and the principles of natural justice."[29]

Fox's India bills were the latest in a series of attempts by members of Parliament, both Whigs and, more often, Tories, to respond to the chaotic situation in India. Some modest prior initiatives had been enacted, but generally to little effect; most, including the more significant pieces of legislation, were defeated, and Fox's bills would meet a similar fate. The general thrust of the legislation was to rein in the Company's activities and to limit its role to a more strictly commercial one, while shifting political control of India to commissioners directly answerable to Parliament. Since the Whigs were concerned about any potential expansions of royal power, the commissioners would, in fact, be appointed by Parliament from among its own membership, a dramatic departure from existing policy. In a work devoted entirely to Burke's views on India, Frederick G. Whelan maintains that Fox's bills amounted to "a relatively radical legislative proposal."[30]

Burke's enthusiastic support for Fox's "relatively radical" legislation stands as one of the many episodes in his career that demonstrate that a simplistic understanding of him as a "conservative" is highly inaccurate. India would be, in fact, not just a passing interest for Burke, but almost an obsession. By the time Fox introduced his bills Burke had become an expert on British activities in India. And the more he had studied the situation the more passionate he had become about the need for reform. His interest in India went beyond the professional and took on a personal quality. In 1780 Burke actually purchased stock in the East India Company in order to become eligible to participate in its deliberations as a stockholder; however, with his meager financial resources he was unsuccessful in influencing policy at that level.[31]

In delving into the Indian question Burke did not just study British activities in India, but India itself, including its culture and religions.

Whelan observes that "Burke was one of the first major European thinkers . . . to have made a serious effort to understand a non-Western civilization and to incorporate his findings into his general political thought."[32] Burke even invited a visiting high-caste Hindu Indian—perhaps the only one in Britain in the eighteenth century—to his home at Beaconsfield, and displayed considerable fascination with him, for which he endured some public ribbing.[33] It is important to recognize that, at this time, the vast bulk of the British people, and even Britain's elites, knew extraordinarily little about the inhabitants of their Indian empire. Shaping public perception of India and its people was therefore a key part of Burke's strategy. India, Burke maintained, consists of "a people for ages civilized and cultivated; cultivated by all the arts of polished life, whilst we were yet in the woods."[34] Although Burke's strong interest in Indian culture is highly atypical for an eighteenth-century Briton, it is fully consistent with his concern for what we call the moral imagination, and for the cultural elements that help shape it. It is also consistent with the strong interest he had demonstrated in the American colonists' worldview, and in the observations he would make in his writings on the French Revolution that good governance requires close attention to human nature.

Burke's concern and respect for the Indians highlights a contrast between liberal and Burkean frameworks. Commentators have long noted connections between liberalism and imperialism; if a liberal society tends to be dismissive of its own traditions in favor of its new "enlightened" understanding of society and government, it is hardly surprising that it would have a low opinion of traditions and cultures elsewhere, and regard less "enlightened" peoples as inferior. Among the more prominent contemporary writers on this phenomenon is Uday Singh Mehta, who explicitly contrasts typical liberal thought with that of Burke.[35] Burke scholar Luke Gibbons picks up on this relationship, although he associates it less explicitly with liberalism per se than with political modernity broadly:

> The Enlightenment, in its dominant American and French forms, had set its face firmly against "first peoples" or vernacular cultures, unless, that is, they were brought within the remit of Romanticism, where they enjoyed a new, sequestered afterlife in the realms of the imagination. . . . The aim . . . was to transform natives into citizens of the world, freed from the limiting horizons of local culture and the encumbrances of time and place. It was this insistence on the politics of place, the lived complexity of recent history and the inherited past, that Burke brought to bear on Enlightenment debates.[36]

The same sort of modern universalism and dismissal of culture and tradition that would contribute to the havoc in France can be seen to support equally disruptive imperialism. Universalism can of course take many forms, including liberalism, Marxism, and various other political ideologies and approaches. One can see Burke's concern regarding universalism all the way back in his comments on the conversion of England in his early *English History*. The Catholic Church represented a form of universalism—although one that was historically grounded, and that was perhaps less overwhelming than the universalism of modernity. Burke, it will be recalled, applauded the pope's efforts to blunt the negative impact of the Church's universalism through the incorporation of local practices and beliefs into Christianity.

As has been observed, Fox's India bill was "relatively radical"; in supporting it Burke had to contend with those resistant to change. A key charge levied by the Company's supporters was that the bill violated the "chartered rights of men." The "charter" in this case was that establishing the Company, and the "men" were the company's officers, directors, and shareholders. Burke rejects this argument, maintaining that "political power and commercial monopoly are *not* the rights of men" and that "these chartered rights . . . do at least suspend the natural rights of mankind at large, and in their very frame and constitution are liable to fall into a direct violation of them."[37] Ironically, years earlier Burke had invoked some of the same rights-based arguments in the Company's defense that he rejects here. Burke's apparent rejection of the Company's "chartered rights" in favor of broader "natural rights" is an anomaly of sorts and will be specifically addressed in chapter 6. For now, it can be noted that Burke neither rejects outright nor broadly embraces a rights-based approach. More generally, it should also be noted that he is clearly willing to change established laws and conventions when their outcome is unjust or undesirable. Burke's position on this issue, and his broader concern for the Indians, is often highlighted by those like O'Brien who characterize him as a fighter for justice and an opponent of arbitrary power.

Burke explains that, in granting such a broad scope of authority to the East India Company, Parliament has overstepped its bounds: "We had not a right to make a market of our duties."[38] Parliament has a duty, a moral obligation, to see that India is justly and effectively governed. Burke suggests that "this bill, and those connected with it, are intended to form the *Magna Charta* of Hindostan."[39] This may seem to be a grandiose claim, but several paragraphs earlier Burke mentions that the "*Magna Charta* is a charter to restrain power," and this is what Fox's legislation would do.[40] Unfortunately, powerful interests opposed the legislation and it failed.

When Fox's bills failed, Burke did not miss a beat. Drawing on his extensive research, and on the 17-volume report of the select committee in which he had participated to investigate matters in India, he turned his attention to pursuing the impeachment of Warren Hastings, the governor-general of Bengal and the most powerful Company official on the subcontinent. This project dominated the latter part of Burke's parliamentary career. In 1787 he would actually succeed in persuading the House of Commons to vote several articles of impeachment against Hastings; the case would, however, be dragged out in the House of Lords until 1795, when Hastings would be exonerated. There is evidence that Burke saw the case as doomed as early as 1785 but that he nonetheless felt compelled to continue, believing that the judgment of history would, ultimately, be on his side.[41] Burke's quest was not an entirely quixotic one, however. While it is clear that he was convinced of Hastings's personal guilt in perpetuating misrule, corruption, and abuse, he was certainly also well aware that these problems predated Hastings and that his removal would not, by itself, greatly improve British governance of India. In indicting Hastings, Burke was indicting the entire system that he had unsuccessfully attempted to reform through Fox's bills. Even an unsuccessful prosecution, then, could help serve Burke's purpose of drawing public and parliamentary attention to the situation in India and encouraging reform. Eventually, of course, British rule in India would be reformed, although the more significant reforms would not occur until long after Burke's death.

When Burke launches into his speeches before the House of Lords on the Hastings impeachment, he offers a rather startling reason for the Lords to vote to convict. It is, in "the interests of our Constitution itself," important to keep the tradition of impeachment alive, and a vote to convict will do so. It has been, Burke explains, 63 years since there has been an impeachment, and the process is in danger of dying out through lack of effective use. This cannot be allowed to happen, since it is the institution of impeachment "that makes England what England is." It is, and should be, an inherently political process reflecting "solid principles of State morality," not simply a legal one. Impeachment is important both as a political mechanism and as one of the elements equipping Britain's moral imagination, since it emphasizes the accountability of political leaders; if it is permitted to die out, Britain will become a different place. Of course, this is a very minor argument that Burke makes; the vast bulk of the material in his speeches before the Lords addresses the specific wrongdoings of Warren Hastings. However, it demonstrates how Burke was always thinking about how government actions might shape the character of the polity by impacting on individuals' perceptions of reality.[42]

Burke's speeches and writings regarding the Hastings impeachment are much more extensive than those regarding the earlier Fox legislation. Much of this material consists of detailed descriptions of particular situations and conditions in India, to build a case that Hastings committed the specific abuses named in the articles of impeachment. On a more general level, however, the thrust of Burke's arguments in the Hastings trial and the thrust of his arguments on the Fox bills are very similar. His political-philosophical standpoint seems to be very much the same in both cases, and much of his more significant language is interchangeable between the two battles. He has very specific ideas regarding India and its governance, which tie closely to his emphasis on the moral imagination.

A major problem with the East India Company is that it is effectively functioning as a government, but it is not a government in anything like the usual sense of the word. It is an alien, for-profit enterprise that controls India but that lacks the usual ties to it. In his speech on the Fox bills Burke compares Britain's conquest of India with previous invasions by the "Arabs, Tartars, and Persians." Although those conquests were bloody, "the Asiatic conquerors very soon abated of their ferocity, because they made the conquered country their own. They rose or fell with the rise or fall of the territory they lived in. Fathers there deposited the hopes of their posterity; and children there beheld the monuments of their fathers." In contrast with such previous invaders, Burke explains,

> Our conquest there, after twenty years, is as crude as it was the first day. . . . Young men (boys almost) govern there, without society and without sympathy with the natives. They have no more social habits with the people than if they still resided in England; nor, indeed, any species of intercourse but that which is necessary to making a sudden fortune, with a view to a remote settlement. . . . With us there are no retributory superstitions, by which a foundation of charity compensates, through ages, to the poor, for the rapine and injustice of a day. With us no pride erects stately monuments which repair the mischiefs which pride had produced, and which adorn a country, out of its own spoils. England has erected no churches, no hospitals, no palaces, no schools; England has built no bridges, made no high roads, cut no navigations, dug out no reservoirs.[43]

Strong connections can be seen between this argument against the manner of rule by the East India Company and Burke's understanding of what creates and sustains a sound moral imagination. Almost nothing exists in the way of social bonds between the young men of the East India Company and the natives of India. It will be recalled that Burke saw that customs could be as important as laws, or even much more important than laws, in constraining behavior. In this case, however, there is no common social structure and, consequently, "no retributory superstitions" to prompt the English to behave charitably toward the Indians. There are no natural affections for the Indian people at work and, likewise, there are no natural affections for the place. Previous conquerors settled in India and raised children there. The ties between the generations—the first generation of conquerors striving to do right by its children, and then their children striving to do right by their ancestors—kicked in. These ties shaped the conquerors' understanding of their world and of their moral responsibilities. What passes for government in India, however, is basically a loosely organized group of young-men-on-the-make, who come there with an aim to make their fortunes as quickly as possible, by whatever means available, and then to return to England. Consequently their relationship to India and its people is purely transactional, and purely exploitative. With neither ancestors nor posterity there the Company's men fail to place their actions within a meaningful moral context that extends beyond their own immediate self-interest.

Much of Burke's concern regarding Britain's Indian policy revolves around these young men of the East India Company. He explains that

> There is nothing in the boys we send to India worse than in the boys whom we are whipping at school, or that we see trailing a pike or bending over a desk at home. But as English youth in India drink the intoxicating draught of authority and dominion before their heads are able to bear it, and as they are full grown in fortune long before they are ripe in principle, neither Nature nor reason have any opportunity to exert themselves for remedy of the excesses of their premature power. The consequences of their conduct, which in good minds, (and many of theirs are probably such) might produce penitence or amendment, are unable to pursue the rapidity of their flight.[44]

Burke is not only concerned about what the East India Company may be doing to the Indians; he is concerned about the formative effect service in the East India Company may have on its own personnel. These young men, who are "without society," fail to develop the kinds of internal checks, or the kind of character, usually developed by young men in Britain. Instead, they become accustomed to exercising arbitrary power over others, facing little or no consequence for unethical or inappropriate conduct. As a result they learn to give rein to a willfulness that under other circumstances people generally learn to constrain.

Burke's motivation here is of course less a concern for the young men per se than a concern for the future of Britain. Whelan maintains that Burke was "determined that British rule should offer an exception to the familiar historical pattern by which imperial states were corrupted into tyrannies by their power and greed."[45] This corruption of the state occurs, in significant part, through the corruption of the moral imagination. The men of the East India Company develop a particular sort of character, and there is no reason to believe that this character changes dramatically once they return to Britain. They became accustomed to ignoring the social structures and conventions of India; similarly, they have little respect for those of Britain. Indeed, they have little respect or regard for other people. They have not learned self-restraint, or the art of setting aside one's ego and of deciphering, and doing, what is truly right. The applicable test for their actions is not, in fact, whether something is right, but whether something is profitable and whether one can get away with it. At a time in life in which they should be learning to check their greed, their experience in India has fed it. Many of these men have quickly accumulated considerable wealth, and with this wealth has come power. The unchecked willfulness of these men is, consequently, in a position to do a great deal of harm. Burke explains that they infiltrate the established families and otherwise gain influence over them; in the process they also gain considerable influence over British politics.[46] Since their governance of India is characterized by oppression and greed, their influence on British politics and society can only be for ill.

In his arguments regarding American policy Burke indicated that if Parliament and the Crown became accustomed to exercising arbitrary power regarding the American colonies, the ultimate result might be tyrannical government at home. His argument in the case of India runs parallel to this, although his concern here seems to be magnified. It is magnified partly because the governance of India is dramatically more tyrannical than the governance of America ever was. It is magnified even more by his realization of how "in-country" experience is shaping Britain's young men and, consequently, British society. Burke's concern here can also be compared to his very early concern about how the arts, especially the theater, were shaping British morality, society, and politics. The basic pattern is the same, in that he sees various influences corrupting the character of the people. Previous chapters have discussed how various aspects of society and culture make up a "wardrobe of a moral imagination" that helps people to keep their moral bearings. Two important manifestations identified by Burke were "the spirit of a gentleman, and the spirit of religion."[47] Such outlooks on life help one to exercise sound moral judgment and to check one's will, in part by contributing to a strong sense of meaningful standards. These "spirits," however, require careful cultivation and development, achieved in part through proper upbringing in good families and through proper socialization. The upstarts from the East India Company often lack such upbringings, and much of their socialization has occurred in the "anything goes" environment of British India. Indeed, it has occurred "without society." It is no wonder that Burke fears that their influence will erode the "spirits" that help blunt the rough edges of politics in Britain and that help make possible a relatively liberal and benevolent state.

Burke's concern about the mentality fostered by the East India Company can be compared to his broader concern about commercial society, expressed in the context of the French Revolution and elsewhere. Writing on Burke, Pocock maintains that "in suggesting that a class brought into being by commerce might destroy itself by attacking the clerical foundations of culture he gave expression to a new problem in social theory."[48] Pocock also recounts David Hume's concern that public credit would be substituted for other property, especially the real property of the landed aristocracy, and would consequently undermine the "natural relations between men."[49] Burke would certainly have been very familiar with this argument and with similar lines of argument. It is important, however, not to put too materialistic a spin on his position. Burke, it will be recalled, was considered to be something of an expert on commercial policy; he was also a Whig, and was certainly not known as an opponent of commerce or of commercial development. His concern is specifically with those approaches to commerce that encourage a shallow, transactional view of human life and human relations. The men of the East India Company think of the people of India as subjects for exploitation, with little or no sense of obligation to them as human beings. Their commercial interests trump the customs, structures, and traditional rules of life in India; they also trump the norms that the Company's officers should have carried with them from Britain. This sense that anything can be bought, and that one's personal self-interest, understood largely in terms of wealth acquisition, should be paramount, continues to rule the Company men once they return to Britain. The sort of commerce that concerns Burke, then, is that which takes the form of naked power relations, not clothed in the "wardrobe of a moral imagination," which would soften those relations with "retributory superstitions," meaningful standards of behavior, and other norms.

It is concern regarding the exercise of arbitrary power that spurs Burke to pursue the Hastings trial for so many years to its unsatisfactory conclusion. Hastings had actually asserted in a letter to William Pitt that he possessed "arbitrary power" and that his use of "despotic" power in India was appropriate.[50] In making his case before the House of Lords, Burke seeks, of course, to demonstrate the truth of certain specific charges that have been made against Hastings. He also, however, endeavors to show more broadly that "no man who is under his [Hastings's] power is safe from his arbitrary will."[51] Burke wishes that Britain's dominion in India "carried with it . . . all the advantage of the liberty and spirit of a British constitution."[52] A system based upon constitutionalism, liberty, and the rule of law is of course the opposite of arbitrary will; it is a spirit of constraint, of standards. Such a principle has not ruled British activities in India, and Hastings maintains that it would in fact be impossible to rule India in this way.

Hastings's argument, Burke states, is "that actions in Asia do not bear the same moral qualities which the same actions would bear in Europe." The men of the East India Company "have formed a plan of Geographical morality, by which the duties of men in public and in private situations are not to be governed by their relation to the great Governor of the Universe, or by their relations to men, but by climates, degrees of longitude, parallels not of life but of latitudes." Burke rejects such geographical morality and maintains that "the laws of morality are the same every where, and that there is no action which would pass for an act of extortion, of peculation, of bribery, and of oppression in England, that is not an act of extortion, of peculation, of bribery, and of oppression in Europe, Asia, Africa, and all the world over. This I contend for, not in the technical forms of it, but I contend for it in the substance." The final qualifying line is important. Burke is emphatically *not* arguing for the simple application of British law and procedures in India, "for if ever there was a case in which the letter kills and the spirit gives life, it would be an attempt to introduce British forms and the substance of despotic principles together into any country." He explains that British laws are not designed for use in the very different context of India, and their selective application under such circumstances simply serves as another means for the officers of the East India Company to tyrannize the local population. The case of the application of British law in India, in fact, can be seen to parallel the French Revolutionary case of the rationalistic adoption of new laws and political paradigms that are not well-rooted in custom, culture, and traditional practice. Without an established framework to give the new laws well-defined meanings, they are subject to arbitrary interpretation and application, and can actually undermine the rule of law.[53]

In 1781 Burke had succeeded in convincing Parliament to enact the Bengal Judicature Act, which, among other things, was supposed to prohibit the application of British law to the Indians where inappropriate. Although Burke was a great lover and admirer of British law, he found the effects of its application by the British judges installed in India to be "arbitrary in the extreme." He speaks of "the incroachments which they made on the most sacred privileges of the people, the violation of their dearest rights, particularly in forcing the ladies before their courts; the contempt that was shewn for their religious ceremonies and mysteries; and the cruel punishments inflicted upon them in case of their disobedience; new, strange, and obnoxious to them."[54]

Although British law may seem on its face to be more desirable than that followed in India, "that which creates tyranny is the imposition of a form of government contrary to the will of the governed; and even a free and equal plan of government, would be considered despotic by those who desired to have their old laws and their ancient system." Consequently, "we must now be guided as we ought to have been with respect to America, by studying the genius, the temper, and the manners of the people, and adapting to them the laws that we establish."[55] It is clear that during the Hastings impeachment Burke continued to hold to this belief. On the first day of the trial Burke remarked, "God forbid we should pass judgment upon people who framed their laws and institutions prior to our insect origin of yesterday! With all the faults of their nature and errors of their institutions, their institutions, which act so powerfully on their natures, have two material characteristics which entitle them to respect: first, great force and stability; and next, excellent moral and civil effects."[56]

Burke displays a humility before the ancient Indian culture that is consistent with that which he displays before the established laws, institutions, and customs of Britain, and is consistent with the horror he would later express at the upending of the established laws, institutions, and customs in France. One may argue, in fact, that it is Burke's perspective that is the truly "universal" one, in contrast with the various forms of hegemonic false universality that have been common in liberal modernity. Burke's appreciation of the effectiveness and morality of Indian law and custom may be compared to contemporary approaches to cross-cultural differences in norms that emphasize the internal coherence of particular cultures and the general goal of "societal viability" that all cultures share.[57]

Burke's argument that, while legal forms vary culturally, there is no such thing as "geographical morality," has often been cited by those advocating a natural law perspective on Burke. Particularly popular is Burke's diatribe against Hastings's claim to "arbitrary power." Peter Stanlis maintains that "Burke's most extended and eloquent attack on Hastings' claim of arbitrary power . . . derives wholly from his ardent faith in Natural Law."[58] Burke argues:

> We [Parliament and the King] have not arbitrary power to give him; because Arbitrary power is a thing which neither any man can hold nor any man can give away. No man can lawfully govern himself by his own will; much less can he be governed by the will of others. We are all born in subjection, all born equally, high and low, governors and governed, in subjection to one great, immutable, pre-existent law, prior to all our devices, and prior to all our contrivances, paramount to our very being itself, by which we are knit and connected in the eternal frame of the universe, out of which we cannot stir.
>
> This great law does not arise from our conventions or compacts. On the contrary, it gives to our conventions and compacts all the force and sanction they can have. It does not arise from our vain institutions. Every good gift is of God; all power is of God; . . . Therefore . . . who . . . would place his own feeble, contemptible, ridiculous will in the place of the Divine wisdom and justice?[59]

This passage, perhaps more than any other in Burke, demonstrates the extent of his traditional Christian and classical orientation and his belief in God-given universal standards. Particularly noteworthy is his observation that one cannot "lawfully" govern even oneself according to one's own will. We are all subject to natural, or divine, law and are not morally free to do whatever we choose. The legitimacy of human laws and institutions arises from their conformity to more basic and universal moral laws or standards. Arbitrary actions are not "lawful" and are not legitimate or defensible. It is, however, very important to note here that, although Burke appeals to a universal or divine standard, he does not hold it up in sharp contradiction to an inferior conventional or "human" standard. Further exploration of his treatment of culturally specific Indian and British standards clarifies his position.

One argument advanced by those favoring the application of British law and legal forms in India was that the local laws, power structures, and customs were despotic. This same argument was advanced during the Hastings trial to defend openly despotic governance by the East India Company. It was generally accepted in Europe that all Asian governments were despotic. The argument of the East India Company's defenders was that, since the people of Asia are accustomed to such governance, they can only be governed in this way. Bengal under Islamic domination was, it was argued, a particularly clear case of tyrannical government. During consideration of the Bengal Judicature bill Burke actually conceded that India's law was inferior to, and more despotic in form than, that of Britain.[60] Even so, he argued, this was the form of law to which the people of India were accustomed, and such law would seem less tyrannical to them than the imposition of an alien legal system. Burke did not hold that the inferiorities of Indian law justified their wholesale replacement with British law. The cultural attunement of Indian law gave it legitimacy, because it created meaningful standards that were widely understood and that prevented the sort of human willfulness that was contrary to universal law. For Burke, it was British law that was being implemented in India with a "despotic spirit." Because British law was not firmly integrated into Indian society but was instead operating in an alien context, it gave free rein to caprice.

Although during the debate on the Bengal Judicature Act Burke concedes the point that British law is superior to Indian law, by the time of the Hastings trial a slight shift has occurred. Burke does not venture into a debate on the question of which form of law is superior, but he is very intent on refuting the common belief that Asian laws, or Asian governments, are necessarily despotic. For an active MP Burke engaged in a remarkable amount of research into the governments, laws, religions, and cultures of Asia. Drawing upon this study, he argues before the Lords that "nothing is more false than that despotism is the constitution of any country in Asia that we are acquainted with"[61] and that the idea "that the people of Asia have no laws, rights, or liberty, is a doctrine that is to be disseminated wickedly through this country."[62] In direct contradiction to Hastings and his supporters, Burke insists that "Oriental governments know nothing of arbitrary power." This is especially clear in the case of Islamic governments (which dominated India):

> To name a Mahometan government is to name a Government by law. It is a law enforced by stronger sanctions than any law that can bind a European Sovereign. . . . The law is given by God, and it has the double sanction of law and of religion, with which the Prince is no more to dispense than any one else. And, if any man will produce the Khoran [*sic*] to me, and will but shew me one text in it that authorizes in any degree an arbitrary power in the Government, I will declare that I have read that book, and been conversant in the affairs of Asia to a degree in vain.[63]

The above remarks may be linked to the observations Burke would later make in the *Reflections* regarding the importance of an established church. It will be recalled that there, Burke explains the importance of religion "sanctifying" government in order to impress a sense of sacred trust upon those in power. Here, the law itself is sanctified. In either case, the effect is to restrain the actions of political leaders and prevent arbitrary rule. What imparts this restraint is a sense of standards greater than one's own will. To use language from Burke's aesthetic thought, these standards may be described as sublime, since they are seen as beyond human control or alteration. In the case of Islamic states Burke explains that sovereigns are clearly understood to be subject to the law. They are, in fact, not even the law's chief interpreters; this function is performed by "that great priesthood established throughout all Asia, whom they call *men of the law*. These men are Conservators of the law."[64] Of course, Burke is not thinking of a radicalized Islamist state or theocracy, but of a traditional Islamic state in which there is a balance of power between secular and religious leaders. This may be roughly compared to the situation in medieval Europe, in which the Church had some ability to check and mitigate the behavior of secular rulers. Even more roughly, it may be compared to the situation in the United States in which the Supreme Court, vested with what is effectively a moral authority to interpret certain texts deemed authoritative, is able to check the other branches of government. The idea is that power is constrained, not simply through formal structures—which cannot operate effectively on their own—but through a particular moral-imaginative framework for thinking about law and about the exercise of power.

Burke makes the broader point that, in the case of *any* government, "law and arbitrary power are at eternal enmity."[65] He uses examples of actual states to show that not only in theory, but in practice, the scope of action of Asian princes is constrained and they do not exercise "arbitrary power." This argument would be paralleled in the *Reflections* by his observation that France was not really an "absolute monarchy" in the fullest sense, since the king was constrained by customs, ancient laws, and various political considerations. It is when traditions and established structures are abandoned—even in favor of an ostensibly more liberal new regime—that the door to arbitrary power is fully opened. Burke's view of Asian regimes is not idyllic; he concedes that corruption is often found in them. But he argues that this does not represent the Asian conception of a proper constitution; rather, it is a deviation from it. Corruption is a problem and a weakness that endangers those regimes, and it hardly makes sense for the East India Company to use the defects in other governments as models for its own practices.

In denouncing "geographical morality" then, Burke does not really reject local standards in favor of a universal standard. Instead, for Burke local standards help to actualize universal standards. They do not necessarily represent the fullest expression of morality, but they help support moral behavior by helping constrain one's will. They serve as expressions of our obligations to one another, and promote a sense of humility through the recognition of an order greater than oneself. It is, in fact, largely through our experience with local standards—and with all the societal elements that embody and express those standards—that we gain a sense of what universal standards are. Rather than contrasting universal standards against local standards, Burke holds up firmly established standards—of any society respectful of tradition—against a lack of standards. Hastings would be a law unto himself, free of the laws and customs of both India and Britain, and this is what Burke cannot stomach. The laws and customs of neither India nor Britain provide justification for Hastings's behavior.

Burke highlights the absurdity of Hastings's position: "Think of an English governor tried before you as a British subject, and yet declaring that he governed upon the principles of arbitrary power."[66] And, "never was there heard . . . such as thing as . . . an officer of government who is to exert authority over the people without any law at all, and who is to have the benefit of all laws, and all forms of law, when he is called to an account."[67] Hastings wishes to claim the benefits, privileges, and protections of a British subject, without meeting the basic obligations of one. More broadly, he expects to be treated according to the laws and moral standards that have been given expression and meaning through human society, while behaving as if he were not a member of human society. Neither British nor Indian laws and customs can constrain him. On the opening day of the impeachment trial Burke states that his summary of Indian history shows that, "through all these revolutions and changes in circumstances, a Hindoo polity, and a Hindoo government existed in that Country, till given up finally to be destroyed by Mr. Hastings."[68] Hastings stands in opposition to human society, and his actions serve to undermine the imaginative framework that provides the structure and meaning needed to support that society. Hastings's actions harm not only the Indian polity, but the British polity as well.

Ireland and Jacobinism

For Burke an even more long-standing concern than India was the cause of Ireland and, particularly, of Ireland's Catholics. This is not surprising, since Burke was an Irishman and his roots were at least partly, and perhaps primarily, Catholic. Writers who emphasize Burke's role as a fighter for justice devote considerable attention to his involvement in Irish policy. Likewise, Burke's writings, speeches, and letters on Irish policy have often been used to bolster a natural law understanding of his thought. Burke had an extensive and long-standing involvement with Ireland. What will be demonstrated here is the extent to which Burke's involvement in Irish affairs can be shown to illustrate a concern regarding the moral-imaginative basis for politics and society.

While Burke's interest in Irish policy was certainly driven by his concern for the people of Ireland, it is striking that in the last years of his political career he came to frame the Irish question in the context of his broader fight against Jacobinism. Writing in 1795 about his views on Irish policy, Burke remarks, "My whole politicks, at present, center in one point; . . . that is, what will most promote or depress the Cause of Jacobinism?"[69] Although Jacobinism had triumphed only in France, Burke recognized it as a dangerous dynamic present throughout the European world and, indeed, as a potential danger to human society everywhere. In another letter that same year he explicitly links his concerns regarding the Protestant Ascendency in Ireland with his concerns regarding India and France:

> I think I can hardly over-rate the malignity of the principles of Protest and ascendency, as they affect Ireland; or of Indianism, as they affect these Countries, and as they affect Asia; or of Jacobinism, as they affect all Europe, and the state of human society itself. The last is the greatest evil. But it readily combines with the others, and flows from them. Whatever breeds discontent at this time will produce that greater master-mischief most infallibly.[70]

In the 1760s Burke employed appeals to natural rights when advocating on behalf of better treatment of Ireland's Catholics, but by the mid-1790s he was basing his arguments on the need to combat Jacobinism. This made good political sense, since by that time events in France had provided a lesson to the British on the dangers of Jacobinism. If sympathy for Ireland's Catholics was lacking in Parliament, and appeals to concepts of rights were falling on deaf ears, fears of revolution might provide a more effective impetus for change.

Circumstances in Ireland had also changed somewhat over the course of Burke's career, making Jacobinism a greater concern. Since the French Revolution, the Society of United Irishmen, a radical Protestant dissenter group with strong antimonarchical and Jacobin leanings, had been established in Ireland. Among other things, this organization promised enfranchisement to Catholics, a position that created the potential for it to blossom into a large and powerful revolutionary group. Elements with Jacobin tendencies also seemed to be emerging among existing Catholic and Protestant organizations, and the potential for revolt, or civil war, seemed to be growing. Moreover, a danger existed that the French themselves, who were now at war with Britain, would lend a hand in such an uprising, making the loss of Ireland a plausible scenario. Although concerns about Irish Jacobinism, and about French influences in Ireland, had existed since at least the early 1760s, the situation was becoming more alarming.

Under the promptings of such fears, a number of reforms, some very short-lived or not fully implemented, were enacted in 1792 and 1793. These included the right of Catholics to establish schools, to practice law, to hold minor offices, and to vote in elections for the nominally independent Irish Parliament, although, to a significant degree, implementation of this last reform was locally thwarted. Burke was dissatisfied with these measures and continued to push for additional reforms in 1795. In Russell Kirk's interpretation, Burke's biggest complaint was the fact that, although Catholics might be permitted to vote for Parliament, they were not permitted to stand for election to it. Burke had worked hard for Catholic enfranchisement, but suffrage was not, in itself, a dominant concern of his. In his view, merely allowing the mass of people to vote did little to bring about good government or effective representation. True reform, in his view, required that Catholics be able to hold meaningful positions in government.[71] It should be noted, however, that a very different interpretation is given by James Conniff, who characterizes Burke's Irish reform efforts as in fact focused on the establishment of broad-based suffrage.[72]

While Burke supported extension of the franchise in Ireland, his support for the franchise, and for the need for Catholics to sit in the Irish Parliament, was not based on a faith in the merits of equal representation. It was, rather, drawn from his moral-imaginative perspective on how society and political behavior are shaped. As Kirk puts it, Burke's concern was that the continued exclusion of Catholics from Parliament amounted to the denial of "aristocratic leadership" to the Catholic community.[73] Burke was an elitist of a sort—but only of a sort. He had denounced as oligarchical earlier efforts to provide a more limited Catholic franchise based on stringent property qualifications. He believed, however, in the need for a well-bred, educated, stable leadership class among the Irish Catholics. The political power exercised by members of the Irish Parliament was, in practice, severely constrained, but they were public figures and in that respect could play an important role in shaping Irish politics and society. Conniff again has a directly opposing view, maintaining that Burke had no interest in an Irish aristocracy. In support for this position Conniff offers this quotation from a private letter of Burke: "The Strength of the Catholicks is not in their dozen or Score of old Gentlemen. Weak indeed they would be if this were the Case. Their force consists in two things: their numbers and their growing property, which grows with the growth of the country itself."[74] This quote, however, is simply a factual observation that, at the moment, the Catholics' political strength lay primarily in their numbers, since they no longer possessed a meaningful aristocracy. It hardly indicates that Burke is uninterested in promoting Irish-Catholic aristocratic leadership.

Burke was in fact very interested in promoting aristocratic leadership, but not for the benefit of an aristocracy. This was one component of a broader concern he possessed for the social and moral, and not just political, state of the Irish Catholics. In part, this was manifested by a concern for the Irish moral imagination. Conniff misses this moral-imaginative dimension of Burke's thought, and therefore states: "It is widely agreed that the French Revolution led Burke to become the leading English spokesman for social stability and political order in his day. Interestingly, there was no similar movement in his views on Irish issues."[75] In the first place, it should be evident from this study that Burke did not suddenly become a "spokesman for social stability and political order" after the French Revolution. More significantly, Conniff seems to believe that since Burke was a "reformist" (in the case of Ireland) he could not have been interested in "social stability" there. Burke, in fact, advocated change largely for the purpose of promoting social stability. A desire for "social stability" is very different from a desire to maintain the status quo. In fact, if the status quo is unstable or potentially so, a desire for "social stability" would be manifested in part as a desire for policy changes, potentially dramatic ones. To have social stability and political order, Burke wanted to promote in Ireland those elements that would help furnish a sound "wardrobe of a moral imagination."

Burke's interest in Irish society—as opposed to just Irish politics narrowly understood—was perhaps heightened by the French Revolution and the growth of Jacobinism but certainly did not begin with it. Similar concerns are found in his unpublished *Tract relative to the Laws against Popery in Ireland,* written in the early 1760s.[76] This work is best remembered for its strong call for justice for Ireland's Catholics, including its brief appeal to natural rights, but its major theme is how public policies have shaped, for the worse, the social and moral fabric of Ireland. For example, the very first issue addressed by Burke is the replacement of the ancient common-law practice of primogeniture with a statutory requirement for the equal division of property among sons. Combined with the land confiscations that had occurred over the years, the effect was nearly to wipe out Ireland's Catholic landed gentry. There may have been a personal dimension to Burke's indignation here since, at least on his mother's side, and possibly on both sides, Burke was descended from such gentry, with family lines tracing back to the Normans.[77] The level of contempt Burke displays for Ireland's "Protestant Ascendency" (or "Anglo-Irish Ascendency") throughout his writings on Ireland, both public and private, may be partly attributable to the fact that the "Catholic gentry . . . looked down on landlords of Cromwellian and Williamite origin as social upstarts."[78] Burke's interest is much more than personal, however. In destroying Ireland's Catholic gentry, the Protestants were depriving Ireland of that key societal element that Burke would, in the *Reflections,* call the "ballast in the vessel."[79] Through systematic leveling the Catholic population was being reduced to a mob; there was no educated, well-established leadership class available to set the tone of discourse and to look out for the common good. The Ascendency certainly could not take the place of such an aristocracy; not only was it Protestant, but it was, in large part, self-interested, relatively unrefined, focused on personal economic gain, and middle-class in character. In 1792 Burke would refer to it as a "plebian oligarchy," which to him was a "monster."[80] Burke draws a sharp distinction between aristocracy and oligarchy throughout his writings on Ireland.

In the 1790s Burke would refer to the Irish Penal Laws as "a machine . . . as well fitted for the oppression, impoverishment, and degradation of a people, and the debasement, in them, of human nature itself, as ever proceeded from the perverted ingenuity of man."[81] It is not just through the elimination of primogeniture that public policy is undermining Ireland's social fabric and the moral resources of its Catholics. Back in the 1760s Burke describes how families and property are undermined by laws that give any child who renounced Catholicism the right to take over family lands. Also, prohibitions on the permanent acquisition of land severely discouraged improvement, as did prohibitions on entry into professions. Education for Catholics was virtually impossible. Catholic grammar schools were, as a general rule, illegal; O'Brien maintains that, when staying with his Catholic cousins in the countryside, Burke himself received some of his early education outdoors at an illegal "hedge school" where students were prepared to disperse should a government official appear.[82] Young Catholic men could not attend college in Ireland or Britain; nor, Burke points out, could they be sent to the continent for an education without, once again, breaking the law and being subject to arrest. Both the barriers to education and the inducements to lawbreaking would certainly contribute to the "debasement . . . of human nature" about which he is so concerned.

The general attack on Catholicism in Ireland, Burke argues in the 1760s, is misguided. It may serve the short-term interest of the Ascendency by keeping Catholics down, but it serves the long-term interest of no one. He grants that, although "the idea of religious persecution, under any circumstances, has been almost universally exploded by all good and thinking men," there may be specific cases in which it is understandable if some may oppose a strange new sect. In such a case the established religion has at least the prejudice of antiquity on its side. The persecution of Catholicism, however, turns the usual order on its head, since "this Religion, which is so persecuted in its Members, is the old Religion of the Country, and the once Established Religion of the State."[83] The disruption of this religion, so firmly integrated into the culture and society, could only have negative consequences. In response to those who claim that Catholicism cannot possibly be socially beneficial, Burke asks, "And was there no civil society at all in these kingdoms before the Reformation?"[84] The question should not be whether or not there are errors in Catholicism, since its practitioners

> received it on as good a footing as they can receive your Laws and your legislative authority, because it was handed down to them from their ancestors. The opinion may be erroneous, but the principle is undoubtedly right; and you punish them for acting upon a principle, which, of all others, is perhaps the most necessary for preserving society, an implicit admiration and adherence to the Establishments of their forefathers.[85]

In opposing the traditional religion in favor of a newer one, the government undermines its own authority, since it undermines respect for the order that has been handed down. Without such respect, a sense of arbitrariness and meaninglessness sets in. Burke's emphasis here on the necessity of respect for the legacy of "ancestors" and "forefathers" so early in his career—and decades before similar language would appear in the *Reflections*—serves to dispel any suspicion that the later prominence of this theme was the product of a "knee-jerk" reaction to the French Revolution.

In his early writings on Ireland Burke hints that attempts at suppression of Catholicism are destructive to religion in general, but this theme emerges more prominently in his later writings on the Irish question. He explains that over the broad sweep of history, the purpose of religious persecution has usually been to bring people into conformity with the established church. Although such persecution is undesirable, it has, at least, a positive intent. That is not the aim in Ireland, however. The laws there essentially amount to the establishment of a "*negative* religion."[86] This is because, in many cases, the laws in Ireland do not follow the usual pattern of discriminating between those who are members of the established church and those who are not. Instead, they discriminate between those who are Catholic and those who are Protestant, with the term "Protestant" employed broadly to cover members of the Anglican Church and virtually all dissenters. Essentially, the laws are structured simply to punish people for being Catholic, not to bring people into another church. For most purposes the authorities do not care what religion one professes, or whether one actually practices in any recognized religious denomination at all; one generally qualifies as "Protestant" as long as one is not Catholic. Burke cannot resist the quip that "a man is certainly the most perfect Protestant, who protests against the whole Christian religion."[87] Hence, one effect of the penal laws is to undermine religion in general. In one open letter he tells the supporters of such laws that "you are partly leading, partly driving, into Jacobinism that description of your people, whose religious principles,—Church polity, and habitual discipline,—might make them an invincible dyke [*sic*] against that inundation."[88] In another late letter he explains that "the seduction of that part of mankind from the principles of religion, morality, subordination, and social order is the great Object of the Jacobins. Let them grow lax, skeptical, careless, and indifferent with regard to religion and . . . Jacobinism . . . will enter into that Breach." Therefore, "the R. C. Religion should be upheld in high respect and veneration."[89] It should not only be tolerated, but should be cherished as a good.

Burke's linkage of a decline of religion with the rise of "Jacobinism" anticipates the observations of twentieth-century thinkers like Eric Voegelin. Voegelin and others have seen social phenomena like the rise of revolutionary totalitarian mass movements in Europe in the early twentieth century as partly attributable to a decline in traditional religiosity.[90] Such movements, which have close relationships to Burke's "Jacobinism," not only have difficulty existing alongside of strong orthodox Christian belief, but also help to fill the gap (or, as Burke says, "enter into that breach") left by the loss of traditional religion. Burke's perception of this phenomenon demonstrates the depth of his understanding of both modernity and the human psyche. Although he failed to achieve all he desired in the area of Irish policy, in his final years he personally assisted in the successful establishment of a national Catholic seminary for Ireland. This effort, like Burke's others, incorporated an anti-Jacobin objective, both by ensuring an adequate supply of priests and by ensuring that they were well educated.

It is in his late writings on Ireland that Burke offers his famous definition of Jacobinism. "What is Jacobinism?" he asks. He answers, "It is an attempt . . . to eradicate prejudice out of the minds of men, for the purpose of putting all power and authority into the hands of the persons capable of occasionally enlightening the minds of the people. For this purpose the Jacobins have resolved to destroy the whole frame and fabric of the old Societies of the world, and to regenerate them after their fashion."[91] In a letter to his son on the subject of Ireland he makes reference to "the new fanatical Religion . . . of the Rights of Man, which rejects all Establishments, all discipline, all Ecclesiastical, and in truth all Civil order."[92] In the final analysis, Jacobinism emerges as a kind of nihilism, since it undermines "all discipline" and "all civil order" by undermining those elements that equip a healthy moral imagination. What most stands against Jacobinism, and for civil order, is "prejudice," that is, those acquired predispositions that provide moral stability and serve as a counterweight to seductive revolutionary rhetoric. Millenarian ideas, in fact, arose in Ireland in 1795–1796.[93] Such ideas, and the irrational hubris which accompanies them, reflect the loss of the anchor in reality provided by a sense of a moral order. In another letter Burke enumerates the three main subjects of Jacobin attack: religion, property, and *"old traditionary Constitutions."*[94] Since public policies toward Ireland have also attacked all of these, government has served to aid the Jacobins in their work. It seems as if the objective of the Ascendency is to transform Ireland's Catholics into an irreligious, propertyless, uneducated, atomized mass, alienated from lawful government and lacking a sound leadership class; such a mob would be ripe for radicalism and rebellion. What is lacking in such a people are those elements that support and build up a sound moral imagination, and it is concern for such elements that provides much of the structure for Burke's writings on Irish policy.

Constitutional Reform

Burke's reformist efforts were not confined to matters concerning such dominions as Ireland and India. In 1780 he introduced legislation for "Economical Reform," by which was meant reform of the Civil List. This legislation, designed to reduce the king's patronage power, curb his influence over members of Parliament, and give Parliament effective control over the civil service, was adopted in 1782. At the same time that Burke was pushing for this reform, however, he was fighting against reform of representation in Parliament. The two reforms might be seen to have similar republican and democratic thrusts, and both enjoyed strong support among the Whigs. In the case of reform of representation, a variety of proposals were on the table, including increasing the number of members, making elections more frequent, and expanding voting rights and making them uniform across England. Almost all proposals included, in some form, reapportionment of parliamentary seats; by this time Britain was becoming full of rotten boroughs and pocket boroughs with tiny constituencies, while the growing cities had relatively little representation. These reforms seem modest compared to the kinds of reforms Burke was advocating for Ireland, yet he stood adamantly against the creation of a parliamentary committee to explore questions in this area.

What seems to drive Burke in his opposition to parliamentary reform is not the substance of the proposals so much as the rhetoric accompanying them. He complains that many of the supporters of the reforms frame their arguments "in the nature of a claim of right, on the supposed rights of man as man."[95] Specifically, they claim that the current structure of the British government violates natural rights. But, Burke points out, the modest reforms that they are publicly advocating would hardly seem to make much difference in this regard. The thrust of their arguments reflects some of the common tenets of Enlightenment liberalism: "that every man ought to govern, himself, and that, where he cannot go, himself, he must send his representative; that all other government is usurpation."[96] The reformed House of Commons, however, would be only one part of a government that still included the king and the House of Lords. Flagrant violations of the reformers' principles would therefore remain. Following the reformers' logic the entire structure of the British government would have to be scrapped. Burke maintains that "the great object of most of these reformers is, to prepare the destruction of the Constitution, by disgracing and discrediting the House of Commons."[97] A major factor behind Burke's opposition to creation of the committee on representation seems to be his fear of lending credence to a line of thought that could take hold of the public's imagination and that, he believed, could play out only in a radical manner.

In some of his late writings on Ireland Burke employs the term "virtual representation" when discussing the inadequacy of political representation there. Virtual representation is a situation "in which there is a communion of interests, and a sympathy in feelings and desires between those who act in the name of any description of people, and the people in whose name they act, though the trustees are not actually chosen by them." He considers virtual representation "to be in many cases even better than the actual."[98] Direct electoral ties, in his view, are less important than common interests and sympathies between representatives and the public. The problem Burke identifies in Ireland is that not only is actual or formal representation inadequate, there is no virtual representation either. Its population is sharply divided, and the interests of the bulk of that population are not represented in government in any way, even informally. This argument explains the apparent discrepancy between Burke's support for reform of representation in Ireland and his opposition to such reform in Britain. In Britain, he maintains, there is no evidence that the interests of any geographic regions or social classes are being ignored; those with a low level of representation appear to receive the same benefits as those with greater representation. The discrepancies in numerical representation are undeniable, "but it is not an arithmetical inequality with which we ought to trouble ourselves. If there be a moral, a political equality, this is the *desideratum* in our Constitution, and in every constitution in the world."[99]

Burke's discussion of "virtual representation" should not be taken as an indication that he is entirely antidemocratic. While Burke was opposed to radical majoritarianism, he was, generally speaking, a strong supporter of the more democratic or republican aspects of the British Constitution. In 1770 he denounced Parliament's practice of refusing to seat elected members it deemed objectionable. There he argued that "the power of the people, within the laws, must show itself sufficient to protect every representative in the animated performance of his duty, or that duty cannot be performed. The House of Commons can never be a controul [*sic*] on other parts of Government unless they are controuled themselves by their constituents."[100] The particular case that helped inspire this writing was not one in which Parliament could be accused of being without cause; the person who had not been seated was John Wilkes, who had been convicted of publishing an inflammatory pamphlet and had fled to France. Burke insists that such "arbitrary incapacitation" of duly elected representatives is unjustifiable, just as he opposes arbitrariness in other cases.[101] There is, of course, really no sharp contrast between a "democratic" Burke here and an "antidemocratic" Burke who opposes reform of representation. His argument that the "power of the people" should be respected in seating elected members is driven by his desire to maintain the integrity of the British Constitution. He knows that where the Constitution really resides is in the moral imagination, and that its integrity depends upon a sense that it is a sacred thing that cannot be ignored. Although there is ample precedent for Parliament's refusal to seat Wilkes, the action comes across as arbitrary since it sets aside a legitimate election conducted according to established law.

In the case of the parliamentary reform proposals, Burke is concerned about the Constitution being undermined in another way. The most vocal supporters of reform of representation essentially claim the existence of a natural right to a particular governmental structure. Someone as knowledgeable as Burke about the historical and geographical diversity of approaches to government would have been struck by the parochial or culturally specific quality of this so-called "natural right." Burke maintains that the idea that people possess a natural right to representative government is, in fact, a concept derived from the British Constitution.[102] That is, the theory has been developed from what has been learned through historical experience. Burke's opponents, however, seem to have forgotten this, and act as if their theory has come from some ahistorical source outside of actual human experience. Even though they have learned from what actually exists, they have come to believe they have nothing to learn from what actually exists, and have moved into an abstract realm.

In focusing on ideal forms of government Burke's opponents have lost sight of the fact that what really matters is how that government acts. Francis Canavan points out that "strangely enough, Burke's extreme reluctance to change existing forms of government was due in part to a conviction that forms were not very important. Any form of government, he felt, could be operated successfully by the right sort of men, and no form was proof against the wrong sort."[103] While Canavan is very correct in noting that Burke emphasizes the character of people, rather than forms of government, this does not mean that Burke considers forms irrelevant. For him forms of government do help to shape people and political discourse, and thereby impact on the quality of governance. The British form has done reasonably well in this area. Burke argues, "To those who say it [the British Constitution] is a bad one, I answer, Look to its effects. In all moral machinery, the moral results are its test."[104] This "effects" criterion Burke sets down for evaluating the British government is the same as that which he cites for evaluating the laws and practices of India.

Burke is no less concerned than his opponents about good government. He realizes, however, that their abstractions will not provide it. By abandoning the historical, they set up a movement toward arbitrariness:

> You admit that there is an extreme in liberty, which may be infinitely noxious to those who are to receive it, and which in the end will leave them no liberty at all. I think so, too. . . . The question is, then, What is the standard of that extreme? What that gentleman, and the associations, or some parts of their phalanxes, think proper? Then our liberties are in their pleasure; it depends on their arbitrary will how far I shall be free. I will have none of that freedom. If, therefore, the standard of moderation be sought for, I will seek for it. Where? Not in their fancies, nor in my own: I will seek for it where I know it is to be found,—in the Constitution I actually enjoy.[105]

Burke understands that for liberty, or for rights, to have any real meaning, there must be standards for those rights that are broadly recognized as greater than the arbitrary will of those in power. His opponents would no doubt agree with him on this point, since they make their claims on the basis of "natural rights," which implies belief in universal and, perhaps, transcendent standards. The problem is that they essentially move these rights into an abstract, ahistorical realm, so that they are no longer tied to a particular society and order. Rights cannot operate effectively as abstract concepts. How does one know precisely what they mean, and how they apply? Who gets to decide what "natural rights" there are? Upon what basis? In their efforts to set rights above the vagaries of human society, Burke's opponents actually eviscerate them, transforming them into little more than matters of whim.

Burke knows that British political ideals arose in a particular social and historical context, and draw their force and meaning from that context. Paradoxically, the best way to set standards above the vagaries of human society is to anchor those standards firmly in that society. His earlier observation about the Americans' tendency to associate liberty closely with the taxation issue because liberty cannot exist in the abstract demonstrates his keen awareness that standards for liberty or for governmental action must be tied to concrete touchstones. It is such touchstones that equip the moral imagination and give meaning to concepts like "liberty." Burke worries about his freedom under a new regime; he feels free under the present regime because he knows "there is an order that keeps things fast in their place: it is made to us, and we are made to it."[106] The people and their governmental structures have grown together and are suited to one another. Laws and political customs form one part of a greater moral-imaginative complex, which shapes the behavior of individuals within government and without. Ordinary people know when the actions of the powerful are out of bounds, and react appropriately. The powerful know too. Everyone has an internalized sense of right and wrong because their perceptions are shaped by a common moral-imaginative framework. The formal checks and balances within government operate effectively because they are tied into this framework. A new scheme, no matter how "rationally" chosen, cannot duplicate this. Burke explains that a nation

> is an idea of continuity which extends in time as well as in numbers and in space. And this is a choice not of one day or one set of people, not a tumultuary and giddy choice; it is a constitution made by what is ten thousand times better than choice; it is made by the peculiar circumstances, occasions, tempers, dispositions, and moral, civil, and social habitudes of the people, which disclose themselves only in a long space of time.[107]

The emphasis on "continuity" is, of course, classic Burke. Throughout this speech he emphasizes the prescriptive nature of the British Constitution, "whose sole authority is, that it has existed time out of mind."[108] Three different but closely related arguments in favor of this constitution can be identified here. One is that it is intimately tied to an established moral-imaginative framework. Another is the traditional conservative argument that the constitution is tried-and-true, reflects accumulated wisdom, and has demonstrated its effectiveness over time. The third argument can be called the "sublime" argument: that the Constitution's age has given it an aura of legitimacy—and perhaps even of sacredness—which strongly discourages its violation. If credence were given to the reformers' rhetoric, this aura would vanish. The adoption of radically new constitutional schemes would create the sense that the rules of government are arbitrary and are open to violation. If abrupt changes can be made once, they can be made again and again. Burke maintains that "as all government stands upon opinion, they [the supporters of the proposals] know that the way utterly to destroy it is to remove that opinion, to take away all reverence, all confidence from it."[109] All regimes, not just the British government, ultimately rest upon public opinion; none can stand long without at least some measure of popular consent. In this particular case, "confidence" and "reverence" are clearly necessary if the rules and freedoms associated with British law are to have real meaning and are to endure. It is Burke's understanding of the role of "opinion" that drives him to oppose reform of representation. The understanding of how political order subsists within the moral imaginations of a people, which here animates a "conservative" Burke, is the same understanding that animates the "liberal reformist" Burke of Irish, Indian, and American affairs.

6 Burke and the Good

IT HAS BEEN SHOWN HOW Burke's political and philosophical thought offers us a model for approaching political, social, and ethical questions centered around the concept of the moral imagination. For Burke, good politics is politics that takes into account how people perceive the world, how they reason, and how they make moral decisions. Political action should be undertaken with consideration of how it may interact with, and shape, the imaginative framework that underlies cognition. Sensitivity to issues of the moral imagination, however, cannot be all that is necessary for good politics; certainly some sort of normative standards must exist that inform political thought. Are there in fact such standards for Burke, and are they "universal"? An effective response to this question is bound up with an understanding of Burke's moral-imaginative approach. The answer to the problem of the relationship of this outlook to universal norms has been hinted at throughout this study, but will be addressed more directly here.

The question of the good is of course central to all moral/ethical thought, as well as to politics, society, and, indeed, virtually all of human existence. We are always trying to determine the right thing to do. In this late-modern or postmodern era especially, the search for the good gets bound up in fundamental questions about the source of morality or of values. One finds, for example, traditional advocates of foundationalist or natural law–based approaches to morality who argue that right and wrong are dictated by God or by a fixed, clearly definable human nature. Others reject such assertions.

In popular discourse one sometimes hears of "moral relativism" versus "moral absolutism." Such terms are highly problematic, so much so that they are not very useful at a philosophic level, but they point to the fact that, even in the popular mind, there is a sense of fundamentally different approaches to morality, and of a sharp divide between them. This is often evoked, either explicitly or implicitly, in contemporary political discourse and debate. Indeed, one can argue that a fundamental characteristic of the contemporary world is a crisis of sorts over the source of values. The question of the good is not only central to contemporary society, but has tended to loom large over many studies of Burke, and animates some of the interest in him. Burke has, in fact, a rather unique and very important approach to the problem of the good, and in uncovering it we illuminate the broader problem in its many manifestations in politics, society, and life.

The question of what is normative for Burke has been both a central one in Burke scholarship and a point of much controversy and confusion. This study has already made reference to the "natural law school" of Burke scholarship. This approach to Burke, which became dominant in the 1960s, arose partly as a reaction against other interpretations of Burke that denied or downplayed any belief by Burke in universal standards. Joseph Pappin refers to such approaches as "utilitarian" interpretations of Burke.[1] This is as good a label as any, although it should be noted that relatively few treatments, such as the classic nineteenth-century study by John Morley,[2] seriously attempt to portray Burke as a true Benthamite in anything like a full sense; more often the "utilitarian" characterizations are more general and vague. Many early to mid-twentieth-century political-philosophical studies of Burke see in him a somewhat confused patchwork of frames of reference. For example, a 1925 work by C. E. Vaughan makes much of Burke's occasional emphasis on "expediency," but also notes Burke's historicist tendencies and his frequent appeal to traditional "moral law."[3] Vaughan sees Burke as a proto-progressive. He finds many inconsistencies in Burke's thought, and Vaughan explains these as arising from the fact that Burke lacked the tools necessary to develop a clear understanding of his own position or to maintain philosophical consistency. This sense that Burke somehow does not quite "get it" pervades much of the twentieth-century literature on him, from detractors and admirers alike.

Like Vaughan, Harold Laski sees a multifaceted Burke. He states that "Burke was a utilitarian who was convinced that what was old was valuable by the mere fact of its arrival at maturity." While Laski repeatedly faults Burke for his conservatism, he praises Burke highly as well, largely for his "liberalism" and for the many occasions in which he was "upon the side of the future." Although Burke is described as a "utilitarian," Laski states that he is *not* a "Benthamite." Burke believes that "particular circumstances must always govern the immediate decision," yet there is "in Burke a Platonic idealism which made him . . . regard existing difficulties with something akin to complacent benevolence." He was also "profoundly religious." Reading Laski, one is almost hard put to identify *any* basic political-philosophical outlook that is *not* ascribed to Burke in some way. It is probably this perceived lack of consistency that prompts Laski to begin his discussion of Burke by stating that "he was a member of no school of thought."[4]

Writing just a few years after Vaughan and Laski, Alfred Cobban maintains that "an inconsistency runs right through" Burke's thought, since Burke is not just a "disciple" but "the greatest of the followers of Locke," yet his thought also often diverges dramatically from that of Locke. Cobban does not really explain why Burke should be regarded as a "disciple" of Locke; he seems to take for granted that, as a Whig, Burke should be so regarded, even though Cobban himself maintains that "Locke's political philosophy is based on individual right," while "Burke begins at the other end with religious obligation," and that "Locke was a theorist of revolution" while Burke was a "conservative." At any rate, although Cobban regards Burke less favorably than does Laski, his overall assessment of Burke is not dramatically different. What Cobban most sees in Burke is an uncomfortable mixture of utilitarianism and Christian natural law, both of which are sometimes trumped by Burke's "doctrine of prescription." Cobban concludes that "the belief that political values are to be judged in their relation with the historical community seemed to us the final teaching of Burke's political theory."[5]

In reading Cobban, or Laski, or Vaughan, or any of a great many treatments of Burke, one can get the impression that, first, Burke is pulled in different directions, and second, more than anything else, he is some sort of "utilitarian" or "pragmatist," if those terms are used in a general sense, rather than as designations of particular well-developed schools of thought. This utilitarianism or pragmatism is seen to be blended with a "conservatism" or preference for what exists, simply because it exists. Burke's appeals to God-given or otherwise universal standards may be sincere, but they are viewed as largely tangential to his thought; it is his "relativism" or rejection of universals in lieu of an emphasis on particulars that is seen to be at the core of his approach to politics and morality and that makes him significant to most scholars. For some Burke commentators this is for the good; for others, such as Leo Strauss, this is very much for ill.

Strauss speaks of Burke's "classical or Thomistic framework," but then argues that he ends up in a place very different from that of true classical or Thomistic thinkers. For one thing, "Burke's opposition to modern 'rationalism' shifts almost insensibly into an opposition to 'rationalism' as such." Consequently Burke ends up denying a meaningful role for human reason in establishing and maintaining a sound political order. And Burke's emphasis on prescription amounts to a rejection of "transcendent standards." If the good is defined as merely that which has existed, one has no meaningful standard for good at all. Burke emerges for Strauss as a sort of proto-Hegelian or extreme historicist. Strauss cites Burke's late private remarks that the French Revolution may turn out to have been decreed by Providence and may represent an unstoppable new order for Europe, and faults Burke sharply for rejecting "resistance in a forlorn position to the enemies of mankind" and for establishing a dynamic that would result in "the supersession of the distinction between good and bad by the distinction between the progressive and the retrograde, or between what is and what is not in harmony with the historical process."[6]

In response to Strauss one may point out that Burke's private remarks are primarily an expression of personal despair at the persistence of the Revolution, mixed with his trademark humility. He does not state definitively that the Revolution was decreed by Providence; he merely points out that it is beyond our ability to know for certain that it is not. Nor does he encourage the Revolution's opponents to give up their fight or surrender to "the historical process," a term that Burke, of course, never uses. Indeed, Burke's career was, in significant part, one of lonely support for lost or unlikely causes. As has been noted, he pursues the Hastings impeachment trial for years after he has concluded that he will not prevail. And he continues to work against the French Revolution even when he is in the despair that Strauss notes, a fact that itself should cast doubt on Strauss's interpretation. Nevertheless, Strauss's portrayal of Burke as an historical determinist and as a moral relativist has been influential.

The "natural law school" of Burke scholarship stands against the above interpretations, maintaining that Burke's thought is in fact centered on transcendent standards. Peter Stanlis perhaps takes the most unflinching position, maintaining that "in every important political problem he ever faced, in Irish, American, constitutional, economic, Indian, and French affairs, Burke *always* appealed to the Natural Law."[7] Stanlis states that "the ethical code of the Natural Law and the legal traditions of the English constitution provided Burke with the normative standards of what government should or should not will." And, since the English Constitution should itself be understood to be based upon natural law, "Burke's attack on the false claims of revolutionary natural rights was a direct defense of the prescriptive English constitution and an indirect defense of the traditional Natural Law." Burke, Stanlis maintains, should be seen as no less than "the foremost modern Christian humanist in politics."[8]

Francis Canavan makes a similar argument. He maintains that "the central idea in Burke's thought . . . was that of order. But this order, as he understood it, was neither wholly natural nor wholly conventional. It was a joint product of God and man, in which the order of society, derived from and reflecting the divinely-ordained order of the universe, was produced, maintained, and improved by the constant exercise of man's political reason."[9] Canavan rejects Strauss's historicist interpretation of Burke, pointing out that "the doctrine of divine providence, as understood in Christian theology, means that history is determined by God, not that God is bound by a law of development immanent in the historical process."[10] Writing more recently in this tradition, Joseph Pappin refutes claims that Burke rejects a meaningful role for reason, arguing that "it does not appear that Burke is any more extreme in his limitation of the scope of reason than Aristotle or Aquinas. They qualify the use of speculative reason and urge its guarded application in the field of politics."[11] Pappin also maintains that for Burke, prescription, prejudice, and expediency "do carry great weight, but they do so only insofar as they are grounded in Burke's metaphysics of a God-centered universe, divinely ordered, purposefully moved, and grounded in the natural law. Burke clearly favors that which is sanctified because it reflects a continuity required by the universe and the social order."[12] One can recognize a role for prescription and expediency without becoming a historical determinist or strict utilitarian. Pappin attempts to address many of the subtleties of Burke's thought while keeping him firmly within the natural law framework.

If one takes Burke's writings at face value, it would seem difficult to deny that Burke's thought is grounded in a concept of a divinely ordered universe that is at least dimly perceptible to human reason. Nevertheless, many Burke scholars find the natural law interpretation to be less than convincing. It does seem to have weaknesses. For one thing, Burke does not invoke natural law very explicitly, and his writing is not particularly Thomistic in flavor. Some other problems with the natural law interpretation have already been alluded to in this study. While Burke's disparagement of "reason" and of "metaphysics" should not be exaggerated or misunderstood, his apparent attacks on such pillars of natural law–type thinking make it difficult to fit him neatly into the natural law camp. Those of the natural law school consequently tend to downplay this dimension of Burke's thought in order to sustain a claim that Burke is a reasonably consistent natural law thinker. As was discussed in chapter 2, Canavan finds Burke's aesthetic theory to be incompatible with his political-philosophical thought, largely because of the "reason" issue. As mentioned in chapter 3, Charles Parkin supports a "natural law" approach by maintaining that Burke stands for "reason" and opposes the "passion" represented by the Jacobins, a position that would appear directly to contradict statements by Burke both on the subject of passion and on that of the Jacobins.

There are, in fact, numerous statements in Burke that may be held up as contradicting a natural law interpretation. Most recent scholars who reject this approach, however, do not develop arguments for some other philosophical basis for Burke's thought. Instead, they avoid the question, or maintain that Burke is a political "pragmatist," not to designate strict adherence to the later philosophical school of pragmatism, but to indicate that he has no coherent normative grounding and essentially follows a "whatever works" approach to politics. Scholars with this perspective often suggest that Burke's references to natural law, natural right, and other frameworks are utilized merely as rhetorically effective devices, not as expressions of Burke's own beliefs. Frank O'Gorman and Christopher Reid[13] essentially portray Burke in this way. Harvey Mansfield, as has been mentioned, maintains that Burke rejects "theory as such."[14] Isaac Kramnick refers to Burke's "basic ideological ambivalence"[15] and instead focuses on psychological factors to explain Burke's positions. James Conniff offers a "progressive" Burke, but this progressivism is not characterized as a systematic philosophical framework. Conor Cruise O'Brien offers the image of Burke as a fighter against abuses of power, but his treatment of Burke, like many recent treatments, is much more biographical and historical than philosophical. Overall, the impression one may get is that Burke really has nothing important to say philosophically, and that he is worthy of study only from a historical or rhetorical perspective. This impression is reinforced by the fact that some general political theory texts fail to include any treatment of Burke, despite his historical stature and his copious, oft-quoted writings.

The confusion and disagreement surrounding the question of what is normative for Burke can be alleviated somewhat if one brings to bear Burke's appreciation of the role of a moral imagination. Although it is not fully articulated, Burke's epistemological and moral perspective is more complex than is usually recognized in scholarly attempts to find a philosophical grounding for his thought. An interpretation that draws upon the concept of the moral imagination and its importance to Burke does not remove all traces of inconsistency from his writings and speeches. However, it does make it much easier to take seriously the theocentric and natural law dimensions of Burke's worldview without finding glaring contradictions in his apparently "utilitarian" or "historicist" leanings. Broadly speaking, Burke can in fact be seen to recognize the world as ordered to a universal purpose, and to believe that human beings must attempt to discern this order as best they can. However, his approach is not best described as Thomistic, at least as Thomism is now typically understood, although it may perhaps be quite Thomistic in a general and, perhaps, medieval sense. As Russell Kirk and others have suggested, there is something premodern about Burke; his perspective has much in common with a medieval Christian and classical one. At the same time Burke brings a late-modern and original understanding to that perspective. Burke's modernity, however, is quite different from that typically associated with, say, the French Enlightenment. Perhaps Burke's understanding could be legitimately described as "postmodern," since his approach is quite different from that of many typical "moderns" of his day. But this term is also problematic, since it implies that Burke can be grouped with the broad school of thought labeled postmodernism. One might suggest that most postmoderns are really hypermodern, and that Burke is a more true postmodern who attempts to move past much of the common thought of modernity, but who also draws heavily upon earlier premodern thought. However one wishes to label Burke's perspective, elements of it, which have been alluded to throughout this study, can now be pulled together and further developed and applied.

Rights and the Universal

Questions about Burke's approach to the good, or whether he is best seen as a "relativist" or as a believer in universal or transcendent standards, often center on Burke's position on rights. There is good reason for this, since the concept of rights ties so closely into these questions and is treated with much apparent confusion by Burke. Burke's nuanced—and perhaps sometimes even contradictory—views on rights illustrate aspects of his unique and complex moral-political perspective. He is well known for his harsh disparagement of doctrines of "rights of men," particularly in the case of the French Revolutionaries and their British supporters, but he often uses the language of rights himself. Kirk and others have seized upon, and strongly emphasized, a distinction in Burke between "rights of men" or "natural rights," and prescriptive "rights of Englishmen."[16] Such a distinction can often be found in Burke, and it does shed light on his perspective, but if an attempt is made to apply it strictly as a political-philosophical doctrine it does not hold up well. For example, in writing on the Popery laws in Ireland Burke maintains that "every body is satisfied that a conservation and secure enjoyment of our natural rights is the great and ultimate purpose of civil society."[17] Such a statement sounds very like the kind of Lockean liberalism underpinning the opening passages of the U.S. Declaration of Independence. These rights are "natural" and, implicitly, universal. They are not identified as specifically British or historical. And, when defending Fox's India bill against charges that it violates the "rights of men" (with the "men" in question being the officers and directors of the East India Company), Burke replies in Parliament that "the rights of *men,* that is to say, the natural rights of mankind, are indeed sacred things; and if any public measure is proved mischievously to affect them, the objection ought to be fatal to that measure."[18] Interestingly, while defending the concept of the "rights of men" here, Burke is also rejecting the claims of the East India Company, which are not actually based on abstract universal "rights of men" at all but on quite specific prescriptive rights they have held. In fact, earlier in his career, when towing the old Whig party line in support of the Company, Burke himself raised the "rights" argument to defend noninterference.

It may be tempting to argue that Burke's position on rights changed over time; as interpretations of rights doctrines became more radical, he became increasingly leery of rights-based claims. It is true that Burke makes freer use of phrases such as "rights of men" and "natural rights" before 1789, and devotes more attention to criticizing rights doctrines after that date. However, even after 1789 Burke does not reject concepts of rights completely. Cobban maintains that "it is not true that Burke changed his opinions fundamentally at the time of the Revolution or at any other time."[19] Another explanation, already mentioned, for Burke's apparently contradictory positions on rights is that he does not, in fact, have anything resembling a political theory at all. He employs the language of rights—somewhat cynically—because of its rhetorical value; it is common currency in late eighteenth-century Britain— "everybody is satisfied" with it so it is therefore effective in argument—but it does not hold any special meaning for him. If he can win fairer treatment for Catholics in Ireland by appealing to accepted concepts of natural rights, he will do so. If he can generate opposition to, or reduce support for, the French revolutionaries and their British supporters by disparaging their radical rights-based framework, he will do so. An explanation such as this, which essentially claims that the writer cannot be taken at face value, is problematic. It creates burdens for demonstrating the insincerity of his positions and for explaining his true beliefs and motivations; such burdens are difficult to carry convincingly in the absence of positive evidence.

Burke's positions on rights are actually not particularly inconsistent, and there is no reason not to take him at his word when he appeals to rights in some cases and rejects them in others. Many commentators on Burke have found this to be the case. Charles Parkin, for example, maintains that Burke clearly accepts the doctrine of "natural rights"; his rejection at times of formulations such as those of "rights of man" springs from the fact that he detects, and rejects, a dangerous tendency of "rights of man" theorists to "assume a direct correspondence between natural and civil rights."[20] A recent commentator, Gary D. Glenn, offers a similar but more nuanced and sophisticated interpretation, finding that "because Burke understands man as by nature political, the rights that may be properly claimed in civil society are political. While rights' origin may be pre-political and therefore transpolitical, their substance in civil society is given shape by prescription."[21] Burke's own rhetoric offers some support for such interpretations. For example, he asks, "how can any man claim, under the conventions of civil society, rights which do not so much as suppose its existence? Rights which are absolutely repugnant to it?"[22] Elsewhere, he states that the "rights of man" cannot be the rights of a people, "for to be a people, and to have these rights, are things incompatible. The one supposes the presence, the other the absence, of a state and civil society."[23] Natural rights do exist, Burke explains, but independently of government or civil society. Since by necessity these rights must be compromised and modified if one is to live with others in civil society, such rights are not fully compatible with government. Therefore, because "government is not made in virtue of natural rights,"[24] it is useless to talk about government with regard to natural rights.

While Burke's argument as described here seems on the surface to be coherent, problems arise if it is taken as the definitive explanation of Burke's perspective on rights. For one thing, in practice it does not prove to be terribly useful in explaining why Burke supports some rights but not others. For example, the "rights" claimed by the members of the East India Company, which are rejected by Burke, would seem on the surface to be the kinds of basic prescriptive property and contract rights that Burke would usually take for granted. Burke's argument that these rights are not applicable in this particular case does not rest on any blanket rejection of natural rights doctrines. More important, the idea that Burke's perspective on rights is defined by a rejection of "a direct correspondence of natural and civil rights" would seem to contradict those statements by Burke that link government or civil society to natural rights. In the above quote attacking the Company, Burke stated explicitly that we should reject public policies that "mischievously" affect natural rights. This is difficult to reconcile with Parkin's argument. And, if Burke holds to a belief that "government is not made in virtue of natural rights," it is hard to explain why he states in another context, "If these natural rights are further affirmed and declared by express covenants, if they are clearly defined and secured against chicane, against power, and authority, by written instruments and positive engagements, they are in a still better condition."[25] Here Burke seems to be saying rather explicitly that government should be in the business of securing natural rights. This 1783 statement could even be understood as implying that he would support the adoption of formal declarations of rights. Of course, Burke would actually denounce such declarations in the French context just seven years later.

It may be helpful to admit that Burke is not as philosophically rigorous or precise in his "rights talk" as he could be. By his own account, Burke was not a "metaphysician." And he was writing as a practicing politician pursuing particular agendas, not as a political theorist. He was not particularly concerned with abstract, technical philosophical questions; consequently his ground shifts somewhat depending upon the particular circumstances he is addressing. This does not mean that his discussions of rights are purely rhetorical, or that his positions are arbitrary. Consistent themes can be identified across Burke's treatments of rights, and they spring from his emphasis on the role of a moral imagination. Burke supports rights when they exist in the proper context; that is, he supports rights that are historically anchored and culturally compatible. This does not simply mean that he is pragmatic, or that he pays attention to historical particulars, as many have observed. There is much more to it than that.

Rights-based frameworks are valid when they are firmly supported by the moral imagination and, in turn, when they contribute to a sound moral imagination because of their historical-cultural ties. Burke rejects the language of rights when it lacks a proper imaginative context to ground it, and when it disrupts or deforms a moral imagination. His biggest complaint about those who engage in "rights talk" is that "their principles always go to the extreme."[26] The principles "go to the extreme" because there is no context to define and delimit them. Our understanding of the world and all its elements derives from the imaginative wholes that we have built up; the meaning of a "right" is dependent upon these wholes. If the proper examples, prototypes, metaphors, and so forth are not present, the practical meaning of a particular right becomes highly fluid. Burke therefore prefers rights that have acquired specific, fairly precise meanings in real-world contexts, and he recognizes those rights only when applied in the proper context. This distinction is not identical with the distinction between "natural" rights of man and "prescriptive" rights of Englishmen, although in practice it may often yield similar results. The critical thing to understand is that Burke is less concerned about the "objective" rights themselves than about our subjective experience of them. So, for example, in the case of the rights newly proclaimed by the Jacobins, Burke finds that "their abstract perfection is their practical defect. By having a right to every thing they want every thing."[27] The Jacobins' emphasis on rights rather than duties feeds the "vanity" that Burke identifies as the chief of the vices. It reshapes the moral imagination, promoting a kind of expansiveness that is directly contrary to the humility and restraint that he sees as a key to morality and to political order.

Burke argues in his *Appeal from the New to the Old Whigs* that, in contrast to the principles of the metaphysicians, his own principles "can never lead to an extreme, because their foundation is laid in an opposition to extremes."[28] Rather than founding government "in imaginary rights of men" Burke would found them "in political convenience, and in human nature,—either as that nature is universal, or as it is modified by local habits and social aptitudes. The foundation of government . . . is laid in a provision for our wants and in a conformity to our duties: it is to purvey for the one, it is to enforce the other."[29] Similarly, he states in the *Reflections* that "government is a contrivance of human wisdom to provide for human *wants.*"[30]

Given such talk of "political convenience" and of government providing for "wants," it is not surprising that Burke is sometimes viewed as a utilitarian, and as one who rejects any moral basis for politics beyond simple utilitarianism. Burke is, however, making important points about how politics works. Most political thinkers, from Aristotle to the social contract thinkers, have agreed that political associations arise to provide for human wants; such a formulation need not, of course, imply a particularly narrow conception of "wants." When used in a political or social sense, the term "wants" is of course often a synonym for "needs," and human needs can be understood to go far beyond basic physical provisions. It was mentioned that Burke argues that the state "is to be looked on with other reverence, because it is not a partnership in things subservient only to the gross animal existence of a temporary and perishable nature. It is a partnership in all science; a partnership in all art; a partnership in every virtue, and in all perfection."[31] For Burke, understanding government in relation to human "wants" is not to diminish reverence for it, and does not require us to lower our political sights. The highest human needs are a "want." Nor is it sacrilege to speak of "political convenience." This is simply a reference to the fact that government should be structured, and should operate, in such a manner that allows it to function best in a given set of circumstances. To ignore "political convenience" in favor of some ideal model is to create a government that is likely to function poorly or to lack the support needed to ensure its stability and continuity. No matter how elevated the intentions, an approach to government that ignores "political convenience" cannot truly be moral in the fullest sense, since it can accomplish no moral goal. Good intentions or lofty objectives are not enough. Burke maintains, in fact, that those who focus on unworkable, idealistic schemes tend to become indifferent about the details of real-world politics and "see no merit in the good, and no fault in the vicious, management of public affairs."[32] The perfect becomes the enemy of the good.

Burke makes numerous references to the importance of sensitivity toward "human nature," in contrast to the simple adoption of formulations of rights. He understands that statements about "rights" are, really, statements about people; it is people who have a physical existence, not rights, and they are the real subjects of our concern. Rights formulations are essentially attempts to recognize and express certain truths about human nature, and about how that nature dictates that people should interact. A potential problem with rights doctrines is that they can be rather blunt instruments by which to approach such truths. Human nature is ultimately mysterious, but subtle knowledge of it, and of how to act with regard to it, can be gleaned in various ways. One benefit of traditional practices, customs, and such is that they tend to incorporate a degree of understanding of human nature, albeit in an incomplete and partly inarticulate or compact form. Rights formulations may likewise contain real, and perhaps profound, information about human nature, but in themselves they do not come close to plumbing its depths or its complexity.

It was observed in chapter 2 that Burke maintains: "That great chain of causes, which linking one to another even to the throne of God himself, can never be unraveled by any industry of ours. When we go but one step beyond the immediately sensible qualities of things, we go out of our depth."[33] This is not an expression of radical skepticism, but a recognition that we must remain humble, and grounded in human experience. Those who overemphasize particular expressions of rights are deceiving themselves that they know much more than they actually do. Moreover, in holding to a rights-based framework in a dogmatic or doctrinaire way these "metaphysicians" actually suppress or blot out a great deal of important knowledge about human nature; a kind of closure to reality occurs. As a result, they can, Burke explains, end up doing terrible things. Burke's belief in the primacy of humility among the virtues therefore supports his cautionary approach to rights.

A simplistic, doctrinaire emphasis on rights not only fails to penetrate far into the mysteries of human nature, it makes the mystery go away. This is perhaps the most dangerous aspect of "rights talk." Human nature, or the human person in the fullest sense, is certainly something that Burke ultimately linked "to the throne of God himself" and that was regarded by him as a proper subject for awe, inspiring reverence and humility. In Burke's aesthetic terminology, the human person would be regarded as sublime. Declarations of rights threaten that sublimity. Recall Burke's observation in his aesthetic writing that one of the characteristics of the sublime was "obscurity." Burke maintained that "hardly any thing can strike the mind with its greatness, which does not make some sort of approach towards infinity" and that "a clear idea is therefore another name for a little idea."[34] An overemphasis on "clear" ideas of rights creates the sense that we know all about human nature; this strips the subject of its mystery, sublimity, and awesomeness. The outcome is to diminish, rather than enhance, the individual's standing and worth. In effect, human beings cease to be regarded as sacred.

Moreover, Burke points out that no sooner are supposedly absolute and inviolable declarations of rights made, than they are compromised or modified or somehow made contingent. He remarks sarcastically in the *Reflections* on the fact that voting rights in France have been made conditional upon the payment of certain fees: "What! a qualification on the indefeasible rights of men?"[35] Five years later, upon being told that the French regime is somehow moderating because it has renounced portions of the *Declaration of the Rights of Man*, Burke responds, "If possible, this their recantation of the chief parts in the Canon of the Rights of Man, is more infamous, and causes greater horror than their originally promulgating, and forcing down the throats of mankind that symbol of all evil."[36] If the *Declaration* is a "symbol of all evil," why is its renunciation even worse than its promulgation? Because this renunciation undermines the entire concept of rights. This is also why Burke treats as so important the "minor qualification" that was attached to political rights. Even though the qualification is minor, it amounts to the "utter subversion" of the Jacobins' principles: "You order him [a citizen] to buy the right, which you before told him nature had given to him gratuitously at his birth, and of which no authority on earth could lawfully deprive him."[37]

In making universal declarations of rights, these rights, and the human beings to whom they adhere, are shifted from a mysterious, sublime realm to the more prosaic domain of human reason and understanding. The subsequent recantation or qualification of those rights completes the process, by shifting rights—and humanity—into the domain of a capricious will. As Burke showed in his discussion of the horse in the *Sublime and Beautiful*, that which is subject to one's will cannot be sublime and cannot have one's full respect. This is, again, the modern problem that Heidegger would call *Zuhandenheit*, applied now to human beings. If something comes to be seen as fully subject to our wills, a loss of meaning occurs and arbitrariness sets in. As was noted above, Burke observes that natural rights "are indeed sacred things." He fears the loss of this sacred quality. Burke remarks of the metaphysicians that "finding their scheme of politics not adapted to the state of the world in which they live, they often come to think lightly of all public principle."[38] Rights are for Burke a dangerous concept, because if rights come to be seen as subject to the will, the whole rights concept is undermined and they become arbitrary. This is to say that they cease to exist in a meaningful way. Rights truly exist only when they are sacred. Getting back to the East India Company, we can easily see that their supposed "rights" are hardly sacred. In reality, these are not "rights" in the large sense at all, but rules and privileges established for the operation of a specific state-sponsored enterprise. They have no bearing on the basic understanding of human nature or society, so Burke feels free to modify them. In invoking "rights of men," the East India Company's supporters are actually helping to undermine the concept of rights by applying it in an inappropriate way.

Burke is comfortable with "rights talk," and uses it himself, when it is applied in a manner that is unlikely to jeopardize the sacredness of the human person. This is one reason why he is comfortable with rights that have become established through long practice. Such rights have acquired relatively precise meanings that are broadly accepted, which have proved workable in practice, and which therefore are unlikely to be suddenly circumscribed. They have become at least somewhat internalized; that is, they are firmly established in the moral imaginations of the public. Because of their long-standing nature, such rights are also unlikely to be seen purely as manifestations of human will, or as arbitrary. They are a part of the landscape, a part of one's inheritance from one's forefathers, and therefore are not seen as something that people "just made up" and can change at will. Through their great age, and/or through their association with idealized figures or periods from the past, they have acquired that implied connection to the infinite that gives them a sublime and sacred quality. At the same time, because of their close connection to a particular network of social and legal practices, such rights have a certain conventional quality. It may seem contradictory to claim that some rights are understood to be simultaneously sacred and conventional, but a sense of a mysterious connection between what is particular and conventional and what is universal and sacred is an important component of Burke's thought.

A common awareness of the partly conventional nature of rights actually helps to protect the sacredness of rights and of the people to whom they adhere. If rights are seen as partly conventional and culture-specific, their specific meanings, that is, the specific interpretations of particular rights, can be subjected to minor modifications over time, without jeopardizing the idea that there is a basic human nature that must be respected. Legal and traditional rights are seen as reflective of an understanding of the human person, which is not arbitrary, but which is imperfect. The result is a strong and somewhat flexible, rather than a rigid and brittle, imaginative framework. Hence, rights can be modified in modest ways without creating a sense that they are merely constructions of a capricious human will. In contrast, the sort of natural rights structure erected by the Jacobins, which may appear to some as stronger than the fuzzy British model, is in fact brittle, and collapses when the Jacobins start to redefine, compromise, or conditionalize the rights.

Human Agency and Morality in the Commonwealth

Burke's understanding of the complex relationship between the conventional and the universal is evident in his observation that "commonwealths are not physical but moral essences. They are artificial combinations, and, in their proximate efficient cause, the arbitrary productions of the human mind."[39] Here he labels commonwealths as "artificial" and "arbitrary," yet he sees no contradiction with the fact that they are also "moral essences." Of course, in using the term "arbitrary" here Burke does not mean it in the sense of "capricious." A commonwealth is "arbitrary" in a manner similar to that in which it is "artificial," in that its precise form is not dictated by nature. It is in part the product of various historical circumstances, and of human will-action operating in the context of those circumstances. If history had played out differently, if certain people had made different decisions at different times, the form of the commonwealth would be different. This "artificial" and "arbitrary" aspect of the commonwealth is not only compatible with the commonwealth being a "moral essence," it is required for it. That which is wholly natural, if the term is used to designate that which arises without human will-action, cannot be moral or immoral; it simply is. It is human beings who possess knowledge of good and evil, and the concept of morality adheres to human thought and action.

Although Burke states in one place that commonwealths are artificial and arbitrary, he states elsewhere that "our political system is placed in a just correspondence and symmetry with the order of the world."[40] This quote is, not surprisingly, a favorite of those who promote a natural law interpretation of Burke. Burke's sense of a universal order and of the relationship of the man-made order to that universal order is, broadly speaking, a form of natural law thinking, and it is an important dimension of his thought. Burke, however, places greater emphasis than most traditional natural law thinkers on the mysterious nature of the relationship between a particular political order and the universal order. He does not claim that one should, or could, achieve a political order "in a just correspondence and symmetry" with the universal order simply by observing the world and then erecting a political order from scratch that is in conformity with the perceived universal order. A sense of Burke's understanding of the actual relationship can be gleaned from the context in which the above quote appears. Here he speaks of "a constitutional policy, working after the pattern of nature" by which "the institutions of policy, the goods of fortune, the gifts of providence are handed down to us." He continues:

> Our political system is placed in a just correspondence and symmetry with the order of the world, and with the mode of existence decreed to a permanent body composed of transitory parts; wherein, by the disposition of a stupendous wisdom, molding together the great mysterious incorporation of the human race, the whole, at one time, is never old, or middle-aged, or young, but in a condition of unchangeable constancy, moves on through the varied tenour

[*sic*] of perpetual decay, fall, renovation, and progression. Thus, by preserving the method of nature in the conduct of the state, in what we improve we are never wholly new; in what we retain we are never wholly obsolete. By adhering in this manner and on those principles to our forefathers, we are guided not by the superstition of antiquarians, but by the spirit of philosophic analogy. In this choice of inheritance we have given to our frame of polity the image of a relation in blood, binding up the constitution of our country with our dearest domestic ties, adopting our fundamental laws into the bosom of our family affections; keeping inseparable, and cherishing with the warmth of all their combined and mutually reflected charities our state, our hearths, our sepulchres, and our altars.[41]

Here the correspondence between the political order and the universal order is linked to a sense of the commonwealth as an inheritance. This can be seen to bolster an understanding of Burke as either a conservative or a historicist. But Burke maintains that "we are guided not by the superstition of antiquarians." He does not believe that the patterns of the past must be adhered to blindly. He is calling for the same humility and respect for the past that has been discussed in previous chapters. This humility and respect is of course seen by Burke as critical to checking the will and minimizing caprice. Moreover, he is calling for a political order and outlook that is integrated into society's broader worldview and into established patterns of life. He emphasizes ties between the political constitution and family affections. Like Aristotle, Burke presumes that families, states, and other forms of association arise after "the pattern of nature" in the sense that human beings have certain basic needs, desires, and inclinations that lead to the development of such associations. This is not to say that precise forms are dictated by nature, or that these associations are not created through human agency. However, they are, or should be, parts of a coherent whole; a sense of continuity should exist between the political order and other dimensions of human life. To maintain a healthy political order, one's sense of that order must be integrated into a coherent, well-developed moral imagination. We are born into particular circumstances and live our lives in the context of those circumstances. Our moral imaginations develop within these contexts, make sense of them, and utilize them to make sense of new experiences. Since our cognitive processes tend to operate through metaphor, analogy, and the imaginative extension of prototypes, a continuity develops in our lives. As a general rule, we function best when such continuity is maintained. The moral imagination grows strong through the reinforcement of our familial and political relations, and a strong, healthy moral imagination creates strong internal checks on capricious, antisocial, or harmful behavior. This is a recipe for a stable and free commonwealth.

Political Truth and the Perception of Reality

One may object that the preceding discussion of Burke's approach to rights and to political order skirts the central question of what is normative for Burke. How does one determine which political actions are appropriate and which are not? The above discussions do, in fact, point toward Burke's answer to these questions. There are no pat formulas that tell us in simple terms whether a particular government structure, change in law or policy, or political action is right or wrong. As the advocates of the "natural law Burke" show, Burke possesses a sense that what is ultimately normative is in fact that which is ultimate, and universal, and absolute. But how can this be Burke's standard when he scoffs at "metaphysicians" and at those who place an excessive emphasis on the use of "reason" to penetrate the absolute? How, for Burke, do we perceive the universal and bring it to bear on real-world circumstances?

On the general problem of morality and the universal, the early twentieth-century literary scholar and social critic Irving Babbitt has observed that "man is cut off from immediate contact with anything abiding and therefore worthy to be called real, and condemned to live in an element of fiction or illusion, but he may . . . lay hold with the aid of the imagination on the element of oneness that is inextricably blended with the manifoldness and change and to just that extent may build up a sound model for imitation."[42] It is with the aid of the imagination that one may perceive, however dimly, what is "abiding" and "real." A similar approach to the universal can be seen in Burke. For example, it will be recalled that Burke regards our forebears, or our impressions of them, as important touchstones for a moral imagination, finding that "under a pious predilection for those ancestors, your imaginations would have realized in them a standard of virtue and wisdom beyond the vulgar practice of the hour: and you would have risen with the example to whose imitation you aspired. Respecting your forefathers, you would have been taught to respect yourselves."[43] Like Babbitt, Burke is calling for us to "build up a sound model for imitation." In building up such a model, we are able to "lay hold of" a deeper reality, and this inspires us to further moral action.

Burke's brief statement on ancestors pulls together many of the elements of his thought that have been discussed in this book. The need for standards, the role of piety in making standards effective, the importance of prototypes in human thought, the role of the imagination in morality, and the human tendency to imitate and to learn through imitation, are all present. All of these elements relate to Burke's understanding of how one may approach the true and the good. He knows that universals are difficult to articulate effectively. Although he does not reject "theory" and "precept," his view is that they can play only a partial role in guiding one to right behavior. It is therefore not surprising that he finds, "History consists, for the greater part, of the miseries brought upon the world by pride, ambition, avarice, revenge, lust, sedition, hypocrisy, ungoverned zeal, . . . These vices are the *causes* of those storms. Religion, morals, laws, prerogatives, privileges, liberties, rights of men, are the *pretexts*. The pretexts are always found in some specious appearance of a real good."[44]

A critical factor in determining whether an action is actually good is whether or not the actor is oriented toward the good. This orientation occurs to a great degree through the building up of the moral imagination. A well-developed moral imagination provides valuable information about what is right, in a form that is often difficult to articulate concisely but is directly accessible. A moral imagination also helps to shape and direct the will; that is, it forms character. Concise articulations of what is good, such as moral precepts or declarations of rights, carry limited meaning in themselves and are subject to interpretation in any number of ways, some of which are truly good and some of which are not. Only if the actor is truly oriented toward the good is it likely that attempts to conform to such codes will yield good results.

An emphasis on the need for an orientation toward the good, and on the inadequacy of moral or political precepts in the absence of such an orientation, is of course not unique to Burke. One may, in fact, go back to Aristotle and find that "to be a competent student of what is right and just, and of politics generally, one must first have received a proper upbringing in moral conduct."[45] Formal study of politics or ethics will not yield desirable results in one who has not already built up the right sort of internal framework. Similarly, Plato, who might be seen by some as the premier "metaphysician," recognizes no less than Aristotle the limited ability of philosophical speculation to shape the human heart. In the *Seventh Letter* he refers to the inadequacy of language to illustrate reality. He also states that no city can know peace if its citizens are brought up to be self-indulgent, and discusses the need for a ruler to "lead the sort of life day by day that would be most conducive to self-control."[46] Perhaps even more noteworthy is the fact that Plato appears to consider the setting, the characters, and the conversation in his dialogues to be no less important in teaching philosophy than the specific doctrines and propositions that are offered. Despite his criticism of poetry, his dialogues are themselves poetic narratives, operating in a manner similar to that in which Burke sees drama, poetry, and literature shaping the individuals who partake of it. For Plato, to study philosophy is to be led along a way; only so much can be directly explained. Burke, well read in classical and traditional Christian literature and philosophy, absorbed and appreciated this recognition of the limitations of intellectual speculation and of the need to cultivate virtue in all aspects of life. Looking at the Christian side of the Western heritage, one sees that in the Christian model of the incarnation the Law is fulfilled not in more laws but in the *person* of Christ. Redemption lay in the "way" of following Christ. Although Burke lived during the Enlightenment, some of his thought is highly reflective of premodern traditions and worldviews.

The idea of morality and politics as a sort of way or path is short-circuited by the metaphysicians whom Burke disparages. Some of his attempts to criticize the metaphysicians on this point, however, have contributed to the confusion in the secondary literature regarding his fundamental approach to politics and morality. He complains, for example, that the metaphysicians "build their politics, not on convenience, but on truth."[47] Burke's apparent rejection of "truth" in favor of "convenience" has contributed to interpretations that he adheres to some sort of utilitarianism, and that he rejects the belief that a greater order exists to which humanity should conform. It is helpful, however, to see this statement in context: "These teachers are perfectly systematic. . . . These teachers profess to scorn all mediocrity,—to engage for perfection,—to proceed by the simplest and shortest course. They build their politics, not on convenience, but on truth; and they profess to conduct men to certain happiness by the assertion of their undoubted rights."[48] What Burke is attacking here is not "truth" per se but the error of ideology, which is partly a form of the error of hubris. "These teachers" have come to believe that they possess perfect or near-perfect knowledge of certain metaphysical truths, and of the precise manner in which to conduct human affairs in conformity to those truths.

Burke's scorn of those who "build their politics . . . on truth" does not constitute a rejection of truth or of its importance. Earlier in the same work, *An Appeal from the New to the Old Whigs,* he criticizes radical majoritarian democracy and the demagogues who expound it by observing that "to flatter them [the people] into a contempt of faith, truth, and justice is to ruin them; for in these virtues consists their whole safety."[49] Then, just a few pages after speaking of the need to uphold "faith, truth, and justice," he makes the apparently contradictory statement that "political problems do not primarily concern truth or falsehood. They relate to good or evil. What in the result is likely to produce evil is politically false; that which is productive of good, politically true."[50] Burke's substitution of good and evil for truth and falsehood as the key political criterion is not so much a "metaphysical" position as an expression of his understanding of how one should approach political problems. Thoughts about the "good" tend to focus on concrete actions and their results; we determine particular actions to be good because we determine that they have specific desirable effects on specific things. In contrast, thoughts about "truth" often tend to be more abstract, and are less likely to focus on actions than on states of being. Even if an abstract conception of a particular truth is "metaphysically" correct, this may provide relatively little information about practical political activity. Conceptions of what is true and of what is good are both subject to error, but because in practice a truth-focused approach is likely to be less contextually grounded, political errors are more likely to arise in that case.

Burke's substitution of good and evil for truth and falsehood is not utilitarianism, if "utilitarianism" is understood to incorporate a rejection of universals. Burke's statement is, above all, a recognition of the epistemological problem of knowing what is true or good. Burke is shattering the myth that those who start from a doctrinaire adherence to an ideology or to a set of universal principles automatically have a handle on "truth," while those who focus more closely on immediate political needs must not. Unless a particular "metaphysician" wishes to claim the benefit of direct, explicit divine revelation, he must admit that he gets at his truth in the same manner as Burke, which is through the knowledge he has built up through experience and learning of various types. Knowledge of the universal is, by necessity, derived from the particular and the historical. Even a past revelation becomes more historical information. Mention has been made of Burke's observation that those who argue for constitutional reform based on natural right theories of representation have derived those theories from their actual experience with the British Constitution. Because Burke realizes that we get at the true and the good, including that which is universally true and universally good, through historical experience and the examination of particulars, he believes that we must continue paying attention to particulars and to history. Not to do so is the height of hubris, because it implies a belief that we have achieved perfect knowledge, or that we have some other source of knowledge to draw upon, such as a form of "reason" that provides illumination in the absence of data. The metaphysicians display such hubris because they have forgotten where their theories come from. They essentially claim a privileged position above the historical flux, which is a position no human can hold.

Burke should not be mistaken as an empiricist in the full-fledged sense, although his thought reflects the influence of the British empiricist tradition. He never maintains that a human being is a *tabula rasa,* and, of course, he does not advocate some sort of scientistic approach to the world in which one considers (or pretends to consider) only a narrow range of observable data. As we have seen, Burke recognizes, even emphasizes, the importance of the character of the observer; internal knowledge is at least as important as new observation. He understands, however, that this internal knowledge has largely been built up from past experience, and that a failure to recognize this basic fact hampers civic discourse and policy making. When the sources of apparently "self-evident" and "universal" truths go unexamined, politics is apt to devolve into a shouting match, and real-world institutions may be held to unachievable, oversimplified, and ultimately harmful standards.

The approach to politics that Burke is criticizing here is essentially a "backwards" approach. Instead of closely observing real people, real circumstances, and real causes and effects, and then building up a theory of governance accordingly, the metaphysician begins with a priori theories, often accepted with little reflection, and then applies them unthinkingly to concrete situations. Burke observes that, in contrast with these naive and arrogant modern theorists equipped with the "metaphysics of an undergraduate," the ancient legislators "had to do with men, and they were obliged to study human nature. They had to do with citizens, and were obliged to study the effects of those habits which are communicated by the circumstances of civil life."[51] Life is mysterious and complex, and real knowledge of politics and morality and right action is not so easily arrived at. The metaphysicians ignore the fundamental epistemological problem. They have developed formulae that offer a convenient framework for understanding reality, but they are mistaking these formulae for reality itself. They treat their partial, rudimentary knowledge as if it were complete and perfect knowledge. Thus the French revolutionaries proclaim in their *Declaration* that "ignorance, forgetfulness or contempt of the rights of man" are "the *only* causes of public misfortunes and the corruption of Governments."[52] Implicit in such a bold declaration is an assertion that the revolutionaries' understanding of core problems of politics and human nature is complete. The contrast with the American constitutional framers, with their famously cautious British attitudes, is dramatic.

As has been noted, Burke finds his opponents "so taken up with their theories about the rights of man, that they have totally forgotten his nature. Without opening one new avenue to the understanding, they have succeeded in stopping up those that lead to the heart. They have perverted in themselves, and in those that attend to them, all the well-placed sympathies of the human breast."[53] What real understanding requires is not a simple formula but a kind of attunement. It was mentioned in chapter 1 of this study that Strauss maintains that for Burke "the good order or the rational is the result of forces which do not themselves tend toward the good order or the rational."[54] Burke's actual position is precisely the opposite. It is the need for "forces" to "tend toward the good order" which is central to his thought. The "forces" of politics are people, and if they do not "tend toward the good order" a desirable outcome is unlikely. Burke recognizes, however, that tending toward the good order is not as easy as some think, and he sees that this problem is often bypassed in the rush to proclaim a universal norm. To achieve the orientation or attunement necessary in order to truly "tend toward the good order" is no easy task, as the ancients knew. It involves the shaping of the whole person, which, Burke finds, is accomplished in large part through the development of a sound moral imagination. The more effectively one's imaginative framework grasps reality, the greater the likelihood that one's actions will be right.

An obvious objection to be raised here is: How does one know whether or not one has a sound moral imagination? That is, even if one grants that a sound moral imagination, or simply sound character, is a key to right action, does this not just push the problem back a step? Not necessarily. One can judge the moral and practical effectiveness of a particular understanding of reality by observing the effects of actions taken based upon that understanding. It will be recalled that Harvey Mansfield complained that Burke does not say "how to be sure of the morality of prudence." There is very little of which one can be completely "sure," and even to approximate certainty regarding "the morality of prudence" on an abstract level is a problematic task. This is why Burke tries not to deal with problems abstractly. The way in which one can get a good idea as to whether certain actions are prudent, or moral, is by observing the effects of those actions. One learns from observing one's own actions and their results, and from observing the actions of others. As a sound moral imagination is built up, one becomes better equipped to determine whether or not actions are sound. For example, one should, in evaluating statements such as the *Declaration of the Rights of Man,* be able through one's intuitive knowledge of the world to get a sense of whether or not it is true that inattention to rights is the "sole cause" of "public misfortunes." Ideological thinkers tend to lack the openness, and the rich moral-imaginative frameworks, necessary to make such determinations accurately. Irving Babbitt's moral outlook, partly influenced by Burke, has been summarized as a belief that "the crux of the ethical life . . . is not acquiring definitive theoretical knowledge of the good, which is beyond man, but the ability to *act* on whatever ethical insight one does have. As man grows in character and performs new good actions, the light of reality streaming forth from these actions will brighten."[55] This understanding can also be seen to be implicit in Burke; he understands political morality to spring from those who continually move toward the good, not those who believe they have seized it.

While the contrast between Burke's approach to the good and that of highly ideological thinkers may be easy to see, with less ideological thinkers the contrast is more subtle. Nevertheless, Burke's thought remains distinctive. Some of the finer points of Burke's approach can be illustrated by its similarities to, and differences from, the view expressed in the following statement from MacIntyre:

> Notice . . . that the fact that the self has to find its moral identity in and through membership in communities such as those of the family, the neighborhood, the city and the tribe does not entail that the self has to accept the moral *limitations* of the particularity of those forms of community. Without those moral particularities to begin from there would never be anywhere to begin; but it is in moving from such particularity that the search for the good, for the universal, consists. Yet particularity can never be simply left behind or obliterated. The notion of escaping from it into a realm of entirely universal maxims which belong to man as such . . . is . . . an illusion with painful consequences. When men and women identify what are in fact their partial and particular causes too easily and too completely with the cause of some universal principle, they usually behave worse than they would otherwise do.[56]

To a large degree this statement is highly Burkean, although MacIntyre, with his differing interpretation of Burke, would very likely not consider it such. Yet there is an implication in this passage that is very un-Burkean; it involves MacIntyre's assertion that "it is in moving from such particularity that the search for the good, for the universal, consists." For Burke the search for the good does, in fact, involve moving from particularity; his reference to the "spirit of philosophic analogy" is just one bit of evidence of this. But

MacIntyre seems to understand this search necessarily to take the form of an intellectual extrapolation from particularity to universal concepts. While the search for the good may take this form in part, for Burke it is primarily experienced through addressing new particularities. In bringing knowledge gleaned form one set of particulars to bear on another set of particulars, a partial grasp of the good—a sense of universals—is developed, but it is largely developed intuitively.

MacIntyre makes reference a few paragraphs later to the "virtue of having an adequate sense of . . . traditions," and states that "in practical reasoning the possession of this virtue is not manifested so much in the knowledge of a set of generalizations or maxims . . . ; its presence or absence rather appears in the kind of capacity for judgment which the agent possesses in knowing how to select among the relevant stack of maxims and how to apply them in particular situations."[57] Burke would of course strongly agree that virtue can be found not in knowledge of maxims but in the capacity for sound judgment. But why must this judgment take the form of selecting among a "stack of maxims"? For Burke, while it may be helpful to make use of appropriate maxims, most judgment, including most moral judgment, does not take this form but occurs on an intuitive level. This is no less true in judgment that involves an "adequate sense of . . . traditions." In fact, if one's sense of a tradition is truly "adequate," the essence of the tradition is internalized and need not necessarily be articulated in the form of maxims. This does not mean that the articulation of traditions is never appropriate, but that maxims are secondary, and are not a requirement for morality. For Burke, moral judgment is always rooted in what we have identified as the moral imagination, or in the imaginative whole that is one's intuitive perception of reality. Writing on the thought of Russell Kirk, W. Wesley McDonald has observed that "Many advocates of natural law take a legalistic and intellectualistic view of morality because they perceive the moral ultimate to be a precept of reason that can be applied to particular cases in a casuistic manner. But, as Vivas pointed out, 'moral law cannot be enacted in advance of experience, enacted into law by decree prior to specific human action.' Man's finite mind is incapable of grasping all the infinite possibilities that will emerge."[58] A keen awareness of the limitations of "moral law" approaches is an important characteristic of Burke, and it contributes powerfully to the sharp distinctions between Burke's thought and that of thinkers like MacIntyre.

An important reason why Burke places humility first among the virtues is that humility is important for developing a sound perception of reality. A lack of humility leads to a kind of closure; hubris blinds one to justice, morality, reality. We learn through experience only if we are willing to concede that we make mistakes. Close observation of the world, including observation of our own actions and their results, builds knowledge and wisdom. This observation often does not take a highly deliberate or intellectual form; it occurs "naturally" in one who is properly oriented, although deliberate efforts to learn are also helpful. Effective observation is made possible in part through a moral imagination, and, in turn, it helps to build up a sound moral imagination. The better developed one's moral imagination, the better able one is to extend metaphorically to new experiences the knowledge gained from old experiences. One builds up an intuitive understanding of universal reality. This sort of understanding is not easily articulated. As Babbitt puts it, the "epistemological problem . . . cannot be solved abstractly and metaphysically, [but] can be solved practically and in terms of conduct."[59] Rather than grasping truth simply by learning some maxim, one moves toward truth, or toward the good, in inarticulate, practical terms through a gradual process of attunement. One develops, in Burke's words, "a moral taste." This is why matters of the imagination, and hence matters of culture, art, religion, tradition, relationships, associations, institutions, and such are so important to Burke. Upon them hinge one's ability to move toward reality, to exercise sound judgment on both a moral and practical level, and to engage in ethical and effective conduct.

Conclusion
Politics, the Moral Imagination, and Burke

WHEN WE IMPROVE OUR UNDERSTANDING of the thought of prominent historical figures, we also—it is hoped—better equip ourselves to address the issues of today. This is especially true in the case of Burke, who approached problems of the modern world in a manner that offers much promise, but has been little understood, developed, or duplicated. An interpretation of Burke's political-philosophical thought that is developed from the "moral imagination" and related concepts not only enhances our understanding of Burke but has broad implications for approaching the political, social, and philosophical questions of the contemporary world. Indeed, it has been suggested here that problems in developing effective interpretations of Burke are reflective of broader problems or limitations in our own thinking. Consequently, problems in interpreting Burke shed light on fundamental issues and problems of contemporary politics and thought.

If there is one conclusion that one may draw from the secondary literature on Burke, it is that he has been difficult to characterize philosophically. In fact, there is no agreement as to whether a coherent political-philosophical approach of any type runs through his works. Even a measure of basic political consistency has not always been recognized among his various positions on matters of public policy. While this book does not purport to represent a fully comprehensive treatment of Burke, it does offer a new way to make sense of him and to resolve some of the apparent inconsistencies in his political thought. In this examination a number of closely linked ethical and epistemological themes have emerged; these will be summarized below.

First, what Irving Babbitt has called "the epistemological problem" is of central importance in understanding Burke. He is keenly aware that there is always a lack of certainty in matters both moral and instrumental. To a degree Burke's views are reflective of British empiricism, and he may have been influenced by the skepticism that was circulating in his day, but his own response is not one of radical empiricism or radical skepticism. Instead, his response is one of humility, of careful attention to particulars, and of interest in matters related to the workings of knowledge and judgment. For Burke, humanity is not blind or helpless, but is always groping along in partial darkness. His skepticism is in some ways postmodern in character, but it could also be seen as premodern, reflecting a classical and traditional Christian sense of humanity's limitations and of the need to avoid the great error of hubris. The metaphysicians whom Burke criticizes are guilty of hubris, and of a failure to recognize fully the epistemological problem and to respond properly to it. One characteristic of this response, humility, can be identified as another major theme in Burke. This theme is widely recognized in the secondary literature, since Burke is quite explicit about humility's central place among the virtues, and about vanity's central place among the vices. The conservatism that is often evident in Burke is partly the result of humility in the face of the epistemological problem.

Closely related to Burke's sense of the epistemological problem is his interest in how people learn and think. For him most learning occurs in a manner that may be called nonrational. That is, people pick up the behaviors and attitudes of those around them without much deliberate thought. They also pick up ideas and understandings of the world from life experience of all sorts. Sometimes these ideas are clearly articulated; more often they are not. The product of much of this learning is what Burke calls "prejudice." This prejudice has a tremendous influence on our opinions and behaviors; "reasonings" are often applied after the fact to justify opinions that have already been reached nonrationally. Burke realizes that we cannot be free of prejudice, so the task becomes one not of eradicating prejudice, but of fostering the right kinds of prejudices. Although politically Burke often stands on the side of reform, he tends to prefer "old prejudices" of the right sort. For one thing, they have stood the test of time and are therefore more likely to offer a better—that is, a more morally sound and practically useful—understanding of the world than is provided by new prejudices adopted with little reflection. More important, old, deep-seated prejudices are usually much more effective than new ones in constraining the will and discouraging capricious behavior.

As developed here, the concept of the moral imagination grows out of Burke's understanding of prejudice and of how we reason or exercise judgment. It also grows out of his early views on the imagination. Burke rejects the old characterization of the imagination as a merely mimetic faculty. Instead, he declares it to be a great creative power. The imagination's power lies primarily in finding resemblances between things; it connects one idea to another and thereby gives meaning and creates a coherent conception of the world. Consequently we have a tendency to think metaphorically. Norms arise through this imaginative process. While this normative role for the imagination is always present, Burke finds it to be most clearly evident in societies lacking in sophisticated philosophical or political-theoretical discourse but possessing rich literary or mythic traditions. The imagination, Burke's thought reveals, plays a crucial role in judgment; sensory data must be made meaningful by the imagination before the "reasoning faculty" can do its work. As we bring contemporary thought to bear on Burke's writings, the model that emerges is one in which we create imaginative wholes. By making connections, a network of meaning is built up that constitutes our sense of reality. It is within this reality that reason must operate. What may, therefore, appear to be a problem with one's "reason" may not be a problem with "reason" per se but with the imaginative framework within which it is functioning. Symbols of various types play an important role in creating frameworks of meaning. The elements that help furnish the "wardrobe of a moral imagination" and supply the "decent drapery of life" are a matter of concern because they are touchstones that add important meaning to our imaginative wholes, enhancing and sharpening our conception of reality and, in the process, building moral character.

The perception of reality that is informed by the "wardrobe of a moral imagination" shapes political behavior in various ways. Because it provides the context within which reason must function, it influences the outcome of our efforts to be rational. Most judgment, however, occurs prior to, or outside of, conscious rational deliberation and conceptualization; a great many judgments, large and small, are made subconsciously or intuitively as we give meaning to new sensory data by fitting these data into our imaginative grasp of the world. Many of these judgments about the world and about our place in it are expressed in the form of intuitions or feelings. Burke greatly values such judgments. He considers feelings, sentiment, and passion to be important, but not foolproof, guides to moral and effective behavior, provided that one has built up the right sort of moral imagination. Unlike those writers who value sentiment but emphasize its instinctive quality, Burke sees it as largely learned. Along with influencing sentiment, the moral imagination influences the will, since it has a normative quality and is a source of internalized standards. One's sense of what one ought and ought not to do under particular circumstances is profoundly shaped by the intuitive mindset that is one's understanding of reality.

An emphasis on standards is another important theme in Burke. Significantly, the kinds of standards that he emphasizes are largely the internalized—and sometimes unspoken—sort. His opposition to the arbitrary exercise of power motivates him to search for constraints on idiosyncratic, selfish willfulness. To have meaningful standards that discourage caprice, Burke believes, one must have a sense of a greater order in which one participates. Ideally, such a sense is supplied by the elements of the wardrobe of a moral imagination. Religion, characterized as the "first prejudice," is especially important to Burke; the "consecration" of the state by religion helps to impress upon political actors the importance of their charge. That which is venerable is also particularly important in contributing to a sense of a moral order. It is in part because of this effect of the venerable that Burke values old customs, traditions, and the like. Without such elements there is no sense of permanence; without a sense of permanence, "all bets are off" and politics and society are plunged into escalating change. Sudden change, made without homage to what has come before, contributes to a sense of arbitrariness and a general loss of meaning.

The problem of meaning emerges as one of the most important in Burke's thought. For Burke meaning is supplied not just through explicit maxims and traditional cultural elements such as customs, religion, and so on, but through literature, theater, and other art forms. It is also supplied through the experiences of daily life, including personal relationships. The development of a sense of meaning is in fact closely linked to what is today often called moral education or political education. It is also inseparable from the central problem addressed by Burke, which is that of building and maintaining a stable and, broadly speaking, liberal or free political order. A sound polity requires for Burke a citizenry with the right sort of character, and an important component of such character is a well-nourished moral imagination.

While the Burke described in this study is, in temperament and in much of his outlook, not unlike the Burke described by those of the "natural law school," it is not precisely the same Burke. Indeed, it has been shown here that one of the things that makes Burke important philosophically is the uniqueness of his approach to politics and, more fundamentally, to morality. A prime representative natural law characterization of Burke is that of Peter Stanlis, who has maintained that "to Burke, no *moral* problem was ever an *abstract* question; he therefore conceived of statecraft as the practical application in concrete human affairs of primary moral principles, clearly evident to man's right reason."[1] Stanlis's point about Burke's rejection of "abstract" approaches to politics or morality, in favor of an emphasis on the "practical" and "concrete," is an important one. And, understood properly, the above statement is not incorrect. Nevertheless, it is problematic. A reader of this statement might find Burke difficult to distinguish from the very "metaphysicians" he opposes. Surely some of the French revolutionaries and their supporters would have claimed that *they* "conceived of statecraft as the practical application in concrete human affairs of primary moral principles." In fact, their principles tended to be highly moralistic in tone and character. (An assertion, for example, that a government is legitimate only if elected through majoritarian democracy, is essentially a moral claim, especially if it is offered with little practical justification. And surely much of the *Declaration of the Rights of Man*[2] could be characterized as the assertion of "moral principles," whether or not those principles are entirely correct.) And, of course, the revolutionaries and *philosophes* certainly believed themselves to be addressing "concrete human affairs."

Stanlis's use of the term "right reason" here is important, and the accuracy of his statement hinges upon it, but this too is somewhat problematic. If a reader does not fully understand or accept a particular conception of "right reason," which is not really articulated by Burke (who does not use the term), what is left is simply "reason," which is clearly not Stanlis's intended meaning. What is problematic about the above characterization of Burke is that he could be viewed as simply a more successful, or more sound, metaphysician. Under this interpretation, both Burke and the metaphysicians he opposes are trying to apply basic moral principles to concrete human affairs. Burke is just better at this than the others. This is partly because his principles are more sound than those of the French revolutionaries and radical Whigs, and partly because he pays more attention to concrete particulars and is more cautious and careful in applying principles. The implication is that Burke is engaged in a sort of casuistry that is in fact most un-Burkean. Certainly, he believes in basic moral principles. And, in statecraft, as in all matters, Burke certainly believes that one should act morally. And he does articulate various principles for application in the business of statecraft. But this does not mean that his chief conception of statecraft is as the "application . . . of primary moral principles," if this statement is understood to mean that, for Burke, an act of statecraft must involve the explicit invocation or articulation of basic principles if it is to be sound.

Burke understands moral principles to be attempts to articulate deeper, mysterious truths that can only be incompletely conveyed. This strong sense of mystery makes him leery of a heavy emphasis on the application of general principles. Remember his youthful remark in the *Enquiry* that "a clear idea is . . . a little idea." Profound truths can only be poorly articulated; they cannot be fully captured by simple maxims. Great truths, in fact, cannot be fully known to human beings. Certainly they are not always "clearly evident," at least not in their deepest sense. However, truths can certainly be known somewhat, and they can often be known on a compact, intuitive level better than they can be rationally articulated. Thus it is not surprising that Burke observes that societies can effectively convey a sense of virtue and vice, and of norms of various sorts, through narratives, long before they have developed philosophical discourse. For him, moral statecraft does not require the deliberate application of clearly articulated moral principles. Principles are often very helpful, but they are derivative; it is the deeper truths that are primary. And these truths become known to us through particulars. This is why Burke tends to shun abstraction, and why he emphasizes close attention to actual situations and to historical experience. Those who start from general principles typically fail to recognize that their principles are derived from what is particular and concrete, and that they are shorthand expressions of deeper and more complex truths. The point Burke makes about the real-world origins of abstract theories of political representation demonstrates his focus on the fact that truths are made known to humankind through particular historical events.

Some might argue from a religious perspective that revealed truths are an exception. In the case of the particular metaphysicians Burke was opposing, this is a moot point, since the Jacobins and sympathetic theorists were generally deistic or atheistic and would not make such religious claims. Burke himself, though widely recognized as sincerely and perhaps even profoundly religious, seems to emphasize the experiential dimensions of religion more than dogma or particular revealed truths. Presumably his sense of mystery and of human limitation applied in this area as well; revealed truths, once expressed in human terms and made a part of human history, would tend to suffer from the same problems as other concise articulations of that which is deeply profound. The articulated truths may be vitally important, but they do not convey so much explicit information that their application becomes automatic in complex concrete situations. Consequently, while Burke accepts basic moral principles, he does not structure his politics around their application. To focus simply on applying principles is to presume that one has very specific knowledge of these principles, and, in particular, that one has highly reliable a priori knowledge of precisely how to apply them in real-world circumstances.

It bears repeating that Burke's position does not constitute a rejection of the idea of the true or the good, or of universals of any kind. Burke is deeply interested in the true and the good and in the problem of getting to them. Since we come to know the true and the good through particulars, he focuses on particulars, of the present and of the past. Principles have a role to play because they are attempts to express knowledge that has already been gleaned, but they are only a part of the puzzle. And even the "rational" analysis of particulars, though very helpful, can only take us partway; Burke took a dim view of technocrats who focused on such analysis but lacked a well-developed, broad-based intuitive sense of the world. For Burke, one cannot simply reason one's way to the true or the good. Instrumental reason is, again, only a part of judgment, and is only a part of how we know things. The material upon which one's reason has to work is the intuitive grasp of reality formed by the imagination. Consequently, movement toward the true and the good occurs in significant part through the development of the moral imagination. What is required is a kind of attunement. The most rigorous analysis and the highest ideals will not yield moral results if they are not employed by one who is internally oriented toward the true and the good. The greatest flaw Burke sees in the metaphysicians is their lack of the right sort of internal orientation.

In stressing the importance of what is often referred to today as "moral education" or "political education" Burke does not emphasize a need for lectures in political or moral principles. In fact, although he certainly does not dismiss such learning, he downplays its importance; recall his claim that theaters can be more powerful moral teachers than churches. When Burke speaks approvingly of the English tradition of education by ecclesiastics, he does not seem to be thinking primarily of the benefits of lectures in religious or moral principles, although he certainly would have expected and approved of such; he seems to be thinking primarily of the *attitude* with which learning was approached, the way of thinking about the world and about one's place in it. It is this sort of unarticulated "nonrational" conveying of truth, this shaping of a worldview, that Burke emphasizes. This is the primary way in which people improve, and this is the primary path to a successful political society that promotes human flourishing.

Burke and the Twenty-first Century

The "Burkean" approach to politics described in this book offers numerous insights for politics today. When observing the American crisis, Burke saw that the colonists and the Tories in Parliament were essentially talking past each other. Subtle but significant cultural differences, or differences in worldview, had developed over time; the difficulty in resolving relatively minor disputes, and the resulting escalation of the conflict, was largely attributable to these differences. The Americans and the Tories were perceiving reality differently; that is to say, their realities were different, and hence their norms and their expectations were different. No real dialogue occurred, merely a shouting match. How often today does politics take a similar form? Discussion and deliberation seem to play relatively minor roles; "reasoned" argument usually changes few minds. This is the case partly because the parties involved are operating within different moral-imaginative wholes; their reason may work fine within their own frameworks, but does not translate well to others'. This does not make communication impossible, but it makes it more complicated than one might think. As Burke observed, it is extraordinarily difficult to convince someone of something that conflicts with his or her existing conception of reality. Highly dubious "truths," however, are readily accepted if they reinforce or confirm one's worldview.

"Politics" narrowly understood is, to a significant degree, secondary or derivative. It is largely the product of the imaginative wholes of a people. Individuals' ordered realities drive their politics; attending to politics therefore requires attending to the moral imagination. One cannot, for example, sustain a liberal order unless citizens' moral imaginations promote public and private behaviors that are compatible with that order. Burke does not, of course, offer any simple formulae for fostering the right kind of moral imagination. He certainly does not display any tendencies toward social engineering, use of propaganda, and the like; such approaches would have clashed with his emphasis on humility. He berates the Dublin theater, but does not call for censorship. He does state that the works of literature held up by prominent elites matter, especially over the long term. The attitudes displayed by those in office toward their forbears, toward traditions, toward religion, and toward the state itself also matter. All aspects of culture and of life experience contribute, positively or negatively, to one's imaginative framework. Because political life and public policy form an important part of that experience, Burke shows that those in government should consider how their actions, or the policies they support, may influence imaginative frameworks and, hence, may shape future political and social life.

Effective statesmanship requires sensitivity to the moral imagination. This involves, for one thing, recognition that people generally do not respond well to merely technical arguments; political proposals and arguments must connect imaginatively as well. W. Wesley McDonald has written that "political and religious movements activate their followers more through their visionary aspects than by reasoned argument. In this sense, imagination, not reason, governs the world."[3] Burkean statesmanship also requires a recognition of cultural differences— including very subtle differences in worldviews among people—and an understanding of how those differences may shape their perception of, and response to, political actions of various sorts. Burke displayed both remarkable sensitivity to subtle cultural differences and remarkable appreciation of very alien cultures. His ethical approach, emphasizing how our understanding of morality is built up from particulars and through the development of the moral imagination, helped him to see the commonalities in morality and politics across cultures, while still recognizing the importance of cultural differences.

A politics of the moral imagination must be one that recognizes the importance of education. As has been noted, Burke decried how the new Rousseau-inspired educational approaches in France yielded youth characterized by a "ferocious medley of pedantry and lewdness; of metaphysical speculations, blended with the coarsest sensuality."[4] This, we can see, is caused by the same quasi-scientific mix of reductionism and ideology that dominates the Jacobins' politics and the emerging society in general. Part of what is lost is "gallantry." There is no sense of meaning, no sense of the sublime; there are no models to inspire and uplift. There is no mysterious sense that life is more than we know, and that we must act in conformity with this belief, striving to elevate ourselves and each other. One contributor to the rise in impoverished thinking may be the sort of educational approaches that suggest, as Oakeshott puts it, that "we should teach children how to use the English language but without encumbering their minds with English literature."[5] The correct sort of culturally rich education, and, as Burke notes, the right attitudes imparted along with such an education, are vital to the preservation of not just a stable and free state, but a livable society.

Burke's perspective helps to illuminate issues of emotion and "reason" in politics. In contemporary political debate, it is often the case that each side will accuse the other of acting emotionally, while claiming reason for itself. The blurring of distinctions between reason and emotion in Burke may offer more effective ways of approaching political debate and disagreement. For Burke, feelings reflect judgments, while reason is strongly influenced by feelings. Judgment, regardless of whether it is expressed through feelings and intuitions or through rational articulation and conceptualization, can be seen to be largely the function of one's moral-imaginative framework. Those who claim simply to be following "reason" have blinded themselves to the fact that one's instrumental reason is only as good as the internal construction of reality upon which it operates. They may tend toward the sort of rationalism that precludes the consideration of opposing points of view, simply characterizing them as "irrational." Believing themselves to be rational, they may be blinded to their own feelings, which are almost certainly influencing their judgments; consequently they do not examine their own feelings critically to determine whether their views and motivations are sound. If the commonality between emotion and reason were widely recognized, political actors would perhaps be both more likely to examine their own feelings and motivations and less likely to dismiss opposing views as emotionally driven and therefore irrational.

An elevation of the recognized role of feelings in politics need not lead to simple emotivism. Indeed, under the model that we have developed from Burke's writings, both emotion and reason may be ill-informed or well-informed. The common dismissal of feelings as irrational, or merely instinctive, is sometimes accompanied by the insulation of feelings from challenge or from rational criticism. Certainly Burke would consider it politically prudent to consider the feelings of various parties when making policy, whether those feelings were entirely justified or not. But he would not consider anyone's feelings to be above reproach and to automatically be worthy of accommodation. For Burke, feelings, no less than judgments expressed rationally, can be more or less correct; they reflect more or less sound character, or, we can say, they reflect more or less sound intuitive judgments based upon a more or less sound imaginative framework.

Burke was writing in the context of emerging political modernity and the emerging liberal order, and his approach to ethics and politics is particularly important in addressing fundamental problems of order and meaning in modern society. As generally understood, modern liberal society is quite "thin," in that it tends to avoid or, at least, to downplay explicit assertions of norms, explicit teleological frameworks, or other explicit conceptions of the good life.[6] In some forms—perhaps its most fundamental or intrinsic forms—liberalism is in fact openly hostile to such norms, frameworks, and conceptions, or at least to their traditional sources. From a Burkean perspective, contemporary liberal society appears highly problematic and precarious. The modern order partially undermined traditional, often largely compact sources of order and meaning; these were partly replaced by the articulation of principles, such as those of liberty and equality. In a late-modern and, increasingly, postmodern age, not only have the traditional and compact sources undergone even more erosion, but the articulated principles of modernity are themselves losing their salience. Increasingly, they appear hollow or arbitrary. Similarly, there is a decline in the degree of shared understandings, or similar worldviews, upon which to base a society and to conduct meaningful argument.

Burke's perspective suggests that, should differences in worldviews grow too large, and/or should the "liberal consensus" become so thin that it degenerates into a pervasive sense of arbitrariness, liberal politics and liberal society will break down. A relatively rich traditional culture not only makes possible the sort of societal consensus, and shared sense of meaning, necessary for a society to function in a nonauthoritarian way; it helps make practical wisdom and good character possible. Individuals well supported by the "wardrobe of a moral imagination" have long-established touchstones that not only provide meaningful standards for their own behavior, but also provide rich perspectives from which to evaluate other individuals, situations, and public policies. As has been noted, we must always have some sort of framework from which to view the world and in which we exercise judgment; those with well-grounded frameworks may be less prone to infatuation with political figures or fads, and less subject to the intoxicating effects of political imagery or rhetoric. They have, in a sense, "seen it all before," and may be less likely to assume that that which appears new is better, or is even really novel. As Burke's discussions of the "metaphysicians" indicate, those with richer moral imaginations may also be less likely to fall into rigid ideological frameworks that warp and unduly constrain their thinking.

Gerald Russello notes that Russell Kirk identified a "new class":

> It had been deprived of all traditional attachments to family, religion, or tradition. As a result, the members of this class were themselves at the mercy of the forces they attempted to control. This new class of administrators,

bureaucrats, and functionaries, whether of the left or the right, had neglected the imagination. They were particularly creatures of their era: "produced by the ideas of the nineteenth and twentieth centuries: vulgarized Darwinism, socialism, vulgarized Freudianism, winds of doctrine of yesteryear."[7]

This "class" is reminiscent not only of Burke's metaphysicians but also of those he identified as "too much confined to professional and faculty habits." Increasingly, such a description may be applied not only to a narrow group of political functionaries, but to broad swaths of the public as well, including many elites of various sorts. The modern scientific method, which shapes so much of the contemporary world, emphasizes the idea that experimental results can be duplicated by anyone following the proper method. Although appropriate for many scientific applications, this approach ignores something emphasized in the ancient and medieval worlds: the idea that wisdom flowed from proper character, from the development of the whole person. Burke strongly recognizes the role played by proper character—consisting in part of a sound moral imagination—in sound judgment and right action. Those who emphasize technical and ideological approaches—characteristics of modernity—at the expense of a richly developed and well-exercised moral imagination become increasingly prone to error, and increasingly vulnerable to ideological fads, just as those who tout their reliance upon "reason" may be in a more precarious position than those who acknowledge their reliance upon intuition and cultural wisdom.

A closely related problem is the predominance of "rights talk" and legalistic approaches to policy making in the contemporary liberal state, and especially the United States. When Burke refers to those of "faculty habits" he is thinking primarily of lawyers of a certain pedantic sort. He speaks negatively of the dominance of the French National Assembly by lawyers, and remarks on how the dominance of American legislatures by lawyers contributes to the revolution, particularly when the Tories in Parliament also insist on approaching problems in a legalistic way. Although Burke emphasizes the importance of rule of law, he finds legalistic approaches confrontational and not conducive to compromise, tending toward the sort of theory-based rationalism that goes to extremes. If mere legalistic approaches by legislatures disturb Burke, he would very likely consider the establishment of sweeping public policies through actual legal processes, rather than legislative processes, particularly dangerous to the social fabric and the long-term health of the state. Burke would likely find the problem compounded in the United States by the strong contemporary emphasis on the brief Enlightenment language found in the first passages of the Declaration of Independence, as representing the entire essence of the United States' identity. The effect is to promote a rationalistic spirit of innovation, leading to confrontation, rather than a spirit of continuity, in which legal and political frameworks accord with well-developed internal moral-imaginative frameworks of the people. To have lasting meaning and force, rights must be culturally embedded, not abstractly applied. A structure of abstract rights is a brittle one that is prone to collapse into brute power politics as soon as the pre-political nature of a right is brought into question. A more solid grounding for a stable free state may be provided by an emphasis on a richer understanding of the source of American identity, recognizing a complex interplay of cultural traditions stretching back many centuries.

Those who lack properly rich, culturally embedded moral imaginations and who rely too heavily on Enlightenment-based structures may be prone to what contemporary British philosopher Roger Scruton labels "oikophobia," defined as "the repudiation of inheritance and home."[8] This is "the disposition, in any conflict, to side with 'them' against 'us,' and the felt need to denigrate the customs, culture and institutions that are identifiably 'ours.'"[9] Burke would not be at all surprised at this phenomenon, since it is a broader expression of one he noted. It will be recalled that he observed that "turbulent, discontented men of quality, in proportion as they are puffed up with personal pride and arrogance, generally despise their own order. One of the first symptoms they discover of a selfish and mischievous ambition, is a profligate disregard of a dignity which they partake with others."[10] Scruton argues that "the oik is, in his own eyes, a defender of enlightened universalism against local chauvinism."[11] While a defense of higher standards is sometimes needed, as Burke himself recognizes, Burke's observations make clear that "oikophobia" results both from ambition and from a kind of cultural alienation. It is a product of a lack of humility, a lack of close social ties and "affections" beginning with our "little platoons," and a lack of proper appreciation of the importance of one's own society and culture. Consequently, one's identity and sense of self-worth becomes wrapped up in a commitment to supposed "higher" ideals, whether those ideals are properly applicable in particular situations or not. Once again one's judgment falls victim to a malformed imaginative framework.

Burke considers religion to be very important to a stable and free state; consequently he would find ominous the increasingly secular nature of contemporary societies. His writings strongly suggest that he places little value on new or personalized religions or on "spirituality" as such, instead emphasizing established traditional religions as necessary for inspiring the right sort of piety and a strong sense of meaningful transcendent standards. His observation that ideological Jacobinism rushes into the breach when traditional religion is absent, and his suggestion that the eradication of traditional "prejudice" leads to the blind following of political leaders, serve as urgent warnings today. But Burke's approach to religion is not dogmatic, and he supports a significant level of religious toleration. He does not feel a need for religious uniformity in the state. From a Burkean perspective, then, a highly secular society may be unsustainable, at least in a form characterized by significant freedom and rule of law, but a state with a highly explicit and specific religious basis may not be the only alternative to such secularism. What matters are the moral imaginations of the citizenry.

Many of the modern problems and conditions that alarmed Burke were still emerging in his day, but have become considerably more serious now. This may suggest that, in today's world, an outlook informed by Burke must be bleak. However, Burke's thought suggests ways to approach and address many contemporary problems, and some dimensions of his thought suggest that the recovery of sources of order and meaning within the context of a liberal state may be achievable. Burke's downplaying of precepts in favor of an emphasis on the more compact moral and political content of various cultural elements suggests that a highly explicit "thick" societal consensus, as it is usually conceived, may not be a necessity for good politics. That is, we may not be faced with a choice between a non-liberal order and one characterized by the sort of radical Enlightenment liberalism that undermines meaning and, ultimately, itself. It may be possible to sustain and enhance a liberal order, if "liberal" is understood to represent an order characterized by significant personal freedom, political equality, limited government, and rule of law, rather than as an order that exists in opposition to its cultural heritage. Burke's wisdom teaches that common understandings of reality and a common political morality do not hinge solely upon what is clearly articulated; they hinge upon all that makes up the wardrobe of a moral imagination. It may still be possible to sustain and foster a rich culture that provides the right sort of moral-imaginative touchstones and thereby contributes to sound character, without relying upon highly explicit teleologies. Broadly speaking, Burke's thought suggests that more resources may exist, or may be made available, for the perpetuation and development of a sound liberal order than may be readily apparent.

Making Sense of Burke

This modest study offers a way of understanding Burke that helps make sense of much that has been found confusing or controversial in him. For example, "Burkean conservatism" is understood in a new way once Burke's interest in conserving the moral imagination is recognized. Indeed, Burke's varied public policy positions, "conservative" and "reformist" alike, take on a new coherence when understood in light of Burke's moral-imaginative orientation. Burke's conservatism is intimately linked to his liberalism; he wishes to conserve and to promote those elements of human life that are likely to help preserve and enhance a free, stable, and predictable political order characterized by limited government, rule of law, and conditions conducive to human flourishing. He knows that such ordered liberty can exist only within the right sort of moral-imaginative context. Burke does not want to stop change, and he is not a reactionary; it is through change that movement toward the good occurs. For him, the mere fact that something exists, or has existed in the past, does not make it good. Traditional elements have value to the extent that they support the right sort of moral imagination; this does not make Burke a simple "traditionalist" as the term is usually understood. Burke's interest can be characterized as one of cultivating the moral imagination, re-creating the framework needed for movement toward the good. This involves creative engagement with the past. One draws upon the past to build up sound models for imitation; traditions help provide standards and help inspire one to do better. New cultural elements also play a role in the ongoing reconstitution of the moral imagination. As Burke himself explains, a sound political actor must be both backward-looking *and* forward-looking.

Just as greater coherence emerges among Burke's various political positions in light of an understanding of his moral-imaginative approach, greater coherence emerges between his aesthetics and his ethical-political thought. Indeed, it becomes clear that there are no really sharp categorical distinctions between the aesthetic and the ethical. This follows from his ethical-epistemological approach; for him, one may develop a kind of "moral taste." Just as Burke emphasizes the intuitive and nonrational in aesthetics, he emphasizes these aspects of moral and political thought. Judgment always involves the imagination. Burke's rejection of classical or neoclassical aesthetics as commonly understood, in favor of a recognition of the immediacy of art, does not constitute a rejection of order. Instead, it is a recognition that perception of order is fundamentally imaginative or intuitive, and that our rational formulations will always be inadequate in describing reality.

The interpretation of Burke offered here partly addresses what has perhaps been the most controversial area of Burke scholarship, which is the relationship of his thought to universals. Controversy on this subject arises in part from modern ways of thinking about morality, which tend to present a stark choice between foundationalism and anti-foundationalism. Burke was one of the first thinkers to address the problem of the "Enlightenment project"; like MacIntyre, Burke suspected that the project of completely rationalizing the basis of order and meaning was doomed to fail. MacIntyre finds that the modern world confronts us with a choice between Aristotle and Nietzsche.[12] For MacIntyre, Aristotle represents, among other things, a metaphysically based teleological view that appears to have proven untenable in the modern world, while Nietzsche represents those attempts to address the modern problem that end in nihilism. MacIntyre favors Aristotle, and attempts to erect a revised Christian-Aristotelian teleology, but concludes bleakly that all we can hope for is "the construction of local forms of community within which civility and the intellectual and moral life can be sustained through the new dark ages which are already upon us."[13] Forced to make the choice, Burke would also, no doubt, take Aristotle over Nietzsche, but Burke's approach to the modern problem may have greater potential that MacIntyre's, in part because it is less intellectualistic and more experiential.

The natural law interpretation of Burke characterizes him as a foundationalist, while "utilitarian," "historicist," or "pragmatist" interpretations usually characterize him as an anti-foundationalist at heart. Burke is in fact both, and neither. Some of the major weaknesses in natural law characterizations of Burke arise from the tendency of much Enlightenment-influenced contemporary natural law thinking to emphasize instrumental reason and a priori principles. This is not to say that natural law thought necessarily conceives of "reason" in a particularly narrow way, or conceives of morality in terms of casuistry. Indeed, one can find in virtually all of the natural law interpreters of Burke clear indications of much richer understandings of both reason and morality. Joseph Pappin especially emphasizes what he calls an "existentialist" dimension of Burke.[14] Nevertheless, many contemporary readers of Burke are dissatisfied with a close identification of his approach with natural law thinking. Readers see Burke's rejection of classical aesthetics and his apparent denunciations of "metaphysics," of "reason," and sometimes even of "truth," and conclude that he is devoid of anything like traditional moral underpinnings. This problem in interpreting Burke can be compared to a broader situation in late-modern discourse. Norms are conceived of in a manner in which weaknesses readily become apparent, and the emergence of such weaknesses causes normativity itself to become subject to a nihilistic postmodern critique.

Burke's thought is broadly compatible with natural law or foundationalist thought in that he believes in a universal theocentric order that may be grasped, if imperfectly, by human beings. What separates Burke from typical foundationalists is his view that universal concepts do not exist in the abstract, outside of history. We come to know universals within historical existence. This does not mean that for Burke truth is something we just make up. He avoids both the hubris of those who claim to have a firm handle on universals and the hubris of those who claim that there are no universals, or who claim that "truth" can be whatever we want it to be. Indeed, the line between the two forms of hubris can be very fine. For example, Burke's metaphysicians claimed to have grasped great truths, but their claims were melded to the arbitrary willfulness of those who recognize no truths beyond those they create. What separates Burke from anti-foundationalists is not just his recognition of universals but his profound sense of mystery and, as an accompaniment to that sense of mystery, his special form of humility. This humility is a recognition of the nature of the human condition. If great truths are sublime, they cannot, by Burke's definition, be fully within our grasp. We can perceive universals, but fuzzily. We recognize that the world is greater than we know.

Despite its classical and Christian roots, the natural law approach as it is typically manifested in the contemporary world tends to be reflective of the "Enlightenment project" of rationalizing morality. Burke's approach is different. With its recognition of the potential for moral bankruptcy in modernity, its downplaying of explicit principles, and its emphasis on the particular, the conventional, and the aesthetic, Burke's approach has what can broadly be called postmodern elements. But there is also a premodern quality to Burke, particularly in his emphasis on the need for an orientation of the whole person toward the good, and in his conception of the good as a way or path. Most important is Burke's emphasis on humility. Burkean humility does not lead to passivity or quietism. Indeed, it is the "metaphysicians," according to Burke, who may become indifferent about real-world politics. Burke's humility promotes the right kind of political and social engagement as one comes to perceive one's obligations. We perceive truth intuitively, and our intuition helps us know the right thing to do.

With experience as an ongoing guide, we develop a sense of universals. This includes the sense that there are, in fact, such things as universals, and that they are important. Movement toward truth occurs through particular real-world actions, as well as through the proper exercise of restraint. The good is realized in practice.

If we are to address the modern crisis effectively, new thinking is needed. Burke's critique of Enlightenment rationalism and abstractionism anticipates postmodernism while offering a way out of the problem of postmodernism. Of critical importance is his understanding of subjectivity. The Western tradition has tended to regard imagination, intuition, feelings, sentiment, and the like as "subjective," while reason, and rational articulations of universals, are regarded as "objective." Burke recognizes, first, that everything experienced or expressed by human beings is, to a degree, subjective. Claims of employing reason, or declarations of universals, do not give one a privileged position above the historical flux. Thus Burke observes that the most high-sounding ideals will often serve as a cover for human vices. There is always the problem of knowing which ideals or standards to employ, and of knowing precisely how to apply them. Our position is always limited and subjective. This is true whether we claim to be relying upon feelings and intuitions, or upon reason and universal precepts. Recognition of this basic fact of human existence does not lead Burke to celebrate radical subjectivity or particularity, or to reject universals. Instead, it leads him to probe more deeply into how we perceive universals. His understanding of the imaginative perception of the universal does not imply an abandonment of objectivity. Real "objectivity," or a workable sense of the true and the good, is achieved through the development of a sound moral imagination, and is confirmed and reinforced through observation of the effects of one's actions in the world. Our subjective sense of what is right thus becomes truly moral in practice, whether that sense is experienced as an act of reason or as a feeling. This contrasts sharply with the false, quasi-scientific objectivity of the "metaphysicians," whose actions rarely yield moral results. It is the proper experience and appreciation of the richness of particularity on a deeply personal level that makes it possible for us to move above and beyond our particular situations and glimpse a broader and deeper understanding of reality.

Burke is not just a critic of Enlightenment rationalism. He is a constructive thinker who offers a way of approaching problems of late modernity, reconciling universality and particularity in a manner that can be effective today. Sincere and thoughtful consideration of Burke's wisdom is a must in addressing problems of contemporary society. His understanding of the imaginative sources of political order, and of how one perceives truth and does good, offers insights that demand incorporation into contemporary political theory and practice. While Burke is justifiably honored for his statesmanship and political insight, for his rhetoric, and for the time-tested soundness of most of his public policy positions, it is his unique moral-imaginative approach to politics and morality that may prove to be his most important and lasting contribution.

Notes

Introduction

1. Burke's biographers disagree as to his date of birth; it has been placed at 1728, 1729, and 1730. Conor Cruise O'Brien argues for 1 January 1729; see *The Great Melody: A Thematic Biography and Commentated Anthology of Edmund Burke* (Chicago: University of Chicago Press, 1992), 3. F. P. Lock maintains that Burke was born in 1730; see *Edmund Burke,* vol. 1: 1730–1784 (Oxford: Clarendon Press, 1998), 16–17.

2. Peter Augustine Lawler, "Conservative Postmodernism, Postmodern Conservatism." *Intercollegiate Review,* v. 38 no. 1, Fall 2002. See also Lawler's *Postmodernism Rightly Understood* (Lanham, MD: Rowman & Littlefield, 1999).

3. Gerald Russello, *The Postmodern Imagination of Russell Kirk* (Columbia: University of Missouri Press, 2007).

4. See, for example, Michael Thompson, Richard Ellis, and Aaron Wildavsky, *Cultural Theory* (Boulder, CO: Westview Press, 1990). Thompson, Ellis, and Wildavsky use a relatively narrow definition of "political culture," but also emphasize the important role played by broader "cultural biases" or "worldviews" in shaping political life.

5. A classic study discussing some particular cultural requirements for a liberal democratic society is Gabriel A. Almond and Sidney Verba, *The Civic Culture: Political Attitudes and Democracy in Five Nations* (Princeton: Princeton University Press, 1963). See also Gabriel A. Almond and Sidney Verba, eds., *The Civic Culture Revisited* (Boston: Little, Brown, 1980).

6. Alasdair MacIntyre, *After Virtue: A Study in Moral Theory* (Notre Dame, IN: University of Notre Dame Press, 1984), 113.

7. See, for example, Immanuel Kant, "A Response to the Question: What is Enlightenment?," in Immanuel Kant, *Practical Philosophy,* trans. Mary J. Gregor (Cambridge: Cambridge University Press, 1996), 11–22.

8. Richard Rorty, *Contingency, Irony, and Solidarity* (New York: Cambridge University Press, 1989), 3.

9. See, for example, David Walsh, *The Growth of the Liberal Soul* (Columbia: University of Missouri Press, 1997).

10. Irving Babbitt titled a chapter "Burke and the Moral Imagination" in *Democracy and Leadership* (Indianapolis: Liberty Fund, Inc., 1979 [1924]). Russell Kirk makes only

brief mention of the concept in his biography *Edmund Burke: A Genius Reconsidered* (New Rochelle, NY: Arlington House, 1967), but it appears more prominently in his later writings and speeches.

11. One work with "imagination" in its title is Gerald W. Chapman, *Edmund Burke, the Practical Imagination* (Cambridge, MA: Harvard University Press, 1967). Chapman does not appear to be using the term "practical imagination" in a philosophical sense, but merely to convey the sense that Burke was both imaginative and practical. A collection of essays edited by Ian Crowe, *An Imaginative Whig: Reassessing the Life and Thought of Edmund Burke* (Columbia: University of Missouri Press, 2005) does not really address the concept of the moral imagination as it is treated here, and devotes relatively little attention to serious study of the idea of the imagination in Burke. A recent collection of essays by Gertrude Himmelfarb, *Moral Imagination: From Edmund Burke to Lionel Trilling* (Chicago: Ivan R. Dee, Publisher, 2007) devotes only one short essay to Burke and, like the vast majority of works with "moral imagination" in their titles, never incorporates a systematic treatment of the subject, or seriously explores its importance to Burke.

12. Friedrich Nietzsche, *The Gay Science,* trans. Walter Kaufmann (New York: Random House, 1974).

13. See for example Rorty, *Contingency.*

14. The works most important in establishing this "school" are probably the following: Peter J. Stanlis, *Edmund Burke and the Natural Law* (Ann Arbor: University of Michigan Press, 1958), and Francis P. Canavan, *The Political Reason of Edmund Burke* (Durham, NC: Duke University Press, 1960). The most important of the more recent works in this tradition is Joseph L. Pappin, III, *The Metaphysics of Edmund Burke* (New York: Fordham University Press, 1993). Other writers in this and other traditions will be discussed in the course of this study.

15. Some works with this perspective are identified and discussed in the Conclusion.

1—The "Burkean" Outlook and the Problem of Reality

1. Harold J. Laski, *Political Thought in England: Locke to Bentham* (London: Oxford University Press, 1950 [1920]), 181.

2. See Russell Kirk, *The Conservative Mind from Burke to Eliot* (South Bend, IN: Gateway Editions, 1978 [1953]).

3. One of the more prominent examples of post-1960s nonconservative American interest in Burke is Stephen K. White, *Edmund Burke: Modernity, Politics, and Aesthetics* (Thousand Oaks, CA: Sage Publications, 1994).

4. A great many of the classic writers on Burke—with varying interpretations of him—have invoked this phrase, ranging from Kirk to Alfred Cobban in his *Edmund Burke and the Revolt against the Eighteenth Century* (London: Allen & Unwin, 1960 [1929]).

5. See, for example, Friedrich Hayek, *The Constitution of Liberty* (Chicago: University of Chicago Press, 1960); and Michael Oakeshott, *Rationalism in Politics and Other Essays* (London: Methuen & Co., 1962).

6. Edmund Burke, *Reflections on the Revolution in France,* in *The Writings and Speeches of Edmund Burke,* Paul Langford, general editor, vol. VIII (Oxford: Clarendon Press, 1989), 138.

7. Frank O'Gorman, for example, states that Burke "wished to restore the traditional constitution of the past, no less and no more." *Edmund Burke: His Political Philosophy*

(Bloomington, IN: Indiana University Press, 1973), 66. Something like this understanding of Burke is also implied in MacIntyre, *After Virtue,* 222.

8. See James Boswell, *The Life of Samuel Johnson, LL. D.* (Chicago: Encyclopædia Britannica, Inc., 1990).

9. James Conniff, *The Useful Cobbler: Edmund Burke and the Politics of Progress* (Albany: State University of New York Press, 1994), 7.

10. See in particular Burke's 1770 *Thoughts on the Present Discontents,* in *Writings and Speeches,* vol. II, as well as the discussion of same in Harvey C. Mansfield, Jr., *Statesmanship and Party Government: A Study of Burke and Bolingbroke* (Chicago: University of Chicago Press, 1965).

11. O'Brien, *Great Melody,* 258–69.

12. One of Burke's sources is no doubt Pope Gregory's letter to Abbot Mellitus (A.D. 601), found in Bede, *A History of the English Church and People (Historia Ecclesiastica),* trans. Leo Sherley-Price, rev. R. E. Latham (New York: Penguin Books, 1982), 86–87.

13. "An Essay towards an Abridgment of the English History," in *Writings and Speeches of Edmund Burke,* Paul Langford, general editor, vol. I (Oxford: Clarendon Press, 1997), 430.

14. J. G. A. Pocock, *Virtue, Commerce, and History: Essays on Political Thought and History, Chiefly in the Eighteenth Century* (Cambridge: Cambridge University Press, 1985), 281.

15. *Writings and Speeches* I, 393.

16. Ibid., 394.

17. Charles Taylor, *The Ethics of Authenticity* (Cambridge, MA: Harvard University Press, 1991), 52.

18. *Writings and Speeches,* VIII, 128.

19. It should be noted that the words "tradition" and "traditional" do not appear in Burke, and he uses a related term, "traditionary," only once.

20. Stephen H. Browne, *Edmund Burke and the Discourse of Virtue* (Tuscaloosa: University of Alabama Press, 1993), 87.

21. Harvey C. Mansfield, Jr., introduction to: Edmund Burke, *Selected Letters of Edmund Burke,* ed. Harvey C. Mansfield Jr. (Chicago: University of Chicago Press, 1984), 8–9.

22. *Reflections,* in *Writings and Speeches,* VIII, 131.

23. For some discussion see Pocock, *Virtue, Commerce, and History,* 198.

24. *Writings and Speeches,* VIII, 130.

25. See Pocock, *Virtue, Commerce, and History,* 281.

26. *Writings and Speeches,* VIII, 130.

27. See, for example, Almond and Verba, *Civic Culture;* Thompson, Ellis, and Wildavsky, *Cultural Theory;* Mary Douglas, *Risk and Blame: Essays in Cultural Theory* (New York: Routledge, 1992).

28. *Writings and Speeches* I, 430.

29. O'Brien, *Great Melody,* xxiii.

30. Speech on Reform of Representation in Parliament, in *Works,* VII, 97.

31. *Writings and Speeches,* VIII, 138.

32. Leo Strauss, *Natural Right and History* (Chicago: University of Chicago Press, 1971 [1953]), 314–15.

33. *Writings and Speeches,* VIII, 217.

34. Ibid., 231.

35. Letter to Richard Shackleton, 1745, in *The Correspondence of Edmund Burke,* vol. I (Chicago: University of Chicago Press, 1958), 50.

36. *A Philosophical Enquiry into the Origin or our Ideas of the Sublime and Beautiful*, in *Writings and Speeches*, I, 224.

37. Oakeshott, *Rationalism*, 105–6.

38. Ibid., 107.

39. Ibid., 114.

40. A Letter from the Right Honorable Edmund Burke to a Noble Lord, on the Attacks made upon him and His Pension, in *Writings and Speeches*, IX, 176–77.

41. Among the writers to use the disparaging term "Cold War Burke" is Conor Cruise O'Brien, in *Great Melody*. In considering this characterization it should be noted that most of the key American Burke scholars of the period, including Peter Stanlis and Francis Canavan, made no overt references to the Cold War in their discussions of Burke.

42. *Reflections*, in *Writings and Speeches*, VIII, 232.

43. For a nice little discussion of the term "ideology," see Terrell Carver, "Ideology: A Career of a Concept," in *Ideals and Ideologies: A Reader*, 6th ed., ed. Terence Ball and Richard Dagger (New York: Pearson Longman, 2006), 3–9.

44. See Claes G. Ryn, *Will, Imagination, and Reason: Babbitt, Croce, and the Problem of Reality* (New Brunswick, NJ: Transaction Publishers, 1997 [1986]).

45. Oakeshott, *Rationalism*, 4.

46. Ibid., 7–8.

47. Ibid., 11.

48. Ibid., 61, 66, 64.

49. *Writings and Speeches*, I, 218.

50. *Reflections*, in *Writings and Speeches*, VIII, 100.

2—Aesthetics, Ethics, and Politics

1. *Reformer* No. 1, 28 January 1748, in *Writings and Speeches* I, 66. Signed "B." No scholarly consensus exists as to whether this passage was written by Burke, by one of his collaborators, or by Burke and others jointly. The editors of the *Writings* attribute it to Burke, but biographer F. P. Lock maintains in *Edmund Burke*, vol. I, that "B" probably designated another contributor, Beaumont Brennan. Because it was the opening statement of a periodical for which Burke appears to have been the primary driver, one might reasonably expect the views expressed to be Burke's. A possibility not addressed by Lock is that Burke might initially have used "B" and then shifted to "AE," which appears in some later issues and which the *Writings* editors and Lock both attribute to Burke. "B" could therefore have stood for Brennan in later issues, but for Burke in the first issues. Clearly the authors did not consider their identification to be important, or they would simply have used their names.

2. See, for example, the discussion of its influence in Lock, *Burke*, vol. I, 107–8 and 118–22.

3. Immanuel Kant, *Observations on the Feeling of the Beautiful and Sublime*, trans. John T. Goldthwait (Berkeley: University of California Press, 2004).

4. O'Brien, *Great Melody*, 39.

5. See Anthony Ashley Cooper (Earl of Shaftesbury), *Characteristics of Men, Manners, Opinions, Times* (Indianapolis: Liberty Fund, 2001); Joseph Addison, *Addison's Essays from the Spectator* (Boston: Adamant Media Corporation, 2001); and Francis Hutcheson, *An Inquiry into the Original of Our Ideas of Beauty and Virtue* (Indianapolis: Liberty Fund, 2004).

6. Laski, *Political Thought*, 181.

7. *Writings and Speeches,* I, 255.

8. Ibid., I, 255.

9. Ibid., I, 255–56.

10. For example, Benedetto Croce, one of the key figures in the development of modern aesthetic theory, associates art with intuition and rejects measurements and other such "physical facts" as constructions of the intellect for utilitarian, not artistic, purposes. See Benedetto Croce, *Guide to Aesthetics* (*Brevario di estetica,* 1913), trans. and intro. by Patrick Romanell (Indianapolis: Hackett Publishing Company, 1995), 10.

11. *Writings and Speeches,* I, 256.

12. Strauss, *Natural Right,* 312.

13. Canavan, *Political Reason,* 40.

14. Ibid., 40.

15. *Writings and Speeches,* I, 272; passage is cited in Canavan, *Political Reason,* 60.

16. Lock alludes to this in *Edmund Burke,* I, 100.

17. Ibid., I, 121.

18. Strauss, *Natural Right,* 312–13.

19. In David Hume, *The Philosophy of David Hume,* ed. and intro. by V. C. Chappell. (New York: Random House [Modern Library], 1963).

20. This is mentioned in *Writings and Speeches,* I, 208n3.

21. Ibid., I, 207.

22. Hume, *Philosophy,* 481.

23. *Writings and Speeches,* I, 208.

24. Hume, *Philosophy,* 487.

25. *Writings and Speeches,* I, 202, 207.

26. Ibid., I, 209.

27. Ibid., VIII, 138.

28. Hume, *Philosophy,* 490–91.

29. See MacIntyre, *After Virtue,* 39.

30. *Writings and Speeches,* I, 198. This is one of many elements of the *Enquiry* that show some likely influence of David Hume, although Burke never cites him. Often the influence is largely superficial. Some limited discussion of the relationship of Burke's thought to that of Hume is provided in chapter 3. For comparison, see David Hume, *A Treatise of Human Nature,* intro. by A. D. Lindsay, 2 vols. (New York: E. P. Dutton & Co. Inc., 1949).

31. *Writings and Speeches,* I, 206.

32. Ibid., I, 201.

33. Thomas Hobbes, *Leviathan* (London and New York: Penguin, 1985), 89. (Emphasis in original.)

34. See Addison, *Addison's Essays.*

35. *Writings and Speeches,* I, 201. This language follows Locke, although there is no reason to believe that Burke adopts Locke's empiricism wholesale. As in the cases of Hume and Addison, the influence is limited and somewhat superficial. For comparison see John Locke, *An Essay Concerning Human Understanding* (New York: Dover Publications, 1959).

36. *Writings and Speeches,* I, 201.

37. Ibid., I, 202, 201, 202 (emphasis in original), 202.

38. Ibid., I, 207.

39. Ibid., I, 197.

40. F. P. Lock, "Rhetoric and Representations in Burke's *Reflections*," in *Edmund Burke's Reflections on the Revolution in France: New Interdisciplinary Essays,* ed. John Whale (Manchester and New York: Manchester University Press, 2000), 24.

41. Lock, "Rhetoric," in *Edmund Burke's Reflections,* 23.

42. See *Writings and Speeches,* I, 208.

43. Lock, "Rhetoric," in *Edmund Burke's Reflections,* 23.

44. *Writings and Speeches,* I, 230, 216, 217.

45. Ibid., I, 230.

46. Friedrich Nietzsche, *Untimely Meditations,* ed. Daniel Breazeale, trans. R. J. Hollingdale. (Cambridge: Cambridge University Press, 1997), 22.

47. *Writings and Speeches,* I, 232.

48. Nietzsche, *Untimely Meditations,* 22.

49. Tracy B. Strong, *Friedrich Nietzsche and the Politics of Transfiguration* (Berkeley: University of California Press, 1975), 140–41.

50. Lock notes its unique significance to Burke in *Edmund Burke,* I, 112.

51. *Writings and Speeches,* I, 231.

52. Ibid., I, 232–33.

53. Ibid., I, 233.

54. Ibid., I, 235.

55. Ibid., I, 235. Burke quotes Job 4:17.

56. Ibid., I, 235.

57. Ibid., I, 238.

58. Ibid., I, 237. Burke quotes Job 39:24.

59. Ibid., I, 237.

60. Martin Heidegger, *Being and Time,* trans. John Macquarrie and Edward Robinson (New York: Harper, 1962).

61. Martin Heidegger, "What Are Poets For?," in *Poetry, Language, Thought,* trans. Albert Hofstadter (New York: Harper & Row, Publishers, 1975), 110, 111, 112.

62. White, *Modernity,* 75 (emphasis in original).

63. White, *Modernity,* 74–75.

64. White, *Modernity,* 32.

65. White, *Modernity,* 75.

66. Eric Voegelin, *The New Science of Politics* (Chicago: University of Chicago Press, 1987 [1952]), 152.

67. *Correspondence* VI, 210, cited in White, *Modernity,* 72.

68. White, *Modernity,* 70.

69. White, *Modernity,* 70. Reference is to Burke's *First Letter on a Regicide Peace.*

3—Reason, Emotion, Knowledge, and Morality

1. Babbitt, *Democracy,* 127.

2. Babbitt, *Democracy,* 34–35.

3. Ryn, *Will,* 144.

4. Knud Haakonssen, introduction to: Adam Smith, *The Theory of Moral Sentiments,* ed. Knud Haakonssen (Cambridge: Cambridge University Press, 2002), xii–xiii.

5. Haakonssen, introduction to Smith, *Sentiments,* xiii.

6. *The Annual Register,* 1759 edition (London: J. Dodsley, 1777), 484. According to F.

P. Lock, Burke was given the book by Hume; Burke wrote the review before he met Smith, and the book prompted Burke to strike up an acquaintance with him. See *Edmund Burke,* I, 186–87.

7. *Register,* 1759, 484. 8. Lock, *Edmund Burke,* I, 187.

9. See, for example, Pappin, *Metaphysics,* 41–42; Peter J. Stanlis, *Edmund Burke: The Enlightenment and Revolution* (New Brunswick. NJ: Transaction Publishers, 1991); Canavan, *Political Reason.*

10. James Conniff, *The Useful Cobbler: Edmund Burke and the Politics of Progress* (Albany: State University of New York Press, 1994), 51.

11. Conniff, *Cobbler,* 50, 49.

12. *Boswell Papers,* XI, 268, cited in Thomas W. Copeland, *Our Eminent Friend, Edmund Burke* (New Haven, CT: Yale University Press, 1949), 167.

13. Ryn, *Will,* 140, 141.

14. *Philosophical Enquiry,* in *Writings and Speeches,* I, 228.

15. "An Appeal from the New to the Old Whigs," in *Works,* IV, 205.

16. Martha C. Nussbaum, *Upheavals of Thought: The Intelligence of Emotions* (Cambridge: Cambridge University Press, 2001), 19. Although this work is of considerable length, it makes no mention of Burke.

17. *Writings and Speeches,* VIII, 131–32 (emphasis in original).

18. In writing *A Vindication of Natural Society,* Burke was probably more concerned with ridiculing, by implication, advocacy of "natural religion," which was much more common than advocacy of "natural society." Those intellectuals who spoke of "natural religion" were, properly speaking, usually drawing a contrast between it and "revealed religion." That is, they contrasted a religion wholly accessible through natural reason with one of revelation, rather than contrasting natural religion with "artificial religion." However, because "revealed religion" generally meant, in practice, traditional Christianity, and because such traditional religion was considered by some to be artificial, a "natural vs. artificial" dimension was present in such arguments.

19. Pappin, *Metaphysics,* 139.

20. Charles Parkin, *The Moral Basis of Burke's Political Thought* (Cambridge: Cambridge University Press, 1956), 22.

21. *Reflections,* in *Writings and Speeches,* VIII, 143.

22. *Writings and Speeches,* VIII, 126–27.

23. Thomas Paine, *Rights of Man, Part I,* in *Political Writings,* ed. Bruce Kuklick (Cambridge: Cambridge University Press, 2000), 72.

24. *Writings and Speeches,* VIII, 129.

25. Ibid., VIII, 128.

26. Hume, *Human Nature,* v. 2, 127.

27. Browne, *Discourse,* 124.

28. Stanlis, *Natural Law,* 182, 188.

29. Benedetto Croce, *The Aesthetic as the Science of Expression and the Linguistic in General,* trans. Colin Lyas (translation of a part of *Estetica,* 1902) (New York: Cambridge University Press, 1992), 55.

30. *Writings and Speeches,* IX, 176–77.

31. Babbitt, *Democracy,* 335–36.

32. A Letter to a Member of the National Assembly, in *Writings and Speeches,* VIII, 316.

33. See, for example, Canavan, *Political Reason,* 63; Pappin, *Metaphysics,* 114.

34. Ryn, *Will*, 32.

35. Parkin, *Moral*, 22.

36. Ibid., 21.

37. *Reflections*, in *Writings and Speeches*, VIII, 137.

38. Ryn, *Will*, 26–27.

39. Babbitt, *Democracy*, 32.

40. Ibid., 350.

41. "Hints for an Essay on the Drama," in *Writings and Speeches*, I, 557.

42. Croce, *Aesthetic as the Science*, 24.

43. Oakeshott, *Rationalism*, 72–73.

44. Pappin, *Metaphysics*, 18.

45. Nussbaum, *Upheavals*, 31.

46. Ibid., 65.

47. *Writings and Speeches*, VIII, 132.

48. Rorty, *Contingency*, xvi.

49. *Drama*, in *Writings and Speeches*, I, 556.

50. Browne, *Discourse*, 29.

51. Ibid., 34.

52. Ibid., 91.

53. Lock, "Rhetoric," in *Edmund Burke's Reflections*, 23.

54. *Writings and Speeches*, VIII, 95.

55. Mark Johnson, *Moral Imagination: Implications of Cognitive Science for Ethics* (Chicago: University of Chicago Press, 1993).

56. Johnson, *Moral Imagination*, 33.

57. Ibid., 10.

58. Ibid., 33.

59. Ibid., 165–66.

60. Ibid., 91.

61. Ibid., 198.

62. Ibid., 199.

63. MacIntyre, *After Virtue*, 216.

64. Ibid., 221.

65. Ibid., 222.

66. *Writings and Speeches*, VIII, 139.

67. Russello, *Postmodern*, 183–84.

68. Alasdair MacIntyre, *Whose Justice? Which Rationality?* (Notre Dame, IN: University of Notre Dame Press, 1988), 353.

69. Speech on Reform of Representation of the Commons in Parliament, in *Works*, VII, 97.

70. *Writings and Speeches*, VIII, 138.

4—Characteristics of a Moral Imagination

1. *Annual Register* 1759, 479.

2. *Reformer* No. 2 (4 February 1748), in *Writings and Speeches*, I, 74 (signed "B"; see note 1 in chapter 2 for a discussion of authorship).

3. *Reformer* No. 3 (11 February 1748), in *Writings and Speeches*, I, 78 (signed "AE";

see note 1 in chapter 2 for a discussion of authorship).

4. *Reformer* No. 1 (28 January 1748), in *Writings and Speeches,* I, 66 ("B").

5. *Reformer* No. 2, *Writings and Speeches,* I, 73 ("B").

6. *Reformer* No. 3, *Writings and Speeches,* I, 78 ("AE").

7. *Reformer* No. 3, *Writings and Speeches,* I, 78 ("AE").

8. *Drama,* in *Writings and Speeches,* I, 561–62. Multiple versions of this painting exist, including one at the Pinacoteca di Brera, Milan, and one at the Pushkin Museum of Fine Arts, Moscow.

9. *Assembly,* in *Writings and Speeches,* VIII, 313.

10. *Reflections,* in *Writings and Speeches,* VIII, 97.

11. Ibid., VIII, 130.

12. Ibid., VIII, 130.

13. Ibid., VIII, 141.

14. *Reformer* No. 11 (7 April 1748), in *Writings and Speeches,* I, 115 (signed "U").

15. *Reflections,* in *Writings and Speeches,* VIII, 142.

16. Ibid., VIII, 143.

17. One place where this perspective is found is in Daniel I. O'Neill, "Burke on the Death of Western Civilization," paper delivered at the 2002 Annual Meeting of the American Political Science Association.

18. *Writings and Speeches,* VIII, 143.

19. Ibid., VIII, 143.

20. *Vindication,* in *Writings and Speeches,* I, 134.

21. Ibid., I, 135.

22. *Reflections,* in *Writings* VIII, 143.

23. Ibid., VIII, 144.

24. Ibid., VIII, 144.

25. Ibid., VIII, 145.

26. Ibid., VIII, 145.

27. Ibid., VIII, 268.

28. Letter to a Member of the National Assembly, in *Writings and Speeches,* VIII, 332.

29. Bruce Frohnen, *Virtue and the Promise of Conservatism: The Legacy of Burke and Tocqueville* (Lawrence, KS: University Press of Kansas, 1993), 23.

30. Ibid., 26.

31. Alasdair C. MacIntyre, *Dependent Rational Animals: Why Human Beings Need the Virtues* (Chicago: Open Court, 1999), 107.

32. *Reflections,* in *Writings and Speeches,* VIII, 88.

33. Pocock, *Virtue, Commerce, and History,* 196–98.

34. Ibid., 236.

35. Michael Freeman, *Edmund Burke and the Critique of Political Radicalism* (Chicago: University of Chicago Press, 1980), 17–18.

36. O'Brien, *Great Melody,* 3–10.

37. Introduction to *Writings and Speeches,* I, 17.

38. *Writings and Speeches,* VIII, 141.

39. Ibid., VIII, 145.

40. Ibid., VIII, 146.

41. Canavan, *Political Reason,* 168.

42. Bruce James Smith, *Politics and Remembrance* (Princeton: Princeton University Press, 1985), 116.

43. Ibid., 116–17.

44. *Reflections*, in *Writings and Speeches*, VIII, 83.

45. Ibid., VIII, 85.

46. Hayek, *Constitution*, 62–63.

47. *Writings and Speeches*, VIII, 85.

48. *Assembly*, in *Writings and Speeches*, VIII, 312, 312, 313.

49. Ibid., VIII, 313 (emphasis in original).

50. Ibid., VIII, 315 (emphasis in original).

51. *Reflections*, in *Writings and Speeches*, VIII, 88.

52. *Assembly*, in *Writings and Speeches*, VIII, 317.

53. Ibid., VIII, 316.

54. Ibid., VIII, 314.

55. Ibid., VIII, 315.

56. *Writings and Speeches*, VIII, 99–100.

57. This is pointed out by Pocock, in *Virtue, Commerce, and History*, 159.

58. *Writings and Speeches*, VIII, 244.

59. Robert Nisbet, *The Quest for Community: A Study in the Ethics of Order and Freedom* (San Francisco: ICS Press, 1990 [1953]), 206.

60. Ibid., 199.

61. *Assembly*, in *Writings and Speeches*, VIII, 315–16.

62. *Reflections*, in *Writings and Speeches*, VIII, 146–47.

63. James Q. Wilson, *The Moral Sense* (New York: The Free Press, 1993).

64. Irving Babbitt, *Democracy*, 133.

5—Moral Imagination and Public Policy

1. O'Brien, *Great Melody*, 107–8; Burke describes his speech in *Correspondence*, I, 232–33.

2. Conniff, *Cobbler*, 185–86.

3. O'Gorman, *Edmund Burke*, 73.

4. See, for example, Lock, *Edmund Burke*, I, 381–98.

5. To Richard Shackleton, 11 Aug. 1776, *Correspondence*, III, 286–87.

6. Lock, *Edmund Burke*, II, 55.

7. Speech on moving Resolutions for Conciliation with America (22 March 1775), in *Writings and Speeches*, III, 135 (emphasis in original).

8. *Writings and Speeches*, III, 119 (emphasis in original).

9. Chapman, *Practical Imagination*, 21–22.

10. *Writings and Speeches*, III, 120.

11. Ibid., III, 120.

12. *Works*, II, 123.

13. O'Brien, *Great Melody*, 95.

14. *Writings and Speeches*, III, 122.

15. Ibid., III, 124.

16. *Speech on American Taxation* (19 April 1774), in *Writings and Speeches*, II, 428.

17. *Taxation*, in *Writings and Speeches*, II, 458.

18. *Conciliation*, in *Writings and Speeches*, III, 146.

19. *Taxation*, in *Writings and Speeches*, II, 458.

20. *Conciliation*, in *Writings and Speeches*, III, 133.

21. O'Gorman, *Edmund Burke*, 73.

22. *Conciliation*, in *Writings and Speeches*, III, 152.

23. Pappin, *Metaphysics*, 18.

24. *Noble Lord*, in *Writings and Speeches*, IX, 157.

25. O'Brien not only emphasizes this point but sees it as a central theme of Burke's entire career.

26. O'Brien, *Great Melody*, 226.

27. Kirk, *Edmund Burke*, 106.

28. O'Brien, *Great Melody*, 304–5.

29. Kirk, *Edmund Burke*, 107.

30. Frederick G. Whelan, *Edmund Burke and India: Political Morality and Empire* (Pittsburgh: University of Pittsburgh Press, 1996), 44.

31. O'Brien, *Great Melody*, 307.

32. Whelan, *India*, 5.

33. Lock, *Edmund Burke*, II, 34.

34. Speech on Mr. Fox's East India Bill (1 December 1783), in *Writings and Speeches*, V, 389.

35. Uday Singh Mehta, *Liberalism and Empire: A Study in Nineteenth-Century British Liberal Thought* (Chicago: University of Chicago Press, 2003).

36. Luke Gibbons, *Edmund Burke and Ireland* (Cambridge: Cambridge University Press, 2003), 232.

37. Fox's Bill, in *Writings and Speeches*, V, 384 (emphasis in original).

38. Ibid., V, 386.

39. Ibid., V, 386.

40. Ibid., V, 384.

41. Browne, *Virtue*, 84.

42. Speech in Opening the Impeachment, First Day (15 February 1788), in *Writings and Speeches*, VI, 272.

43. Fox's Bill, in *Writings and Speeches*, V, 401, 402.

44. Ibid., V, 403.

45. Whelan, *India*, 4.

46. *Writings and Speeches*, V, 403.

47. *Reflections*, in *Writings and Speeches*, VIII, 130.

48. Pocock, *Virtue, Commerce, and History*, 281.

49. Ibid., 203, 250.

50. Kirk, *Edmund Burke*, 117.

51. Speech in Opening, Second Day (16 February 1788), in *Writings and Speeches*, VI, 372.

52. *Writings and Speeches*, VI, 315.

53. Opening, Second Day, in *Writings and Speeches*, VI, 346.

54. Speech on Bengal Judicature Bill (1) (27 June 1781), in *Writings and Speeches*, V, 141.

55. Ibid., V, 141.

56. *Opening, First Day*, in *Works*, IX, 382. The passage quoted here varies significantly from the version found in *Writings and Speeches*, VI, 304–5, but the general sentiment is the same in both versions.

57. See, for example, Charles Lockart and Gregg Franzwa, "Cultural Theory and

the Problem of Moral Relativism," in *Politics, Policy, and Culture,* ed. Dennis J. Coyle and Richard J. Ellis (Boulder, CO: Westview Press, 1994), 175–89.

58. Stanlis, *Natural Law,* 33.

59. Opening, Second Day, in *Writings and Speeches,* VI, 350–51.

60. Bengal (1), in *Writings and Speeches,* V, 141–42.

61. Opening, Second Day, in *Works,* IX, 454. (This sentence is not included in the *Writings* version.)

62. Opening, Second Day, in *Writings and Speeches,* VI, 363.

63. Ibid., VI, 353.

64. Ibid., VI, 353 (emphasis in original).

65. Ibid., VI, 351.

66. Ibid., VI, 347.

67. *Works,* IX, 461. The quoted passage varies significantly from its equivalent in *Writings and Speeches,* VI, 352, but the general sentiment is the same.

68. Opening, First Day, in *Writings and Speeches,* VI, 312.

69. Letter to William Smith, Esq., on the Subject of Catholic Emancipation (29 January 1795), in *Writings and Speeches,* IX, 661.

70. Second Letter to Sir Hercules Langrishe, on the Catholic Question (26 May 1795), in *Writings and Speeches,* IX, 667.

71. Kirk, *Edmund Burke,* 144–45.

72. Conniff, *Cobbler,* 251–65.

73. Kirk, *Edmund Burke,* 145.

74. To Richard Burke, Jr., 3 January 1792, in *Correspondence,* VIII, 11, quoted in Conniff, *Cobbler,* 268.

75. Conniff, *Cobbler,* 257.

76. For issues regarding the dating of this work, see O'Brien, *Great Melody,* 40, n1.

77. Ibid., 15–19.

78. Ibid., 45.

79. *Writings and Speeches,* VIII, 102.

80. Letter to Sir Hercules Langrishe, on the Subject of the Roman Catholics of Ireland, in *Writings and Speeches,* IX, 600.

81. *Langrishe,* in *Writings and Speeches,* IX, 637.

82. O'Brien, *Great Melody,* 21.

83. Fragments of a Tract on the Popery Laws, in *Writings and Speeches,* IX, 465.

84. Ibid., IX, 468.

85. Ibid., IX, 466.

86. *Langrishe,* in *Writings and Speeches,* IX, 605 (emphasis in original).

87. *Writings and Speeches,* IX, 608.

88. Second Langrishe, in *Writings and Speeches,* IX, 668.

89. Letter to Smith, in *Writings and Speeches,* IX, 663.

90. See, for example, Voegelin, *New Science.*

91. Letter to Smith, in *Writings and Speeches,* IX, 661.

92. Letter to Richard Burke, Esq., on Protestant Ascendency in Ireland (1793), in *Writings and Speeches,* IX, 647.

93. O'Brien, *Great Melody,* 531.

94. Second Langrishe, in *Writings and Speeches,* IX, 669 (emphasis in original).

95. Speech on a Motion for a Committee to Inquire into the State of the Representation of the Commons in Parliament (7 May 1782), in *Works,* VII, 92.

96. Ibid., VII, 93.

97. Ibid., VII, 101.

98. *Langrishe,* in *Writings and Speeches,* IX, 629.

99. Representation, in *Works,* VII, 98.

100. *Thoughts on the Cause of the Present Discontents,* in *Writings and Speeches,* II, 300.

101. Ibid., II, 300.

102. Speech on Reform of Representation, in *Works,* VII, 97.

103. Canavan, *Political Reason,* 165.

104. *Works,* VII, 96.

105. Ibid., VII, 100.

106. Ibid., VII, 101.

107. Ibid., VII, 95.

108. Ibid., VII, 94.

109. Ibid., VII, 91.

6—Burke and the Good

1. Pappin, *Metaphysics,* 22.

2. John Morley, *Burke (*New York: Harper and Brothers, 1879).

3. C. E. Vaughan, *Studies in the History of Political Philosophy before and after Rousseau* (Manchester: The University Press, 1925).

4. Laski, *England,* 155–56, 149, 161, 179, 178, 148.

5. Cobban, *Revolt,* 40, 95–96, 53, 258.

6. Strauss, *Natural Right,* 296, 313, 319, 319, 318.

7. Ibid., 83 (emphasis in original).

8. Ibid., 52, 53, 84.

9. Canavan, *Political Reason,* 81.

10. Ibid., 180.

11. Pappin, *Metaphysics,* 19.

12. Ibid., 41.

13. Christopher Reid, *Edmund Burke and the Practice of Political Writing* (New York: St. Martin's Press, 1985).

14. Mansfield, introduction to Burke, *Selected Letters,* p .4.

15. Isaac Kramnick, *The Rage of Edmund Burke: Portrait of an Ambivalent Conservative* (New York: Basic Books, 1977).

16. Kirk, *Edmund Burke,* 152.

17. *Popery,* in *Writings and Speeches,* IX, 463.

18. Fox's Bill, in *Writings and Speeches,* V, 383.

19. Cobban, *Revolt,* 40.

20. Parkin, *Moral,* 12.

21. Gary D. Glenn, "Natural Rights and Social Contract in Burke and Bellarmine," in *Rethinking Rights: Historical, Political, and Philosophical Perspectives,* ed. Bruce P. Frohnen and Kenneth L. Grasso (Columbia: University of Missouri Press, 2009).

22. *Reflections,* in *Writings and Speeches,* VIII, 110.

23. *Appeal,* in *Works,* IV, 188.

24. *Writings and Speeches,* VIII, 110.

25. Fox's Bill, in *Writings and Speeches,* V, 383–84.

26. *Appeal,* in *Works,* IV, 206.

27. *Reflections,* in *Writings and Speeches,* VIII, 110.

28. *Works,* IV, 206.

29. Ibid., IV, 206–7.

30. Ibid., VIII, 110 (emphasis in original).

31. *Reflections,* in *Writings and Speeches,* VIII, 147.

32. *Writings and Speeches,* VIII, 114.

33. *Philosophical Enquiry,* in *Writings and Speeches,* I, 238.

34. Ibid., I, 235.

35. *Writings and Speeches,* VIII, 222–23.

36. Fourth Letter on the Proposals for Peace with the Regicide Directory of France, in *Writings and Speeches,* IX, 101.

37. *Reflections,* in *Writings and Speeches,* VIII, 223.

38. *Writings and Speeches,* VIII, 114.

39. First Letter on a Regicide Peace, in *Writings and Speeches,* IX, 188.

40. *Reflections,* in *Writings and Speeches,* VIII, 84.

41. *Writings and Speeches,* VIII, 84.

42. Irving Babbitt, *Rousseau and Romanticism* (1919; New Brunswick, NJ: Transaction Publishers, 1991), lxxv–lxxvi.

43. *Writings and Speeches,* VIII, 86.

44. Ibid., VIII, 189–90 (emphasis in original).

45. Aristotle, *Nichomachean Ethics,* trans. Martin Ostwald (New York: Macmillan Publishing Company, 1962), 1095b.

46. Plato, *Seventh Letter,* in *Collected Dialogues,* ed. Edith Hamilton and Huntington Cairns (New York: Pantheon Books, 1961).

47. *Appeal,* in *Works,* IV, 206.

48. Ibid., IV, 206.

49. Ibid., IV, 162.

50. Ibid., IV, 169.

51. *Reflections,* in *Writings and Speeches,* VIII, 231.

52. *The Declaration of the Rights of Man and of the Citizen* (26 August 1789), trans. Thomas Paine, in *Classics of Modern Political Theory: Machiavelli to Mill,* ed. Steven M. Cahn (New York: Oxford University Press, 1997), 663 (emphasis added).

53. *Reflections,* in *Writings and Speeches,* VIII, 115.

54. Strauss, *Natural Right,* 315.

55. Ryn, *Will,* 26–27 (emphasis in original).

56. MacIntyre, *After Virtue,* 221 (emphasis in original).

57. Ibid., 223.

58. W. Wesley McDonald, *Russell Kirk and the Age of Ideology* (Columbia: University of Missouri Press, 2004), 76–77, citing Eliseo Vivas, "Animadversions upon the Doctrine of Natural Law," *Modern Age* 10 (Spring 1966): 155.

59. Babbitt, *Rousseau,* lxxvi.

Conclusion

1. Stanlis, *Natural Law,* 83 (emphasis in original).

2. *Declaration of the Rights of Man and of the Citizen,* in Cahn, ed., *Classics,* 663.

3. McDonald, *Russell Kirk,* 61.

4. *Assembly,* in *Writings and Speeches,* VIII, 317.
5. Oakeshott, *Rationalism,* 107.
6. See, for example, Taylor, *Ethics.*
7. Russello, *Postmodern Imagination,* 193.
8. Roger Scruton, *The Need for Nations* (London: Civitas, 2004), 36.
9. Ibid., 36.
10. *Reflections,* in *Writings and Speeches,* VIII, 97.
11. Scruton, *Need,* 37.
12. MacIntyre, *After Virtue.*
13. Ibid., 263.
14. Pappin, *Metaphysics.*

Bibliography

Aarsleff, Hans. *The Study of Language in England, 1780–1860*. Princeton: Princeton University Press, 1967.

Addison, Joseph. *Addison's Essays from the Spectator*. Boston: Adamant Media Corporation, 2001.

Almond, Gabriel A., and Verba, Sidney. *The Civic Culture: Political Attitudes and Democracy in Five Nations*. Princeton: Princeton University Press, 1963.

———, eds. *The Civic Culture Revisited*. Boston: Little, Brown, 1980.

The Annual Register, various years. London: J. Dodsley, 1777.

Aristotle. *Nichomachean Ethics*, trans. Martin Ostwald. New York: Macmillan Publishing Company, 1962.

———. *The Politics of Aristotle*, ed. and trans. Ernest Barker. New York: Oxford University Press, 1958.

Ayling, Stanley. *Edmund Burke: His Life and Opinions*. New York: St. Martin's Press, 1988.

Babbitt, Irving. *Democracy and Leadership*. Indianapolis: Liberty Fund, Inc., 1979 [1924].

———. *Rousseau and Romanticism*. New Brunswick, NJ: Transaction Publishers, 1991 [1919].

Babbitt, Susan E. *Impossible Dreams: Rationality, Integrity, and Moral Imagination*. Boulder, CO: Westview Press, 1996.

Baker, Keith Michael, ed. *The French Revolution and the Creation of Modern Political Culture* (4 vols.). New York: Pergamon Press, 1987–1994.

Baldacchino, Joseph. "The Value-Centered Historicism of Edmund Burke." *Modern Age* 27, 2 (Spring 1983).

Ball, Terence, and Richard Dagger. *Ideals and Ideologies: A Reader*, 6th ed. New York: Pearson Longman, 2006, 3–9.

Bede. *A History of the English Church and People (Historia Ecclesiastica)*, trans. Leo Sherley-Price, rev. R. E. Latham. New York: Penguin Books, 1982.

Blakemore, Steven. *Intertextual War: Edmund Burke and the French Revolution in the Writings of Mary Wollstonecraft, Thomas Paine, and James Mackintosh*. Madison, NJ: Fairleigh Dickinson University Press, 1997.

Boswell, James. *The Life of Samuel Johnson, LL. D.* Chicago: Encyclopædia Britannica, Inc., 1990.

Bromwich, David. *A Choice of Inheritance: Self and Community from Edmund Burke to Robert Frost.* Cambridge, MA: Harvard University Press, 1989.

Browne, Stephen H. *Edmund Burke and the Discourse of Virtue.* Tuscaloosa: University of Alabama Press, 1993.

Burke, Edmund. *The Correspondence of Edmund Burke.* 10 vols. Chicago: University of Chicago Press, 1958–1978.

———. *The Works of the Right Honorable Edmund Burke.* 12 vols. Boston: Little, Brown, & Company, 1865–1871.

———. *The Writings and Speeches of Edmund Burke.* Paul Langford, general editor. 8 published vols. (I–III, V–IX). Oxford: Clarendon Press, 1981–2000.

Canavan, Francis P. *Edmund Burke: Prescription and Providence.* Durham, NC: Carolina Academic Press, 1987.

———. *The Political Reason of Edmund Burke.* Durham, NC: Duke University Press, 1960.

Chapman, Gerald W. *Edmund Burke, the Practical Imagination.* Cambridge, MA: Harvard University Press, 1967.

Cobban, Alfred. *Edmund Burke and the Revolt against the Eighteenth Century.* London: Allen & Unwin, 1960 [1929].

Cone, Carl B. *Burke and the Nature of Politics.* 2 vols. Lexington: University of Kentucky Press, 1957 and 1964.

Conniff, James. *The Useful Cobbler: Edmund Burke and the Politics of Progress.* Albany: State University of New York Press, 1994.

Cooper, Anthony Ashley (Earl of Shaftesbury). *Characteristics of Men, Manners, Opinions, Times.* Indianapolis: Liberty Fund, 2001.

Copeland, Thomas W. *Our Eminent Friend, Edmund Burke.* New Haven, CT: Yale University Press, 1949.

Coyle, Dennis J., and Ellis, Richard J., eds. *Politics, Policy, and Culture.* Boulder, CO: Westview Press, 1994.

Croce, Benedetto. *The Aesthetic as the Science of Expression and the Linguistic in General* (Part 1 of *Estetica*), trans. Colin Lyas. New York: Cambridge University Press, 1992.

———. *Guide to Aesthetics* (*Brevario di estetica*, 1913), trans. Patrick Romanell. Indianapolis: Hackett Publishing Company, 1995.

Crowe, Ian, ed. *The Enduring Edmund Burke: Bicentennial Essays.* Wilmington, DE: Intercollegiate Studies Institute, 1997.

———, ed. *An Imaginative Whig: Reassessing the Life and Thought of Edmund Burke.* Columbia: University of Missouri Press, 2005.

De Bruyn, Frans. *The Literary Genres of Edmund Burke: The Political Uses of Literary Form.* New York: Clarendon Press, 1996.

The Declaration of the Rights of Man and of the Citizen (26 August 1789), trans. Thomas Paine, in *Classics of Modern Political Theory: Machiavelli to Mill,* ed. Steven M. Cahn. New York: Oxford University Press, 1997, 663–64.

Douglas, Mary. *Risk and Blame: Essays in Cultural Theory.* New York: Routledge, 1992.

Freeman, Michael. *Edmund Burke and the Critique of Political Radicalism.* Chicago: University of Chicago Press, 1980.

Frohnen, Bruce. *Virtue and the Promise of Conservatism: The Legacy of Burke and Tocqueville.* Lawrence: University Press of Kansas, 1993.

Frohnen, Bruce P., and Grasso, Kenneth L., eds. *Rethinking Rights: Historical, Political, and Philosophical Perspectives.* Columbia: University of Missouri Press, 2009.

Gibbons, Luke. *Edmund Burke and Ireland.* Cambridge: Cambridge University Press, 2003.

Hampsher-Monk, Iain. Introduction to *The Political Philosophy of Edmund Burke*, ed. Iain Hampsher-Monk. New York: Longmans, 1987.

Harris, Ian. Introduction to *Pre-Revolutionary Writings / Edmund Burke*, ed. Ian Harris. New York: Cambridge University Press, 1993.

Hayek, Friedrich. *The Constitution of Liberty.* Chicago: University of Chicago Press, 1960.

Heidegger, Martin. *Being and Time,* trans. John Macquarrie and Edward Robinson. New York: Harper, 1962.

——. *Poetry, Language, Thought,* trans. Albert Hofstadter. New York: Harper & Row Publishers, 1975.

Himmelfarb, Gertrude. "Judging Richard Posner." *Commentary* 113, 2 (February 2002): 37–44.

——. *Moral Imagination: From Edmund Burke to Lionel Trilling.* Chicago: Ivan R. Dee, Publisher, 2007.

Hobbes, Thomas. *Leviathan.* London and New York: Penguin, 1985.

Hume, David. *The Philosophy of David Hume,* ed. V. C. Chappell. New York: Random House (Modern Library), 1963.

——. *A Treatise of Human Nature,* intro. A. D. Lindsay. 2 vols. New York: E. P. Dutton & Co. Inc., 1949.

Hutcheson, Francis. *An Inquiry into the Original of Our Ideas of Beauty and Virtue.* Indianapolis: Liberty Fund, 2004.

Johnson, Mark. *Moral Imagination: Implications of Cognitive Science for Ethics.* Chicago: University of Chicago Press, 1993.

Kant, Immanuel. *Observations on the Feeling of the Beautiful and Sublime,* trans. John T. Goldthwait (Berkeley: University of California Press, 2004).

——. *Practical Philosophy,* trans. Mary J. Gregor. Cambridge: Cambridge University Press, 1996.

Kirk, Russell. *The Conservative Mind from Burke to Eliot.* South Bend, IN: Gateway Editions, 1978 [1953].

——. *Edmund Burke: A Genius Reconsidered.* New Rochelle, NY: Arlington House, 1967.

Kramnick, Isaac. *The Rage of Edmund Burke: Portrait of an Ambivalent Conservative.* New York: Basic Books, 1977.

Laski, Harold J. *Political Thought in England: Locke to Bentham.* London: Oxford University Press, 1950 [1920].

Lawler, Peter Augustine. "Conservative Postmodernism, Postmodern Conservatism." *Intercollegiate Review* 38, 1 (Fall 2002).

——. *Postmodernism Rightly Understood.* Lanham, MD: Rowman & Littlefield, 1999.

Ljungberg, Carl Johan. "The Liberalism of Edmund Burke: The Idea of the Constitution." Ph.D. dissertation, The Catholic University of America, 1983.

Lock, F. P. *Edmund Burke,* Volume I, 1730–1784. New York: Clarendon Press, 1998.

——. *Edmund Burke,* Volume II, 1784–1797. New York: Clarendon Press, 2006.

Locke, John. *An Essay Concerning Human Understanding.* New York: Dover Publications, 1959.

MacIntyre, Alasdair. *After Virtue: A Study in Moral Theory.* Notre Dame, IN: University of Notre Dame Press, 1984.

——. *Dependent Rational Animals: Why Human Beings Need the Virtues (The Paul Carus Lectures).* Chicago: Open Court, 1999.

——. *Whose Justice? Which Rationality?* Notre Dame, IN: University of Notre Dame Press, 1988.

Mansfield, Harvey C., Jr. Introduction to Burke, Edmund, *Selected Letters of Edmund Burke,* ed. Harvey C. Mansfield, Jr. Chicago: University of Chicago Press, 1984.

——. *Statesmanship and Party Government: A Study of Burke and Bolingbroke.* Chicago: University of Chicago Press, 1965.

McCue, Jim. *Edmund Burke and our Present Discontents.* London: Claridge Press, 1997.

McDonald, W. Wesley. *Russell Kirk and the Age of Ideology.* Columbia: University of Missouri Press, 2004.

Mehta, Uday Singh. *Liberalism and Empire: A Study in Nineteenth-Century British Liberal Thought.* Chicago: University of Chicago Press, 2003.

Millies, Steven P. "'A Relation Between Us': Religion and the Political Thought of Edmund Burke." Ph.D. dissertation, The Catholic University of America, 2001.

Morley, John. *Burke.* New York: Harper and Brothers, 1879.

Musgrave, William R. "That Monstrous Fiction: Radical Agency and Aesthetic Ideology in Burke." *Studies in Romanticism* 36 (Spring 1997).

Nietzsche, Friedrich. *The Gay Science,* trans. Walter Kaufmann. New York: Random House, 1974.

——. *Untimely Meditations,* ed. Daniel Breazeale, trans. R. J. Hollingdale. Cambridge: Cambridge University Press, 1997.

Nisbet, Robert. *The Quest for Community: A Study in the Ethics of Order and Freedom.* San Francisco: ICS Press, 1990 [1953].

Nussbaum, Martha C. *Love's Knowledge: Essays on Philosophy and Literature.* New York: Oxford University Press, 1990.

——. *Upheavals of Thought: The Intelligence of Emotions.* Cambridge: Cambridge University Press, 2001.

Oakeshott, Michael. *Rationalism in Politics and Other Essays.* London: Methuen & Co., 1962.

O'Brien, Conor Cruise. *The Great Melody: A Thematic Biography and Commentated Anthology of Edmund Burke.* Chicago: University of Chicago Press, 1992.

O'Brien, Karen. *Narratives of Enlightenment: Cosmopolitan History from Voltaire to Gibbon.* New York: Cambridge University Press, 1997.

O'Gorman, Frank. *Edmund Burke: His Political Philosophy.* Bloomington: Indiana University Press, 1973.

O'Neill, Daniel I. "Burke on the Death of Western Civilization." Unpublished paper delivered at the 2002 Annual Meeting of the American Political Science Association.

Paine, Thomas. *Political Writings,* ed. Bruce Kuklick. Cambridge: Cambridge University Press, 2000.

Pappin, Joseph L., III. *The Metaphysics of Edmund Burke.* New York: Fordham University Press, 1993.

Parkin, Charles. *The Moral Basis of Burke's Political Thought.* Cambridge: Cambridge University Press, 1956.

Plato. *Collected Dialogues,* ed. Edith Hamilton and Huntington Cairns. New York: Pantheon Books, 1961.

———. *The Republic,* trans. Desmond Lee. New York: Penguin Books, 1987.

Pocock, J. G. A. "Burke and the Ancient Constitution: A Problem in the History of Ideas." *The Historical Journal* 3, 2 (1960): 125–43.

———. *The Machiavellian Moment: Florentine Political Thought and the Atlantic Republican Tradition.* Princeton: Princeton University Press, 1975.

———. *Virtue, Commerce, and History: Essays on Political Thought and History, Chiefly in the Eighteenth Century.* New York: Cambridge University Press, 1985.

Reid, Christopher. *Edmund Burke and the Practice of Political Writing.* New York: St. Martin's Press, 1985.

Rorty, Richard. *Contingency, Irony, and Solidarity.* New York: Cambridge University Press, 1989.

Russello, Gerald. *The Postmodern Imagination of Russell Kirk.* Columbia: University of Missouri Press, 2007.

Ryn, Claes G. *Will, Imagination, and Reason: Babbitt, Croce, and the Problem of Reality.* New Brunswick, NJ: Transaction Publishers, 1997 [1986].

Scruton, Roger. *The Need for Nations.* London: Civitas, 2004.

Smith, Adam. *The Theory of Moral Sentiments,* ed. Knud Haakonssen. Cambridge: Cambridge University Press, 2002.

Smith, Bruce James. *Politics and Remembrance.* Princeton: Princeton University Press, 1985.

Stanlis, Peter J. *Edmund Burke and the Natural Law.* Ann Arbor: University of Michigan Press, 1958.

———. *Edmund Burke: The Enlightenment and Revolution.* New Brunswick. NJ: Transaction Publishers, 1991.

Strauss, Leo. *Natural Right and History.* Chicago: University of Chicago Press, 1971 [1953].

Strong, Tracy B. *Friedrich Nietzsche and the Politics of Transfiguration.* Berkeley: University of California Press, 1975.

Taylor, Charles. *The Ethics of Authenticity.* Cambridge, MA: Harvard University Press, 1991.

———. *Human Agency and Language (Philosophical Papers I).* Cambridge: Cambridge University Press, 1985.

Thompson, Michael, Richard Ellis, and Aaron Wildavsky. *Cultural Theory.* Boulder, CO: Westview Press, 1990.

Tivnan, Edward. *Moral Imagination: Confronting the Ethical Issues of Our Day.* New York: Simon & Schuster, 1995.

Trilling, Lionel. *The Liberal Imagination: Essays on Literature and Society.* New York: Viking Press, 1950.

Vaughan, C. E. *Studies in the History of Political Philosophy before and after Rousseau.* Manchester: The University Press, 1925.

Voegelin, Eric. *The New Science of Politics.* Chicago: University of Chicago Press, 1987 [1952].

Walsh, David. *The Growth of the Liberal Soul.* Columbia: University of Missouri Press, 1997.

Welsh, Jennifer M. *Edmund Burke and International Relations: The Commonwealth of Europe and the Crusade against the French Revolution.* New York: St. Martin's Press, 1995.

Whale, John, ed. *Edmund Burke's Reflections on the Revolution in France: New Interdisciplinary Essays*. Manchester and New York: Manchester University Press, 2000.

Whelan, Frederick G. *Edmund Burke and India: Political Morality and Empire*. Pittsburgh: University of Pittsburgh Press, 1996.

White, Stephen K. *Edmund Burke: Modernity, Politics, and Aesthetics*. Thousand Oaks, CA: Sage Publications, 1994.

Wilkins, Burleigh Taylor. *The Problem of Burke's Political Philosophy*. Oxford: Oxford University Press, 1967.

Wilson, James Q. *The Moral Sense*. New York: The Free Press, 1993.

Wood, Neal. "The Aesthetic Dimension of Burke's Political Thought." *The Journal of British Studies* iv, 1 (1964): 41–64.

Index